ROUTLEDGE LIBRARY EDITIONS: BRITISH IN INDIA

Volume 18

PALACES OF THE RAJ

PALACES OF THE RAJ
Magnificence and Misery of the Lord Sahibs

MARK BENCE-JONES

Routledge
Taylor & Francis Group

LONDON AND NEW YORK

First published in 1973 by George Allen & Unwin Ltd

This edition first published in 2017
by Routledge
2 Park Square, Milton Park, Abingdon, Oxon OX14 4RN

and by Routledge
711 Third Avenue, New York, NY 10017

Routledge is an imprint of the Taylor & Francis Group, an informa business

British Library Cataloguing in Publication Data
A catalogue record for this book is available from the British Library

ISBN: 978-1-138-22929-7 (Set)
ISBN: 978-1-315-20179-5 (Set) (ebk)
ISBN: 978-1-138-29336-6 (Volume 18) (hbk)
ISBN: 978-1-138-29342-7 (Volume 18) (pbk)
ISBN: 978-1-315-23206-5 (Volume 18) (ebk)

Publisher's Note
The publisher has gone to great lengths to ensure the quality of this reprint but points out that some imperfections in the original copies may be apparent.

Disclaimer
The publisher has made every effort to trace copyright holders and would welcome correspondence from those they have been unable to trace.

PALACES

OF THE

RAJ

MAGNIFICENCE AND MISERY
OF THE
LORD SAHIBS

MARK BENCE-JONES

London
GEORGE ALLEN AND UNWIN LTD
RUSKIN HOUSE   MUSEUM STREET

First published in 1973

This book is copyright under the Berne Convention. All rights
are reserved. Apart from any fair dealing for the purpose of
private study, research, criticism or review, as permitted
under the Copyright Act, 1956, no part of this publication may
be reproduced, stored in a retrieval system, or transmitted, in
any form or by any means, electronic, electrical, chemical,
mechanical, optical, photocopying, recording or otherwise,
without the prior permission of the copyright owner. Enquiries
should be addressed to the publishers.

© George Allen & Unwin Ltd, 1973

ISBN 0 04 954017 3

Printed in Great Britain
in 12 point Barbou type
by W & J Mackay Limited, Chatham

To my Father and Mother
who first took me to India

ACKNOWLEDGEMENTS

Unpublished Crown copyright material in the India Office Library or India Office Records transcribed or reproduced in this book appears by permission of the Controller of Her Majesty's Stationery Office. In this connection, I would like to express my thanks to the India Office Library staff, particularly to Dr Richard Bingle, Mrs M. Archer and Miss P. M. Harrold, for their help and for the cheerful forbearance with which they endeavoured to satisfy my apparently insatiable demands for abstruse material.

I would like to thank the following who have kindly given me permission to quote from unpublished letters, and other manuscript sources: Lord Elphinstone (Elphinstone Collection); Lord Strachie (R. Strachey Collection); Sir John Lawrence, Bt, O.B.E. (Henry Lawrence Collection); Sir Richard Temple, Bt, M.C. (Sir Richard Temple Collection); Miss Elizabeth FitzRoy (Journal of Yvonne FitzRoy); Mr J. C. Lyall (A. C. Lyall Collection); Mrs. L. W. Smith (Harcourt Butler Collection).

Then there are those who provided illustrations, lent me books and papers, and gave me personal reminiscences – as well as hospitality, which made researching in various parts of the country not only easy for me, but a great pleasure. To each of the following I am indebted on one or more, or – as is frequently the case – all of these counts: the Marquess of Dufferin and Ava; Doreen, Lady Brabourne, C.I.; Sir Gilbert Laithwaite, G.C.M.G., K.C.B., K.C.I.E., C.S.I.; Mr A. R. Astbury, C.S.I., C.I.E.; the Master of St Benet's Hall, Oxford; the Broadlands Archives; the proprietors of *Country Life*; Miss Denise Dane; Mrs de Montmorency; Mr Giles Eyre; Miss Violet Stuart Fraser; Dr B. B. Gaitonde, Director of the Haffkine Institute, Bombay; Mr Charles Harding; Miss Pamela Maclagan; Mr Philip Mason, C.I.E., O.B.E.; Captain Peter Montgomery; Mrs Gervas Portal; Lieutenant-Colonel R. B. Sleeman, O.B.E., M.C.; Mr John Teed; Mrs Harold Temple-Richards; Miss Ann Wright.

I feel especially grateful to the late Lady Maclagan and the late Mrs A. R. Astbury, who gave me the benefit of their wonderful memories of India shortly before they died. But for Mrs Astbury and her husband, Mr A. R. Astbury, this book might not have been written; for it was they who encouraged my father and mother to go to India, nearly forty years ago. I remember them clearly from when I was three years old, and when I saw them again, early in 1972, having not seen them during the intervening period, they seemed hardly to have changed at all.

Last, but by no means least, comes my gratitude to members of my family. To my wife, Gillian Bence-Jones, for accompanying me to many Indian buildings in hot weather. To my father and mother, to whom I owe the good fortune of a childhood spent in the India of the Raj; to my father, also, for his help and encouragement in the early stages of this book, which he did not live to see finished; and to my mother for checking my script. To my uncle and aunt, Commander and Mrs Scott-Lewis, for looking up elusive names and dates, and copying the plan of Government House, Calcutta.

This plan, and the plan of the Viceroy's House, New Delhi, are based on plans in published works, but have been simplified; the plan of Government House, Madras is a simplified copy of a plan by the architect, John Goldingham, in the India Office Library, which has been altered to show how the centre of the house was actually built. The other plans in this book are based only on memory, and so may not be quite accurate, or in scale. Where I am frankly uncertain as to the shape or arrangement of part of a building, I resort to broken lines: the breaks represent gaps in my memory, and in the memory of other people who knew the houses, and in no way reflect on the draughtsman who produced the final version of the plans. In fact, the plans are merely intended to help the reader to find his or her way about the houses in the pages of this book and would not be recommended to anyone wishing to emulate the Commissioner of Police who, when testing the security arrangements of the Bombay Government House during the Mutiny, succeeded in appearing by the Governor's bedside at six one morning disguised as a sweeper.

CONTENTS

Himalayas

LAHORE • SIMLA •
(PETERHOF)
(VICEREGAL LODGE)

NAINI TAL •

NEW DELHI •

LUCKNOW •

Himalayas

ALLAHABAD •

Ganges

BARRACKPORE •
CALCUTTA •

• BOMBAY
(PARELL)

• POONA
(DAPURI)
(GANESH KHIND) • HYDERABAD

MADRAS •

ILLUSTRATIONS

All prints except numbers 1, 9 and 25, from India Office Library

INTRODUCTION

THERE were Governors and Governors' Palaces in the days of
Pontius Pilate; there still are, although Imperialism has become a
dirty word. But never did the concept of Viceroyalty rise to such
a pitch as during the British Raj in India, when rulers of high integrity
– and for the most part, high ability – followed one another in a setting
which might be described as the Court of the Great Mogul run with the
quiet precision of the Court of St James's. The story of the Indian
Government Houses and Residencies is thus not only the story of the
houses themselves, and of the men and women who lived in them,
but it is the story of a Viceregal way of life, unequalled in any other
time or place; of how it evolved and was maintained, often in adverse
conditions.

Before taking a closer look at some of these houses, we should see
them in the context of the history of British India as a whole. Government House, Madras, and Parell, near Bombay, were both Governors'
houses in the early days when the sole object of the East India Company
was trade. British India then consisted of the three settlements of
Madras, Calcutta and Bombay, each of which had a few minor settlements dependent on it, and each of which was in charge of a Governor
or President – hence the term Presidency, which continued to be applied to the provinces of Madras and Bombay until the end of the Raj.

The house which grew into Government House, Madras, was bought
in 1753 by Governor Thomas Saunders, to replace a previous house de-
stroyed by the French during their occupation of Madras from 1746 to
1749. It was the aggressive policy of Joseph-François Dupleix, Governor-General of the French possessions in India, which caused the British
to take sides in the war then raging between rival Nawabs. Thanks to
the brave leadership of the young Company servant, Robert Clive,
whom Saunders put in command of the force which, in 1751, captured
and held Arcot in the face of tremendous odds, the British emerged as

the real victors in this war, becoming, as though by accident, the dominant power in southern India.

In Calcutta, the Government House was newer than those in Madras and Bombay, the reason for this being that the original Governor's house was burnt by the Nawab of Bengal, Siraj-ud-daula, when he seized Calcutta in 1756, an event chiefly remembered on account of the Black Hole. To recover Calcutta, and to obtain satisfaction from the Nawab for the losses he had caused the Company, Clive and Admiral Watson were sent to Bengal with troops and ships. The first object was easily achieved, but Siraj-ud-daula proved difficult in the matter of compensation, so that, in the following year, Clive joined with some of his chief subjects in a conspiracy to overthrow him. The conspiracy was successful and, after the Battle of Plassey, Siraj-ud-daula was replaced by a new Nawab who became a puppet of the British. From 1765 onwards, the British were the masters of Bengal.

The three Presidencies were originally independent of each other, but in 1774, the Governor of Bengal, Warren Hastings, became Governor-General, with power over the Governors of Madras and Bombay. Hastings and his two immediate successors lived in a comparatively modest Calcutta house, but the Earl of Mornington, afterwards Marquess Wellesley, who was Governor-General from 1798 to 1805, replaced it with a palace. Wellesley planned a second palace at Barrackpore, fifteen miles up river from Calcutta, but in the end the Governor-General's country retreat here was less grandiose, and dated from the time of the Marquess of Hastings, formerly Earl of Moira, who was Governor-General from 1814 to 1823 – a nobleman frequently confused with Warren Hastings.

Between 1765 and 1849, the whole of India came under the power of the British East India Company. This was due not to any deliberate policy of conquest, but to repeated attempts at solving the frontier problem, each of which took the British flag a little further north and west, until it eventually reached the Khyber and the Arabian Sea. Of the numerous independent states which had arisen out of the ruins of the Mogul Empire, many came peacefully under British protection. Others were reduced in the campaigns of such generals as Coote, Harris, Lake, Gough and Napier. The hardest to defeat were Mysore, ruled by Hyder Ali and his son, Tipu Sultan; and the kingdoms of the Marathas, those fierce warriors from western India. Wellesley, with his brother Arthur, the future Duke of Wellington, as one of his commanders, waged a successful war against Tipu Sultan. He also reduced the Marathas, whose power was finally broken in the time of Lord Hastings, when Poona, their former capital, became British territory, and was placed under the jurisdiction of the Governor of Bombay.

At first, there was no question of the newly-acquired territories being formed into new provinces. They were, like Poona, simply added to the Presidencies of Madras or Bombay, or to the territories administered directly by the Governor-General in his capacity as Governor of Bengal. By 1834 the latter extended as far into Hindostan as Agra, so it was decided to create a separate administration for what became known as the North-Western Provinces. The head of the new administration was not a Governor but a Lieutenant-Governor; he was, nevertheless, in the words of one holder of the office, 'a lofty provincial swell' who kept up considerable state. To the Indians, he was the 'Lord Sahib', a title originally confined to the Governor-General, who was usually a peer, and then applied to all Governors and Lieutenant-Governors, regardless of whether they were peers, knights or commoners. There was no permanent Government House in the North-Western Provinces until 1869, the provincial capital having been moved from Allahabad to Agra and then finally back to Allahabad after the Mutiny. In 1854 the remaining territories administered by the Governor-General were handed over to a Lieutenant-Governor of Bengal, leaving the Governor-General free to concentrate on the business of ruling India, which had become as much as he could possibly manage.

In the first half of the nineteenth century, when the Raj consisted less of territories under direct British rule than of self-governing Indian states under British influence, the key figure was not so much the Governor or Lieutenant-Governor as the Resident. Theoretically a kind of ambassador, the Resident tended to become the chief power in the State to which he was accredited. Not only did he represent the might of British India, but in certain states, such as Hyderabad, he controlled a British garrison, established there by agreement with the Indian ruler. As an outward sign of the Resident's power, the Residency was usually a fine house – at Hyderabad, it was a palace. The most important Residencies, apart from Hyderabad, were at Lucknow, capital of Oudh, and, after 1846, at Lahore, capital of the Sikh kingdom of the Punjab. There was also a Resident at the court of the descendant of the Moguls, who reigned as titular King of Delhi with a pension from the British, although Delhi itself was under direct British rule.

During this period of expansion and consolidation, the Government
Houses and Residencies sheltered many giants. At Government House,
Calcutta, there was Wellesley himself, and, later, Dalhousie. In the
middle of the period there was Lord William Bentinck, who, with the
help of Macaulay, brought about great advances in administration and
justice. At Government House, Madras, there was Sir Thomas Munro,
at Parell, Mountstuart Elphinstone and Sir John Malcolm. At Hyderabad Residency, there was Sir Charles Metcalfe, who later became the
first Lieutenant-Governor of the North-Western Provinces. At Lahore,
there was Henry Lawrence and his brother, John.

Wellesley, Bentinck and Dalhousie were noblemen who had been
sent out from England to be Governor-General; the others had all
spent the best part of their lives in India. From the time of Wellesley onwards, no former Indian Civilian became Governor-General or
Viceroy, with the exception of John Lawrence. As the century progressed, it likewise became the custom for the Governors of Madras and
Bombay to be sent out from home. That these noblemen and politicians
were, until 1858, the servants of a trading company, albeit a company
enjoying a prestige in the City of London second only to that of the
Bank of England, might seem anomalous. It must be remembered,
however, that successive legislation brought the East India Company
increasingly under the control of the British Government, so that eventually the Directors were only the nominal masters of India, the real
master being the President of the Board of Control, who was equivalent
to the Secretary of State of later years. The rule of the Company was
finally ended in 1858, when India came under the Crown and the
Governor-General was given the additional title of Viceroy. It was not
until 1877 that Queen Victoria was proclaimed Empress of India, at the
instigation of Disraeli.

The reason for the ending of Company rule was, of course, the
Mutiny, which broke out in May 1857. The stirring events of that year
did not much affect the Government Houses at Madras and Bombay,
and the Governor of Bombay's monsoon Government House at Poona;
but Government House, Calcutta, was the scene of many crucial meetings between the overworked and careworn Governor-General, Lord
Canning, and such military commanders as Outram, Havelock and Campbell. Hyderabad Residency was attacked, but the attackers were driven
off, while the Residency at Lucknow was besieged for three months.

At the outbreak of the Mutiny, Oudh was no longer an Indian State, but had, in the previous year, become a province of British India under a Chief Commissioner, the office being held at the time by Henry Lawrence, formerly of the Punjab, who was to die a hero's death in the Lucknow Residency. Lord Dalhousie's annexation of Oudh was one of the chief causes of the Mutiny, though it was justified by the ineptitude of the former rulers. A few years earlier, Dalhousie had annexed the Punjab, but there, the situation was saved by the statesmanship of Henry and John Lawrence. Having at first been ruled by a President of the Board of Administration, and then by a Chief Commissioner, the Punjab was raised to being a Lieutenant-Governor's province in 1859; and Henry Lawrence's old house at Lahore became Government House.

After the Mutiny, Delhi was transferred from the North-Western Provinces to the Punjab, at the same time as the court was abolished, the last King, who threw in his lot with the insurgents, having been deposed and exiled. The Punjab also included the hill station of Simla, which became the official summer headquarters of the Government of India in 1864. A permanent Viceregal Lodge was built at Simla in the eighteen-eighties, to replace a rather makeshift dwelling. Provincial Governments followed the example of the Government of India and moved every summer to the Hills; the Lieutenant-Governor of the Punjab becoming the Viceroy's neighbour at Simla, the Lieutenant-Governor of the North-Western Provinces going to his own hill station of Naini Tal, where a Government House was built in the eighteen-seventies. In 1877, the Lieutenant-Governor of the North-Western Provinces acquired a third Government House, at Lucknow, the successor to the battle-scarred Residency, for in that year Oudh was placed under his jurisdiction.

This was the set-up of British India in the second half of the nineteenth century. It was a more peaceful age; the fighting now took place outside India – in Afghanistan, where Roberts fought his memorable campaign, or in Burma. The great men were no longer Founders but Guardians, to use the distinction of Mr Philip Mason's admirable books.[1] Typical of them was Sir Alfred Lyall, a poet as well as an administrator, who was Lieutenant-Governor of the North-Western Provinces from 1882 to 1887; and his brother, Sir James, a very successful Lieutenant-Governor of the Punjab. When the North-Western Provinces and the Punjab were governed by the Lyalls, the brilliant,

[1] *The Men who Ruled India:* Vol. 1, *The Founders,* Vol. 2, *The Guardians* by Philip Woodruff (Philip Mason) (Cape 1953, 1954)

cultured and charming Lord Dufferin was Viceroy; it was the real heyday of the Raj. It was also the India of Kipling, who was then a young journalist in Lahore.

There was a sadness about the Viceroyalty of Lord Curzon, at the turn of the century; for the dynamic young Viceroy alienated the Indian Civil Service and quarrelled with the Commander-in-Chief, Lord Kitchener. Curzon started the process which continued during the remaining years of the Raj of separating various territories from existing provinces and putting them under new administrations. After he had formed the North-West Frontier Province out of part of the Punjab, the North-Western Provinces became known as the United Provinces. In 1921, all Lieutenant-Governors were raised to being Governors, even those in charge of provinces which had only recently been set up.

The most important change in the present century was the transfer of the Imperial Government from Calcutta to Delhi in 1912, following the great Durbar held by George V, the only British Sovereign to come to India as King-Emperor. From then until 1929, when Lutyens' Viceroy's House was ready for occupation, the Viceregal Court occupied temporary quarters. The former province of Bengal, with its Indian Civilian Lieutenant-Governor, was replaced by a new Presidency, governed, like Madras, and Bombay, by a politician from England, who took over Government House, Calcutta.

Thus did the Palaces of the Raj grow up all over India. The monarchs who reigned in them fell into three or four distinct groups. There was, first of all, the Viceroy or Governor-General, who was usually a leading statesman of his day. Governing India might not have required greatness; but the job was more arduous and difficult than any other job to which a British public servant could aspire, and of all those who took it on, only Auckland and Ellenborough, and perhaps Amherst and one later Viceroy, were not up to it.

There might seem little difference between the Viceroy and the Presidency Governor; both were drawn from the ranks of the British political aristocracy. But while the Governorships of Madras and Bombay – and Bengal after 1912 – had much of the glory of the Viceroyalty, with less of the hard work, they seldom attracted statesmen of the first calibre. Wilfrid Scawen Blunt's description of a Victorian Governor of Madras as 'a thin, sickly, querulous man, out of temper with everything around him, yet paid ten thousand a year by the Madras Indians for ruling them' was certainly unfair as applied to the Governor in question; yet it is indicative of what the Presidency Governor could be like at his worst: a political hack, who obtained his Governorship as a reward for services to his Party, and regarded it as a poor consolation for the seat in the Cabinet which he had hoped to get. Fortunately, however, there was also a good type of Presidency Governor; a younger man, with a particular interest in the Empire, for whom a Governorship afforded an opportunity to leave Westminster and embark on an Imperial career. Thus, Lord Brabourne became Governor of Bombay at the age of thirty-eight, and then went on to be Governor of Bengal. Lord Willingdon, having been Governor of Bombay and then of Madras, became Governor-General of Canada before returning to India as Viceroy. He and Bentinck were the only two British rulers of India who had previously been Presidency Governors. Another good type of Presidency Governor was not so much a politician as a Colonial administrator, who had already governed territories elsewhere in the Empire. Thus Sir William Denison became Governor of Madras after being Lieutenant-Governor of Van Diemen's land and Governor of New South Wales; Sir Philip Wodehouse was Governor of British Guiana and of the Cape before becoming Governor of Bombay.

Obviously different from the Viceroy and the Presidency Governor was the Lord Sahib who belonged to the Indian Civil Service. He had grown up in a harder school, having served in India from his youth. He spoke the languages of the country. To have become the head of a province marked him out as a man of outstanding merit; he had risen to the very top of an exceptionally talented Service. The Lord Sahib might previously have been Resident in Hyderabad or one of the many other States which remained under Indian rule. Latterly, however, the Resident tended to constitute a fourth type, more diplomat than administrator, having spent the greater part of his career in the Indian States.

Apart from the odd brilliant exception like Malcolm Hailey, who went on from governing the Punjab to governing the United Provinces, the Indian Civilian Lord Sahib lived under the shadow of impending retirement. It was different with the Viceroy, or the Presidency Governor; for him, the end of his term of office meant a return from exile, to friends, estates and perhaps a further advancement in his political career. But for the man who had spent the best years of his life in India, it was exile to have to return home; and he bade farewell to the greater part of his earthly glory when he finally descended the steps of his Government House.

Even if the former Governor went back to a high position at home, it was never quite the same as ruling a province the size of England, Scotland and Ireland put together, with a population of twenty million. As well as the power, there was the panoply; the retinue of Secretaries and ADCs, the servants that outnumbered the grandest ducal household of Victorian England many times over. There was the feeling of being a King, of being received and entertained as royalty by the Indian Princes. Last but not least, there was the pleasure of living in a Government House.

The Indian Government Houses and Residencies might not have been up to the palaces and mansions of Europe, yet they were all impressive and commodious, and some were of real architectural distinction. Each had a charm of its own; many of them had been enlarged and altered at various times, acquiring the air of an old country house which has grown through the centuries. With Lord Sahibs and Lady Sahibs changing every five years, even their recent past became lost in legend, so that a wing added fifty years before could seem as old and mysterious as it would have done in England if it dated from the time of Charles I. The ravages of the Indian climate, and the new Lady Sahib's almost invariable habit of changing the decorations from what they were under the previous regime, meant that the past was even more quickly buried. Other influences, however, helped to preserve it. Government Houses, like ancestral homes, had their old retainers who were determined to resist all change. Then there was ancient furniture and relics such as, in a private house, would probably have been thrown out by one generation or another, but which, being Government property and under the control of the Public Works Department, was left undisturbed. If it was banished to the lumber-room by one Lady Sahib, it was brought out again by the next.

There was also a certain continuity in the fact that the incoming Lord Sahib and Lady Sahib had probably been on friendly terms with several of their predecessors, and had stayed at their Government House in the past. Many Viceroys and Governors had forebears or relatives who had also reigned at an Indian Government House – perhaps the same one. The fourth Earl of Minto, Viceroy from 1905 to 1910, was the great-grandson of the first Earl, who was Governor-General a century earlier. Two Earls of Elgin, father and son, were Viceroys; the first soon after the Mutiny, the second in the eighteen-nineties; while Lord Hardinge of Penshurst, Viceroy from 1910 to 1916, was a grandson of Viscount Hardinge, Governor-General from 1844 to 1848. Lord Dalhousie's daughter, Lady Susan Ramsay, returned to India when her husband, Robert Bourke, afterwards Lord Connemara, became Governor of Madras. When Curzon took away the North-West Frontier territory from the Punjab, he aroused the indignation of Lady Young, the Lieutenant-Governor's wife, even more than of her husband, for the Punjab had also been her father's kingdom. Miss Pamela Plowden, daughter of a Resident at Hyderabad, married the second Earl of Lytton who was Governor of Bengal in the nineteen-twenties and whose father, the first Earl, was Viceroy some fifty years earlier.

The English country gentleman's habit of speaking of a fellow-landowner on the other side of the county as his neighbour was carried to its ultimate extreme among the Government Houses of India. Sir Richard Temple, when he was Lieutenant-Governor of Bengal, spoke of the Lieutenant-Governors of the North-Western Provinces and the Punjab as 'my neighbours', one of them being five hundred miles away from him, the other more than a thousand. In fact the world of the Government Houses and the principal Residencies, which included the Secretaries and ADCs as well as the Lord Sahibs and Lady Sahibs and their families, was very much like a county in that everybody knew everybody else and exchanged visits across the length and breadth of the great Indian subcontinent. It was a world almost as far removed from the ordinary sahibs and memsahibs as the old European Royal cousinhood was from lesser mortals; though this was due to circumstances rather than to any deliberate exclusiveness on the part of the Lord Sahibs and Lady Sahibs, who, with few exceptions, were far too genuine and intelligent to be affected by the proverbial snobberies of British–Indian life.

And in their grand surroundings, the inhabitants of the Government Houses suffered from the heat, the mosquitoes and the germs as much as everybody else did; perhaps even more so, on account of their high position. 'Dysentery . . . does not sort well with opening railway bridges in the hot weather,' Sir Alfred Lyall observed ruefully to his brother. The humbler sahib and memsahib did not have to face crowds and an official reception, looking immaculate and elegant, after two days and two nights in an Indian train. Before air-conditioning, the white and gold train of the Viceroys was no more impervious to heat and dust than any ordinary first class carriage.

And if discomfort served as a bond between the Government House world and the rest of British India, still more so did death. India took its toll of Lord Sahibs and Lady Sahibs, just as it did of all the others who came here from Europe in the days when medical science was less advanced. Apart from those who actually died in India, there were those like Dalhousie and Canning whose health was so shattered by the time they returned home that they did not survive long. Henry Lawrence and his successor, John Sherbrooke Banks, were killed while defending the Residency at Lucknow. Sir Henry Durand, Lieutenant-Governor of the Punjab in 1870, lost his life when the howdah in which he was riding was crushed going under a low arch. Lord Mayo, who was Viceroy at the same time, fell to the dagger of an escaped convict in the Andaman Islands.

Mayo was alone among Viceroys and Governors in being assassinated; unless we count Sir Michael O'Dwyer, who was shot dead by an Indian fanatic in London, many years after his retirement. That none of the others suffered a similar fate – though there were attempts on the lives of one or two of them from 1912 onwards – can be taken as a sign of the popularity of the Raj; for until the troubles of the three decades before Independence made it necessary to take greater precautions, the security arrangements of Viceroys and Governors were not very elaborate. Statistically, the Viceroy of India was no more likely to be assassinated than the Prime Minister of Great Britain; and he was three times safer in this respect than the President of the United States.

It would now be fashionable to say that the world of the Government Houses and Residencies was out of touch with the 'real India'. In fact, the social segregation of the British from the Indians which was so unfortunate a characteristic of the Raj in its later years, occurred lower down in society. The doors of the Government Houses were always open to Indians, just as much as they were to Europeans. If they opened more readily to the Chiefs and landowners than they did to the new intelligentsia, the same could have been said of any European Court before 1914. Nor did the intelligentsia constitute the real India, which lay out in the *mofussil*, where the peasants walked behind their oxen. The Chiefs and landowners would have been closer to it; the Governor, if he was an Indian Civilian, would have been closer still, for he would in that case have spent some years as a District Officer, listening daily to the peasants' troubles and sorting out their problems.

I

GOVERNMENT HOUSE
MADRAS

ALTHOUGH historically speaking a backwater after 1800, Madras
has always been, in the British mind, the epitome of India. It was
here that the first foundations of the Raj were laid in the military exploits of Clive, Stringer Lawrence and Coote; it was here that
the early Anglican missionaries gathered the impressions which they
retailed to their countrymen at home, who thus identified India with
the Coast of Coromandel – the 'coral strand' of which Reginald Heber
sang while still in his Shropshire rectory, having himself not yet answered the call of the missions. Generations of British in India, who
never went near Madras, heard all about it from Madrassi servants;
their children were brought up on its lore by Madrassi *ayahs*, so that
they almost felt as if they had lived there in a previous incarnation.
Then again, most curries are labelled Madras, even though they may
bear scant resemblance to the magnificent dish found at the peak of its
excellence at the Madras Club.

As the most traditional city of British India, it was fitting that Madras
should have possessed the most traditional of Government Houses: the
finest surviving example of a 'garden house', the country residence of a
rich or important European, or Indian of European tastes, in the eighteenth century. The true garden house did not just have a garden in the
suburban sense, but a sizeable domain. While many of these 'country
seats' in the neighbourhood of Madras lost their grounds as the city
spread outwards, Government House kept its seventy-five acres,
though it was no longer in the country but in the busy quarter of Tripli-
cane, separated from Fort St George, the original English settlement
and the official seat of Government, by the Cooum River, flowing

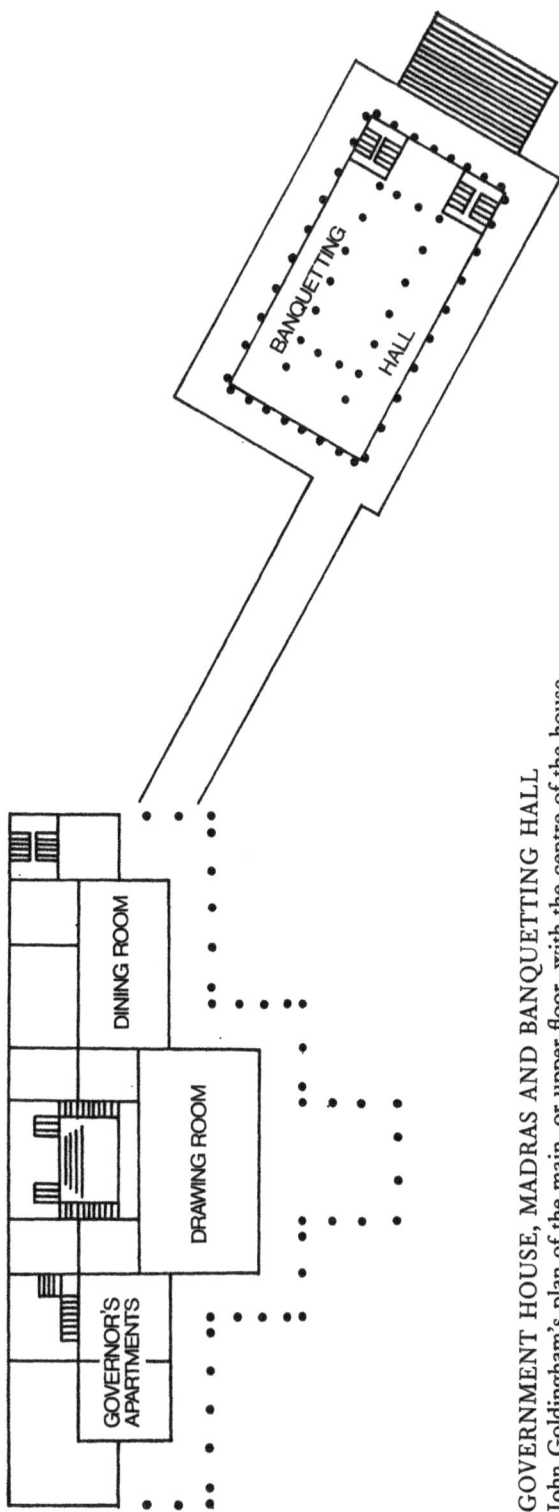

GOVERNMENT HOUSE, MADRAS AND BANQUETTING HALL
John Goldingham's plan of the main, or upper floor, with the centre of the house altered to show the staircase and drawing room as actually built.

sluggishly into the sea in patches of silver and brown, and the open *maidan* of the Island. Outside its gate, at the beginning of Mount Road, the broad, dusty thoroughfare leading to St Thomas's Mount, the traditional site of the Apostle's martyrdom, were all the noises of an Indian city, and also the smells – added to the effluvia of the river mud; an endless stream of humanity, a stopping place for bullock carts with attendant hawkers of rice cakes, bananas, oranges and betel-nut. Through the gate and past the sentries lay another world: a park shaded with groves of the sweet-scented wild date and other palms, with tamarinds and pepul trees and banyans; where the only sounds were birdsong and the undertones of the falling surf, the shore being only half a mile away.

The house turned its back on the town and faced the sea across lawns and a lotus-covered lake. It rose, widespread but rather insubstantial among the trees consisting, as it seemed, of nothing but pillars: three tiers of them, dazzlingly white against the dark intervening spaces. For it was surrounded on three sides by verandahs, which, when the cane *tatties* or sun-blinds were down, formed cool, shadowy perspectives where servants with scarlet and gold sashes over their white Maratha petticoats moved noiselessly along the polished marble floor or stood in pairs by the fanlighted doorways, ready to open a leaf each to the Lord Sahib or Lady Sahib or any of the other Masters or Madams who inhabited the house.

While it was enlarged and altered at various times in its history, Government House incorporates in its structure a house that is known to have been in existence as far back as 1746, when it belonged to a rich Portuguese merchant named Luis Madera. In 1753, Governor Thomas Saunders bought it from Madera's widow to take the place of the old Governor's Garden House which had been demolished by the French during their occupation of Madras from 1746 to 1749. The house was thus lived in by Governors of Madras from the very moment when the English, having been no more than merchants, became the dominant power in southern India – for it was Saunders who gave the young Robert Clive the chance of commanding the expedition to Arcot, and who backed him throughout his subsequent campaigns.

Clive must have been a guest at the house before he left for England early in 1753, Saunders having rented it for a year previous to buying it. He would also have visited it when it was occupied by Saunders' two immediate successors. The first of these was George Pigot, who led a gallant defence against the Comte de Lally and some of the best regiments of France when they besieged Madras in the winter of 1758-9. During this siege the French captured the Garden House and tried to demolish it, pulling down most of the pillars of the verandah. But before they could complete the work of destruction, they were driven away. This was not the only time the Garden House fell into the hands of an enemy: in 1767 it was seized by Hyder Ali's raiders, the Governor and his Council escaping down the Cooum River in a boat which happened to be handy.

Two years after they had besieged Madras, Lally and some of his officers returned to the Garden House as prisoners, having been defeated by Coote. The damage done by their countrymen had not yet been repaired; but, with the chivalry of those days, they were given such rooms as were still intact and also allowed to ask for whatever food and drink they wanted, regardless of cost. As though in revenge, they consumed far too much, which aggrieved the English. The house was repaired in 1762 and Pigot, a rich bachelor of easy morals, lived there in Oriental luxury, while remaining English enough to keep a pack of hounds, as well as a menagerie of more exotic beasts. He also had a very English love of gardens, adding to the grounds of the Garden House, in which the chief feature was then, as afterwards, the lake; employing a European gardener and twenty Indian gardeners, together with ten 'weeders'.

After living grandly in England for some years, during which time he obtained an Irish peerage, Pigot was obliged for financial reasons to return to Madras as Governor in 1775. A quarrel arose between him and his Council which grew so violent that the Council decided to depose him by force. One night, as he was approaching the gate of the Garden House in his chaise, he was held up at pistol point by a group of officers and taken as a prisoner to a house at St Thomas's Mount. Here he remained in captivity for some months, until, having got sunstroke while gardening and fallen dangerously ill, he was brought back to the Garden House, where – in spite of being nursed devotedly by his natural daughter – he died.

The house was enlarged by Pigot's successor, the notorious 'Nabob' Sir Thomas Rumbold, and again by the military engineer, Archibald Campbell, who was Governor from 1785 to 1789. It was not, however, until the opening years of the new century that it grew into its present size. By then, the Governor was Clive's son, Edward, the second Baron

Clive, the first wealthy aristocrat to occupy the post. Although India was very much in his blood, he had never been there before, and was unused to its discomforts. He found the Garden House 'insufficient either for the private accommodation of my family and staff, or for the convenience of the public occasions inseparable from my situation'. While living there, he was obliged to hold his entertainments at the Fort, or even at the Pantheon, the public assembly rooms. This make-shift arrangement was hardly in accordance with his ideas of British dignity and the honour of the name of Clive; it would have appealed still less to his wife, a daughter of the Earl of Powis. And so, in 1800, he embarked on a scheme to turn the Garden House into Government House – a setting for grand entertainments as well as a permanent resi-dence for the Governor, who had hitherto moved between it and a house in the Fort. He employed as architect John Goldingham, a mathe-matician who had worked in Madras as a surveyor and astronomer, and whom he now appointed Civil Engineer. It could have been Golding-ham's bent for astronomy which recommended him to Lord Clive, whose mother was a keen amateur astronomer, and whose uncle was Nevil Maskelyne, the Astronomer Royal.

Goldingham almost doubled the length of the house, constructed the immense two-storeyed verandah along the main front and round the sides, and remodelled the interior. The entrance hall was beneath a central pediment. From the far end of a long, pillared hall a handsome double staircase with wrought-iron balustrades led up to the Governor's private apartments, and to the two great reception rooms, which were loftier than the rooms on either side of them, rising into roof pavilions above the main skyline. The principal rooms and the staircase were adorned with delicate plasterwork; the walls and pillars being finished in *chunam*, a stucco made of burnt sea-shells which polished like marble, and which was also used for the exterior of the house.

The improvements of Lord Clive and Goldingham extended beyond the house to the grounds, which were landscaped in accordance with fashionable taste. Various out-offices were erected, including a farm yard, stabling for 200 horses and quarters for the Governor's Body-guard; together with a building for Lord Clive's natural history collec-tion and, most spectacular of all, a detached Banquetting Hall in the form of a Tuscan-Doric temple flanking the main front of the house. Raised on a platform with a great ceremonial flight of steps, it not only served as a room for large functions but was also in the nature of a temple of military glory. Trophies of arms in the pediments at either end commemorated the battle of Plassey and the more recent victory over Tipu Sultan at Seringapatam; helmets and urns, symbolising the spoils of war, decorated the frieze; while inside hung a series of full-length portraits of Coote, Cornwallis, General Sir William Medows and other famous soldiers.

The Banquetting Hall was inaugurated in October 1802 with a grand ball to celebrate the Peace of Amiens. The guests, who included all the ladies and gentlemen of the settlement and the officers of the Fleet and Army, were enthralled by what was described at the time as 'the most magnificent and beautiful specimen of architecture which the science and taste of Europe have ever exhibited to natives of India'. Certainly the room must have looked splendid, with its two tiers of glistening columns and its array of lustres.

The Directors of the East India Company were less enchanted when they heard of Lord Clive's great project and its cost. 'It by no means appears to us essential to the well-being of our Government in India that the pomp, magnificence and ostentation of the Native Governments should be adopted by the former; the expense to which such a system would naturally lead must prove highly injurious to our commercial interests' they wrote, Lord Clive having, it seems, justified his expense on the grounds that it was necessary to keep up with the Nawab of Arcot, who had recently built himself a magnificent new palace in the European style nearby at Chepauk. The Directors were not the only critical voice. 'Architects say it requires a new roof, and several other alterations, to render it tolerable to an eye of any taste', a visitor to Madras in 1811 wrote of the Banquetting Hall. Bishop Heber, who saw it in 1826, thought it 'in vile taste'.

To Mountstuart Grant Duff, a Governor of the eighteen-eighties, the architecture of Government House was 'as anomalous as the church in Langham Place'. By that time, however, Goldingham's design had been obscured by later additions. Macaulay's brother-in-law, Sir Charles Trevelyan, added an extra storey to one side of the house during his brief reign as Governor from 1859 to 1860. A typically Indian porte-cochère – with a verandah over it – masked the original pediment. The extra storey did away with two of the three roof pavilions, which meant that the great drawing room at the top of the stairs lost half its height. It was redecorated in the style of a Victorian club house, with dark wooden pilasters.

In other rooms, Goldingham's delicate plasterwork fell a prey to the Madras climate. Yet some of it survived, on the staircase, in the Banquetting Hall, and elsewhere; while the ravages done by Time to the original decorations were redeemed by the building up of a splendid collection of portraits. In the drawing room was a Hoppner of the Duke of Wellington, a portrait of Clive after Nathaniel Dance and a full-length by Sir Thomas Lawrence of the beautiful Lady Munro, who was so loved by everyone in the settlement that they subscribed to have this portrait painted when her husband, Sir Thomas Munro, was still Governor. An impressive group depicting the installation of the last titular Nawab of Arcot greeted the arriving guest in the Lower Hall, and there were more portraits of Nawabs at the top of the stairs. The military heroes in the Banquetting Hall, 'fast going to decay in the moist sea breeze', when Heber saw them, managed to survive and were joined by other Madras worthies, as well as by George III, Queen Charlotte and Queen Victoria. But while the interior of the Banquetting Hall remained unaltered, the exterior became less classical and more Indian with the addition of an arcaded verandah in 1892; though this afforded an excellent place for sitting out during a ball.

If the house displayed numerous architectural solecisms, it was, none the less, entirely suited to its purpose and to the climate; cool and airy, always catching the sea breeze – the Governor's bedroom had as many as twelve doors and windows. Its chief defect was shortage of accommodation, even after the addition of the extra storey. Staff and guests had to overflow into the Marine Villa and the ADC's Bungalow, or, when there was a large party, into tents on the lawn. Seldom were there no guests staying, particularly when the illustrious sportsmen of Europe became increasingly attracted to the big game of the Madras Presidency and the neighbouring state of Mysore. In the early eighteen-sixties, Sir William Denison entertained Prince Frederick of Schleswig-Holstein, and also those bright sparks of the British sporting set, Harry Chaplin and Sir Frederick Johnstone. Grant Duff entertained various travelling royalties, including Duke Paul of Mecklenburg-Schwerin and Don Carlos, the romantic claimant to the Spanish throne; though unfortunately the latter had lost his voice and could only speak in a whisper. A more unusual guest at this time was the veteran Austrian statesman, Baron Hübner, who regaled his host and hostess with memories of Metternich. Apart from such distinguished guests who came privately, there were the periodic Viceregal influxes, as well as visits by three successive Princes of Wales. A group photograph taken during the second of these Royal visits, when the future King George V and Queen Mary stayed with Lord and Lady Ampthill in 1906, shows a house party of thirty strong, not counting the Ampthills' three small sons, who stand smartly to attention dressed in miniature Governor's Bodyguard uniforms.

A Royal or Viceregal visit meant that the round of balls, dinners and receptions at Government House was even dizzier than ever. At any time, however, when the Governor was in residence, the pace was fast enough; so that the history of the house, from the time of the second Lord Clive until the end of the Raj, reads mainly as one long chronicle of entertainments, interrupted neither by the Mutiny, nor by any of the other stirring events of nineteenth century India, which were far away. Madras may have been 'The Benighted Presidency', but the city of Madras was smarter socially than any other British Indian city. Yet even here, the ladies seemed wanting in '*usage du monde*' to someone like the beautiful and accomplished Lady Canning, who was a close friend of Queen Victoria and had been familiar with the court of Louis Philippe: 'They just stuck in their foreheads and chins', she recalled, 'and never stirred when introduced.'

Following Lord Clive's ball for the Peace of Amiens, we hear of a splendid dinner given by the next Governor, Lord William Bentinck, given in honour of that early fashionable tourist, Lord Valentia, who thought that he and his fellow-guests 'looked like pygmies' in the lofty Banquetting Hall. A less exalted traveller, Mr James Wathen, attended a ball at Government House a few years later, and expressed himself 'much gratified by the appearance of a great number of my lovely countrywomen who displayed their charms to great advantage in the mazes of the sprightly dance'.

Mrs J. C. Maitland, in her *Letters from Madras*, quotes an Indian newspaper's account of a ball at Government House in the eighteen-thirties: 'The Nawab entered with a grand *suwarree* of a hundred guards, and a hundred lanterns all in one line, and appeared like a man of penetration. The English danced together pleasantly after their fashion, shaking each other's hands, and then proceeded to make their supper, when the respectable natives all retired'. By 'respectable natives' the paper meant, of course, the higher caste Hindus, who were unable to eat what Mrs Maitland called 'our pariah food.' This was only one of the problems attendant on inviting Indians to Government House balls.

1   Government House, Madras, and the Banquetting Hall, about 1807.

2   Government House, Madras, towards the end of the nineteenth century.

3   Government House, Calcutta, from the east, about 1820. The Governor-General, Lord Hastings, driving in the carriage.

4   Government House, Calcutta, the south front, about 1870.

There was also the question of the wives, who were not usually brought by their husbands, but who often came incognito with the servants to watch the fun. Lady Hobart, in the eighteen-seventies, refused to invite Indians to balls unless they brought their wives with them. As a consolation for those whose principles forbade this, she gave an Indian-style entertainment with music and fireworks; she also gave parties specially for Indian ladies.

Then there was the problem of the Prince of Arcot, whose ancestors had been the East India Company's theoretical overlords at Madras, and whose more recent forebears had kept up considerable state as titular Nawabs; but who by the second half of the nineteenth century had diminished in grandeur, while remaining very conscious of their dignity. When Prince Azim Jah, no longer the glittering potentate of a hundred guards but 'an elderly man in a tumbled and rather dirty white muslin dress' with a handful of followers as shabby as himself, arrived at the Queen's Birthday Ball in 1861, he became 'as sulky as a bear' because Mr Morehead, the Councillor standing in for the Governor, who had fever, met him at the top of the Banquetting Hall steps instead of at the bottom. He was already in a bad mood, believing that the Governor had invented his illness to slight him. This same Prince of Arcot stayed away altogether from a subsequent ball because the Governor had warned him that he would be unable to come down the steps to meet him owing to a sprained ankle. He later seems to have grown less touchy, contenting himself with publishing a pamphlet on his ancestors, with details of the various occasions when former Governors invited them to breakfast. Early in the present century a Prince of Arcot boosted his morale by purchasing a Rolls-Royce, the first ever to be seen in Madras. It is said that when he tried it out he was bitterly disappointed, for it was quite silent. 'Nobody will know I am coming!' he lamented. However, a local mechanic was able to loosen a few screws – surely unbeknown to the gentlemen in Derby – and the Prince was happy.

The Prince of Arcot was not the only Indian prince to attend the Government House balls. There were others, more colourful and less difficult to handle. Young Ella Druitt, who lived at Government House in 1872 and 1873 when her father was physician to Lord Hobart, was impressed by their cloth of gold tunics and diamond head-dresses at the first ball she attended. There were other 'dark people' there, no less colourfully clad; while the fashionable European ladies and the officers

33

in exotic Indian army uniforms made a wonderful sight as they waltzed languidly round the Banquetting Hall floor, which had been polished beforehand by fifteen men sitting on their heels, using coconuts cut in halves. Poor Ella, who had taken such trouble to look nice, getting her *ayah*, Rachel, to braid her hair, soaking herself in ammonia and glycerine to reduce her mosquito bites, felt rather dowdy in that brilliant crowd; her skirt was 'very scanty', and the bottom flounce nearly got torn off. She must surely have looked better on a subsequent occasion when she wore a Turkish dress, though less gorgeous than Lady Hobart in her Indian dress of soft white silk with 'real gold spots' and a 'real gold fringe'. Ten years later Mrs Grant Duff excelled this by coming to one of her fancy dress balls as Starlight, with powdered hair and a dress of silver and diamonds. That particular ball was attended by two Maharanis of Travancore, an unheard-of event which caused much surprise.

The Grant Duffs were partial to fancy dress; they gave one ball to which everybody had to come in Indian materials. At another, their party appeared as the Court of Louis Treize, with Mrs Grant Duff as Anne of Austria and the ADCs as the Three Musketeers. Colonel Herbert impersonated his own ancestor, Clive, copying the portrait in the drawing room; while Miss Gordon, the granddaughter of Sir Walter Scott's secretary, came as The Cloud with the Silver Lining. These costumes, however, caused less of a sensation than did the newly-invented electric lights which, cunningly concealed in bouquets of flowers, illuminated the supper tables at a ball given in the following year, 1886, during the visit of the Viceroy and Vicereine, Lord and Lady Dufferin. That night, the Southern Cross was clearly visible to the guests as they strolled to and fro between the house and the Banquetting Hall; as though the heavens were competing with the Government House electrician in honouring the Viceregal pair. It was March, and already getting hot; there was a large bank of ice at one end of the dance floor, surrounded by ferns. Lady Dufferin found it particularly pleasant to dine in the open verandah, beneath the swinging *punkahs*. This was the usual venue for the smaller Government House dinners, when the monsoon was not raging; the larger parties – like the Scotch dinner in December 1884 when six pipers played – took place in the Banquetting Hall. In a single season the Grant Duffs gave dinner to 1,089 people, not including their own party and house guests.

More austere among the Government House entertainments were

the weekly 'public breakfasts' which any gentleman in the settlement could attend by merely writing his name in the book; their purpose being to enable the Governor to talk informally with his civilians and officers. Then there were the garden parties, a military band playing beneath a wide-spreading banyan tree. A smaller company attended the Government House amateur theatricals, which recalled the long-vanished theatre built in the grounds by a temporary Governor named Whitehill in 1780. Everybody, according to Ella Druitt, wept 'for sorrowful emotion' at *Maître Jacques*; while Sheridan's *Critic* made the audience 'cry with laughter'. During Ella's stay there was also a concert – the Overture from the *Magic Flute* and selections from Mendelssohn's *Midsummer Night's Dream* – as well as a 'grand entertainment' by a Japanese juggler, when the programmes were printed on blue and white satin edged with lace. At the dinner beforehand a musk rat ran into the room and up the dress of one of the young ladies who had to be washed and 'deluged in cologne' before she was fit to rejoin the company.

The festivities of Government House were not entirely limited to fashionable society. Ella mentions a large party given by Lady Hobart for orphans; while Lady Denison describes a visit to the Bodyguard Lines during *Mohurrum*, the yearly commemoration of the death of Hassan and Hussein, a period of fasting and mourning among the stricter Shiah Muslims, but in the Madras of the eighteen-sixties, a saturnalia for the whole populace. There was a vast crowd of Indians in a tent illuminated with candles and blue lights, at one end of which stood a representation of the tomb of Hassan and Hussein made of paper and talc. People sang, acted and performed gymnastic feats; sweetmeats were handed round and the Governor and his party were decked with garlands and had rose water and attar of roses poured onto their handkerchiefs. The most spectacular – as well as the most democratic – entertainment of all was during the visit of Albert Edward, Prince of Wales, in 1875, when the surf was illuminated by thousands of floating lights, lit by men with torches who dashed through the breakers in flimsy catamarans and *masula* boats. The Prince's host at Madras was the last Duke of Buckingham and Chandos, the only Ducal Governor India ever had; whose fortune, though depleted by his father, was large enough for him to revive, at Government House, something of the lavish hospitality of his forebears at Stowe.

Much of the Prince of Wales's time at Madras was spent in receiving visits from the potentates of southern India. He received some of them ceremonially, and others in private, including the widowed Maharani of Tanjore, who talked to him and shook his hand through a hole in a screen, since no man was supposed to look on her face. The more formal audiences were similar to those held by the Governor when he was alone in his glory, and not overshadowed by a Royal Personage. The second Lord Clive's ideas of grandeur, which had so dismayed the gentlemen of Leadenhall Street, became the accepted rule with the growth of British power. Sir William Denison found Madras very different from his previous Government House in Australia. No sooner did he call 'Peon!' than a servant was at his elbow; when he walked in the park, a man followed him with an umbrella; when he rode, a syce ran behind him. There were, at that time, 205 servants at Government House; many of whom, according to the time-honoured custom, slept on mats in the verandahs and passages. They ranged from the army of butlers and *khitmagars* with scarlet and gold sashes down to the 'dreadful looking harridans' – as Sir William unkindly called them – who made the beds; and, still further down the hierarchy, the lowly but indispensable sweepers. As well as the servants, there was the Governor's Bodyguard, who originally wore a Hussar uniform in dark blue and silver, but later changed to a Lancer full dress of scarlet with yellow facings.

Grant Duff was once reminded of his own sublimity by receiving a petition addressed to 'The Almighty God, care of the Rt Hon Mountstuart E. Grant Duff, Governor of Madras'. To most of the thirty-five million inhabitants of the Madras Presidency the Governor *was* next to God; separated from Him only by the Viceroy and the Sovereign who were figures so remote as to constitute no barrier. The Governor was the Lord Sahib, regardless of whether he was a peer, a knight, or indeed plain Mr Grant Duff. Yet Government House was never quite as formal as the Viceregal court. When Sir William Denison had to act as Viceroy following the death of Lord Elgin, he felt oppressed by the atmosphere of Calcutta: the sentries at the top and bottom of his private stairs, the custom by which his Staff kept silence at breakfast unless spoken to by him. He thought the Madras Government House was four times as comfortable as Wellesley's great palace, where he passed a lonely Christmas, longing 'for a child to romp with'.

While the Viceroy spent long hours at his desk, the Governor of Madras, with his less arduous duties, was able to enjoy some of the simpler pleasures of life. Early in the morning – and at other times of the day during the brief 'cold weather', which was like a hot European summer, with a delicious breeze – Grant Duff botanized in the park, marking the trees and shrubs with labels. After lunch he sat quietly in the verandah – 'I have right before me the Bay of Bengal, covered with white horses, while the surf booms like the roar of a great city' – and threw food to the kites; he never tired of watching 'the perfect grace, strength and amiability to each other' of these birds. He went walking in the cool of the evening and after dark; on one such walk, the full moon rising out of a bank of clouds reminded him of 'a scene for the opera – nothing but the prima donna wanting'.

For those not burdened with the cares of office, or with the multitudinous activities of a Governor's wife, the life at Government House was a delicious combination of gaiety and leisure, of Eastern magnificence and the joys of an English country house party. One can imagine what it must have been like for Ella Druitt, the doctor's daughter straight from England, to find herself in such a world. Her stay began inauspiciously: on the way from the ship to Government House, when she was all set to be presented for the first time to Lady Hobart, wearing 'the light coloured dress with violet trimmings, absolutely the *only* decent thing I had left, what did that naughty little Topsy do but misbehave herself in my lap'. However, Lady Hobart was very understanding and allowed Ella to retire at once to her room, where she waited until her trunks arrived and she was able to change into 'a white dress trimmed with lace'.

She soon became quite at home, and found it easy to pick up the local Indian language; her father attributed this to her knowledge of Latin. She also learnt to ride, though not without falling off and giving herself a black eye. The time went quickly, because it was generally too hot to hurry, so that any occupation was very time-consuming. She tried to make friends with the antelopes in the park; she watched the many strange birds and listened to their song; she sat languidly while Topsy chased squirrels and lizards on the verandah. Then came the excitement of a new ADC, the 'young, handsome, very merry' Captain Foot, who sang, danced, acted, in fact did 'everything to perfection'; he could even play the penny whistle. We do not, however, know if Ella was paid serious attentions by either this paragon or any of the multitude of other young eligibles in Madras; though marriage must surely have been the object of her journey to India with her father, since her mother stayed behind in England. Her father's description of her in a letter to her mother as 'plump and in good condition, but dreadfully bitten by mosquitoes' suggests no outstanding beauty; but at any rate her charms were such as appealed to an elderly Armenian jewel dealer named Mr Araboun, who, having seen her at a ball, called on her afterwards and with many 'gallant speeches' gave her a verse on scented paper:

> 'In the assemblage of beauties where many are seen
> Isabella Druitt is surely the queen.
> Her head so beautiful with loveliness crowned
> Embellish a face with mildness adorned.
> Her figure so graceful with complexion bright
> Shows her at once a perfection at sight'.

Reading it, while Mr Araboun watched her, she found it hard not to laugh. However, she expressed her appreciation and Mr Araboun called again, this time bringing her a diamond ring. Rather surprisingly, her father let her keep it. 'I think India is a very nice place to come to,' she declared with some smugness, when writing of this gift to her mother.

The particular chapter in the history of Government House described in Ella's letters ended tragically in 1875 when Lord Hobart was struck down by typhoid. Immense and sorrowful crowds lined his funeral route from Government House to St Mary's Church in the Fort, where he was buried alongside Pigot and two other Governors, Sir Thomas Munro and Sir George Ward, both of whom died of cholera – the latter within a few weeks of assuming office in 1860. Sudden death always lurked behind the grandeur and gaiety of nineteenth-century India, even at Government House, Madras. Grant Duff received a stark reminder of this when his African valet, to whom he was much attached, fell a victim to the same dread disease. Yet Government House saw less sorrow than would be expected, considering the length of its history. For this reason, and also perhaps because Madras is noticeably free of that rather sinister melancholy which, elsewhere in India, is never far below the charm, the house kept a cheerful atmosphere. It was, however, the scene of a different sort of domestic drama in the time of Grant Duff's successor, Lord Connemara, an Irishman of magnificent looks who was over-fond of the fair sex. One night Lady Connemara, no longer able to stand her husband's infidelities, fled from

Government House and took refuge at the hotel now called the Conne-mara; in fact it is said to have so named itself in honour of having sheltered the Governor's wife.

Just as the house could not be wholly insulated from human tragedy, so was it not entirely cut off from the real India outside its gates. Sir William Denison, taking his morning stroll in the town immediately behind Government House, found himself among a mass of low huts, where men, women and children swarmed. He had never before realized that Indians lived in such cramped conditions; he afterwards recalled that the huts were quite clean, but that 'the alley was awful'. Sixty years earlier, Lord Clive had complained of the noise from some of these huts which were then even closer; at his orders, the main road was moved further back, the huts cleared away and the people com-pensated.

The road, however, was still close enough for the inhabitants of Government House to hear the noise whenever there was an Indian festival. Lady Denison has left an account of one *Mohurrum*. A sound of drumming grew louder as night fell, swelling into an uproar. The glare of red lights reflected on the wall of the room in which the Governor's wife and her small son were sitting; so they went to watch from a verandah. The road was lit up in red and blue, and there was a babel of sound: drums, squeaking fifes, Indian music, shouts, roars, cries of all sorts; and over it all, the starry tropical night. 'Mamma, do you think the people ought to make that tiger music on Sunday?' asked her son, and she agreed that 'they *were* sad sounds for a Sunday evening, so different from the quiet of an English town at such times'.

The proximity of Government House to the teeming centre of the town may have been why Sir William Denison – and sixty years later, Lord Willingdon – considered turning it into offices and living per-manently at Guindy, the Governor's country residence six miles away to the south. But somehow they never brought themselves to abandon the old house. It has, however, been abandoned in favour of Guindy by the present-day Indian Governors, and given over to the State Legisla-ture. The people of Madras are conservative, and have an affection for the monuments of British rule; the house and Banquetting Hall are well maintained. The portraits in the Banquetting Hall remain undisturbed, as does the statue of George V outside the main gate; though the trophies of Plassey and Seringapatam have been replaced by the arms of the new India.

But while those now responsible for Government House treat it with respect, it has the forlorn air of a house no longer lived in. Worse, a skyscraper has gone up in the middle of the park. So let us leave the house not in the present but in the golden afternoon of the Raj, when it was described in a charming book on South India illustrated in colour by Lady Lawley, whose husband was Governor from 1906 to 1911. The sun is beginning to go down and the breeze quickening. In a brilliantly polished landau drawn by prancing horses, the Governor sets out for his drive. On the box sits Adam, the head coachman, resplendent in scarlet and gold livery; other servants, also in scarlet, perch behind; behind again clatters a mounted escort of the Bodyguard, their accoutrements glinting in the westerly sun. Muniswami, the head butler, a rotund, grey-moustached figure who has served many Governors and waited on Lord Roberts, is left standing at the top of the steps under the porte-cochère. As the noise of the cavalcade dies away, the boom of the surf and the song of the birds can be heard once again. The potted palms and chrysanthemums grouped around the bases of the columns quiver slightly.

2

GOVERNMENT HOUSE
CALCUTTA

FROM at least the time of Clive, the English Governor in Calcutta kept up a certain state. He was attended by *chobdars* or mace bearers; he had a mounted bodyguard; there were always many guests at his table. When, however, the young Irish peer, Richard Wellesley, Earl of Mornington, arrived in Calcutta as Governor-General in 1798, bringing with him stores, carriages and baggage valued at £2,000, he invested his office with a Viceregal grandeur quite unknown to his predecessors, setting the tone for all those who came after him, despite the attempts of some of them – and also of the commercially-minded East India Company Directors – to revert to the old simplicity.

Less than a month after his arrival, Mornington decided that the existing Government House, which was no different from the mansions of the leading Calcutta citizens, was unworthy of his station. So he ordered that it should be pulled down and a palace erected on the site, which was to be enlarged by the purchase and clearance of adjoining properties. He employed as architect Lieutenant Charles Wyatt of the Bengal Engineers, whose relationship to the great family of architects has not been established. Building commenced in 1799, by which time the Governor-General was engaged in a more serious matter, the war against Tipu Sultan. Tipu was defeated and killed, Mornington being created Marquess Wellesley as a reward for this success, in which his younger brother, Arthur, the future Duke of Wellington, played a prominent part. The palace that was rising up in Calcutta thus became a symbol of the growth of British power.

It was finished four years later, at a cost of £63,291. The Directors

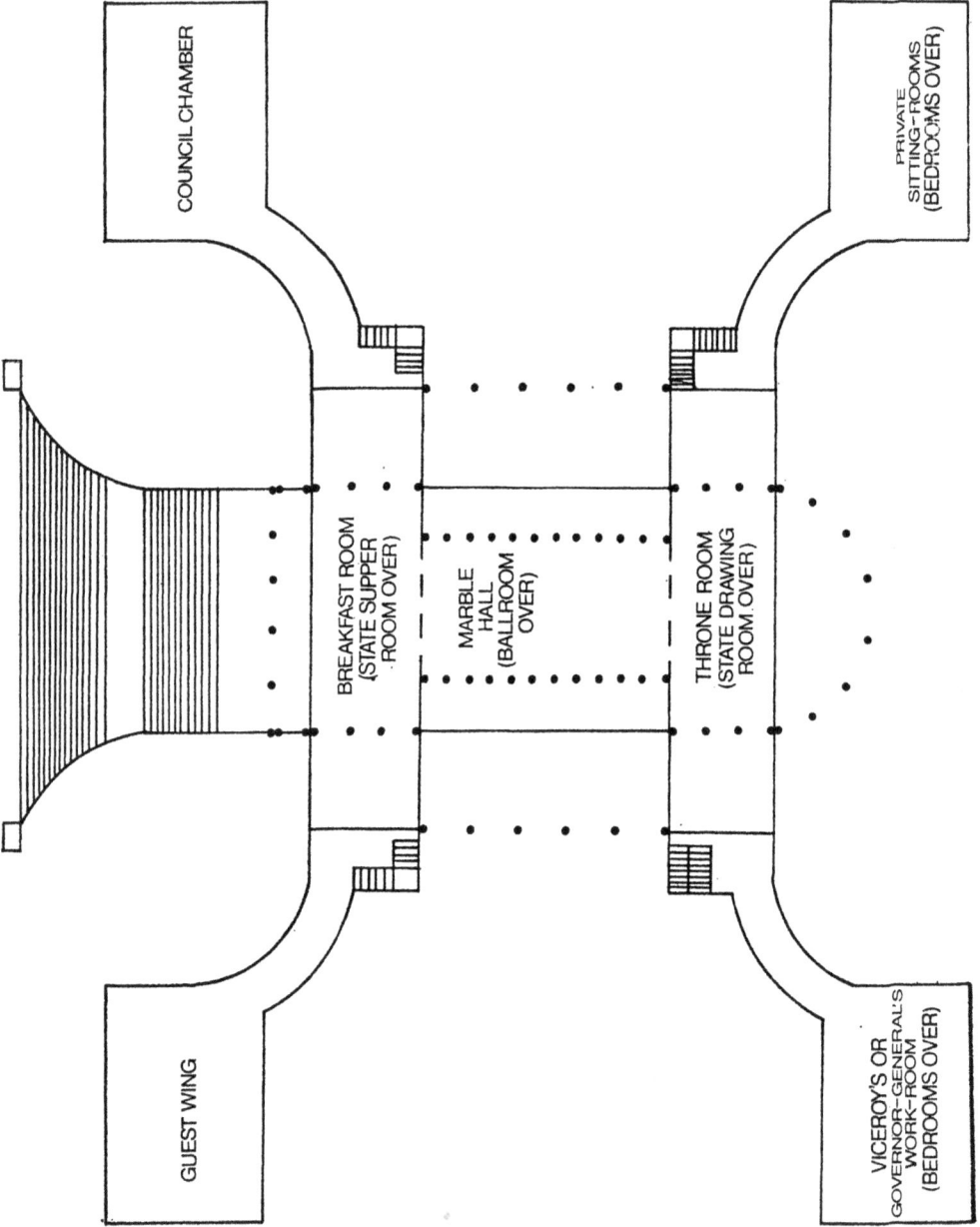

COUNCIL CHAMBER

PRIVATE
SITTING-ROOMS
(BEDROOMS OVER)

BREAKFAST ROOM
(STATE SUPPER
ROOM OVER)

MARBLE
HALL
(BALLROOM
OVER)

THRONE ROOM
(STATE DRAWING
ROOM OVER)

GUEST WING

VICEROY'S OR
GOVERNOR-GENERAL'S
WORK-ROOM
(BEDROOMS OVER)

regarded this sum as excessive, and punished Wellesley's extravagance by recalling him; but even in those days, it was remarkably little for what is probably the finest governor's palace in the world. The splendour of its Ionic façades is matched only by the admirable simplicity of its great rooms. It is a house ideally suited to the climate, catching the breeze from all four quarters thanks to its plan, which is, as is well known, an adaptation of the plan of Kedleston Hall in Derbyshire, a central block containing the state apartments joined to four wings by curving corridors. The corridors and wings are of the same height as the central block and treated continuously with it, creating a far more palatial effect than at Kedleston, where they are subordinate.

Despite this and other notable differences, Government House is popularly believed to be an actual copy of the Derbyshire mansion; and the story is told that when the resemblance was pointed out to Lord Curzon, whose home Kedleston was, he remarked, with his celebrated short 'a', that whereas the pillars at Kedleston were of alabaster, those at Government House were only of lath and plaster. One doubts if Curzon, who was second to none in his admiration of Government House, and who, from an early age, was fully versed in the points of resemblance, as well as the obvious differences, between it and his own home, ever made this remark; he would, moreover, have known that the pillars supporting the ceilings at Government House were not of lath and plaster but of brick covered with *chunam*.

During the first half of the nineteenth century, Government House dominated the Calcutta scene in a way that no other building did; standing stark behind its railings, in grounds that were devoid of even a single tree. It made an impressive showing from all four sides; gleaming white or ochre, depending on what colour it had been painted after the last monsoon. From Tank Square, later called Dalhousie Square, the business centre of the town, its main portico and the immense flight of steps which each new Governor-General or Viceroy would ascend in state could be seen through the northern entrance to the grounds. From the opposite direction, the south front with its dome could be seen at a great distance, facing across the open space of the Maidan towards Fort William. The east front, flanked by a pair of arched gateways crowned with lions, dominated Old Court House Street, the thoroughfare joining the business quarter with the fashionable residential neighbourhood of Chowringhi; while the west front formed a background to the forest of masts on the Hughli.

The ceremonial steps on the north front led up to the first of the three great state apartments which, on each of the two main floors, filled the entire centre block. This was known as the Breakfast Room, since it was originally used for the Governor-General's 'Public Breakfasts', informal male gatherings where business could be talked. Its proportions were those of a gallery, more than a hundred feet long, each end being screened by columns. A room of similar size and proportions, which in later years was the Throne Room, balanced the Breakfast Room in the south front; and the two were joined by the much broader Marble Hall, running from north to south, with two rows of Doric columns and windows on either side giving onto verandahs. There were three similar rooms on the floor above, that over the Marble Hall being the Ballroom, with Ionic columns instead of Doric. The two southern wings contained the private apartments of the Governor-General or Viceroy and his family; one of the two northern wings contained the Council Chamber, while the other was for guests.

As well as being practical, the plan was spacially effective, with vistas in all directions: broad straight vistas through the main rooms, curving vistas along the corridors where the ceiling beams, high overhead, made strange angles and shadows. Though there were simple coffered ceilings in the Ballroom and some of the other state apartments, the Marble Hall and most of the lesser rooms had ceilings of painted beams. Originally, the ceilings of the Marble Hall and Ballroom were adorned with canvases of gods and goddesses by an artist named Creuse; but these were soon eaten by termites. The Calcutta climate made for austerity, with white as the prevailing colour, and acres of uncluttered floor; gleaming grey marble in the lower storey, polished teak upstairs.

The furnishings were always sparse, though there was enough to prevent the house from seeming empty: a fascinating and ever-growing series of portraits; statues of Wellesley and Dalhousie facing each other from either end of the Breakfast Room; busts of the Twelve Caesars ranged along the walls of the Marble Hall; a magnificent collection of lustres, some of them from Constantia, the palace of the French military adventurer, General Claude Martin, at Lucknow. Wellesley himself contributed a gilded seat that had belonged to Tipu Sultan; Lord Mayo imported Louis Seize chairs and settees for the State Drawing Room, adjoining the Ballroom; Lord Dufferin adorned the same room with mirrors from the palace of the deposed Burmese King, Theebaw.

At times, however, the furnishings of Government House were decrepit. Lord Dalhousie, on his arrival in 1848, reported that one of the beds had collapsed through 'sheer age'. There was also a shortage of linen, china and plate, together with a complete dearth of books. Each Governor-General or Viceroy was expected to bring plate of his own, and, moreover, was charged customs duty on it, Lord Canning having to pay as much as £400.

The earlier inhabitants of Government House did without a garden, being surrounded by bare grass and expanses of gravel – which Lord Hastings, in 1818, imported all the way from Bayswater. Lady Amherst, the wife of the next Governor-General, laid out some magnificent flower beds; but they were swept away by her successor, Lady William Bentinck, who thought flowers unwholesome. There were further attempts at gardening by Emily and Fanny Eden, who kept house for their bachelor brother, Lord Auckland; and when Lady Canning arrived here in 1856 she found 'Cape jessamine as high as shrubbery laurels', strongly scented roses, oleanders, euphorbias, and other flowers. But save for a few scattered palms there were still hardly any trees, so that, at the time of the Mutiny, passers-by could see, through the railings, the solitary figure of Lord Canning, pacing quickly round and round, the only exercise he permitted himself during those anxious months.

It was only after 1870 that a definite scheme of planting was put in hand by Lord and Lady Mayo, and continued by their successors, Lord Northbrook and Lord and Lady Lytton, so that by the 'eighties there was a thick screen of trees, palms and bamboos to give seclusion, together with shady walks by ornamental pools and a raised mound. The immediate surroundings of the house remained open and formal, broad expanses of lawn, gravel and flower-bed liberally sprinkled with guns captured in various campaigns; the most spectacular of which was Chinese, mounted on a fearsome iron dragon.

Soon after Government House was finished, it was visited by Lord Valentia, who thought it 'a noble structure, although not without faults in the architecture'. He considered the money it had cost to have been well spent: 'India is a country of splendour, of extravagance and of outward appearances . . . the Head of a mighty Empire ought to conform himself to the prejudices of the country he rules over . . . in short, I wish India to be ruled from a palace, not from a counting-house.' A writer of the eighteen-twenties described Government House as 'a most august and beautiful fabric', while an architectural expert of fifty years later, when taste had so much changed, believed that there were 'few modern palaces of its class either more appropriate in design, or more effective in their architectural arrangement and play of light and shade'.

The Amir of Afghanistan, Dost Mohammed, who came to Calcutta as a refugee in the time of Lord Auckland, asked if there was really in Europe a larger palace than Government House. And to show what sort of impression the house made on a less exalted Oriental, there is the account of a Malay *munshi*, who in 1810 attended one of the Public Disputations of the short-lived College of Fort William, held here in the presence of the Governor-General and some of the Calcutta élite. The susceptible Malay quite lost his heart to a bevy of pregnant English ladies, imagining them to be the wives of the Governor-General; this may have added to the enthusiasm with which he wrote of the occasion.

'How beautiful is this palace, and great its extent – who can describe it! Who can relate the riches of this country, and, above all, the beauty of the palace! When I entered the great gates, and looked around from my palanquin (for in this country even I, Ibrahim, the son of Candu the merchant, had my palanquin) and when I beheld the beauty and extent of the compound, the workmanship of the gates . . . on the tops of which lions, carved out of stones, as large as life, seem small, and as if they were running without fearing to fall, I thought that I was no longer in the world I had left in the east . . . The floors of the great hall are of black stone, polished and shining like a mirror, so that I feared to walk on them; and all around, how many transparent lustres and branches for lights were suspended, dazzling and glistening so that I could not look for long upon them! Until I arrived at the second storey, the stairs were all of stone, which formed part of the wall, and had no support. I then entered the great hall where all the Tuans were assembled . . . at the end of the hall is a throne, superlatively beautiful, supported by four pillars of gold, and having hangings of the colour of blood, enriched with golden fringe . . .'

There was, nevertheless, plenty of criticism of Government House, both at the time when it was built, and afterwards. Bishop Heber felt that it 'narrowly missed being a noble structure'. The fact that none of the four interior stairs was of a grandeur commensurate with such a palace – though they were hardly 'dingy' and 'miserable' as Sir Charles

D'Oyly described them in a satirical verse – was generally regarded as a grave defect; while there were those who objected to the dome as being merely, as D'Oyly put it, 'a wood box perched up alone, To aid proportion and for dumpiness to atone', not covering any domed apartment.

And while the house was basically practical, there were many who found it inconvenient. Emily and Fanny Eden complained of being 'far as the poles asunder'; for their rooms were in opposite wings, separated by the length of two corridors and by the echoing space of the state apartments in between. When they made the long pilgrimage to visit each other at night, they were liable to trip over sleeping servants, like 'bales of living white muslin'. During a large evening levee held by Lord Dufferin, the ladies of the house-party, except for those fortunate enough to be sleeping in the wing where they had been sitting, found themselves cut off from their bedrooms by crowds of gentlemen in all the intervening apartments.

If the Viceregal family lived entirely in the south-west wing, they had to be content with a sitting-room on the second floor, which made Lady Canning feel as though she was 'recovering from a long illness'; for the lower floor of this wing was taken up with the Governor-General's or Viceroy's work-room. If, like the Dufferins, they packed themselves into the other 'elephant's paw' on this side of the house, it meant that the Viceroy slept a Sabbath day's journey away from where he worked – no little hardship since he usually had to work until well into the small hours. So while the Vicereine generally slept above her husband's work-room in the south-west wing, she had her sitting-room on the lower floor of the south-east wing opening on to a verandah under the colonnade, where convolvulus entwined itself round the bases of the pillars and green parakeets nested in the capitals. Lady Canning found it a difficult room to arrange, for it had nine doors, of which all but one were always left open; and she knew from bitter experience that no chairs or sofas would be sat on unless they were 'under the influence of the line of *punkahs* along the centre'. However, she managed to avoid what she regarded as the stereotyped Indian arrangement of 'round tables in the middle, chairs all round, and an ottoman beyond on each side'; and with the help of chintz, blue Sèvres, miniatures and prints of the Royal children she was able to make the room 'pretty and cool and English'.

While the family could in this way have a comfortable sitting-room, they had no private dining room, but were obliged to eat in the Marble Hall or in the adjoining Throne Room whether they were on their own or entertaining a banquet of a hundred guests. Then, for all its vast size, the house was short of bedrooms. The north-west wing afforded spacious accommodation for one or two honoured guests; a few more could be fitted in with the family on the south side; but a large party overflowed into tents on the lawn, as usually happened in India. Another Indian custom, the separation of the kitchen from the rest of the house, to keep away the heat and smell of cooking, was here taken to extremes; for the kitchen was not just outside the house but outside the grounds, in one of the narrow and inevitably squalid streets that flanked the northern approach. 'The kitchen is somewhere in Calcutta, but not in this house' was Lady Dufferin's trite comment soon after her arrival. The food had to travel 200 yards in *dhoolies* or boxes on poles carried on men's shoulders. Servants' quarters, stables, coach houses and the Private Secretary's office were relegated to neighbouring premises. It was not until the opening years of the present century that Lord Curzon cleared these streets and erected ranges of offices on their site.

Later again, when the house was the residence of the Governor of Bengal, the western aisle of the Marble Hall was screened off to form a kitchen; so that the Governor and his guests dined to the smell of cooking and the noise of clattering plates. This ghastly expedient not only made the room lopsided, but deprived it of its remaining light; for by that time three *malis* or gardeners and their families had somehow acquired squatters' rights on the verandah at the other side, blocking it up with coconut matting to form their dwellings. Only after Lord Brabourne had become Governor in 1937, and his wife had encountered a ragged little boy with advanced measles running about in the Marble Hall itself, were the *malis* housed more suitably elsewhere. The Brabournes also moved the kitchen into an addition on the west side of the house, and were thus able to restore the Marble Hall to its original beauty.

Lord Curzon was the great modernizer of Government House. He replaced the old green-painted wooden tubs with fixed baths, though there had in fact been hot and cold running water for the past twenty years. The house had been lit by gas since as far back as 1857 – its advent serving to distract Lord and Lady Canning from the Mutiny, which was then raging – but in Lord Curzon's time it was first lit by electricity. He

5   Government House, Calcutta, the Marble Hall. From a photograph taken during the Viceroyalty of the ninth Earl of Elgin, 1894–1899.

6   Barrackpore, the House, with the reach of the river and the Temple of Fame in the foreground, 1825.

7   Barrackpore, elephants and bodyguard in the Park, 1820.

8   Barrackpore, the Menagerie.

also introduced electric lifts – one of them, a magnificent overgrown bird cage of wrought iron, still survives – and electric fans, while keeping the old hand *punkahs* in the Marble Hall and the other state apartments, preferring their 'measured sweep' to what he called 'the hideous anachronism of the revolving blades'.

A peculiarity of Government House remarked on by many was the fact that the normal entrance was by a door in a dark tunnel beneath the great ceremonial steps, which served as a porte-cochère; the steps themselves were only used by the Governor-General or Viceroy on his state arrival or departure, and by visiting potentates. The door led into a low and dimly lit hall beneath the Marble Hall, which made Miss Emma Roberts, a visitor of 1835, feel as though she was 'on the point of being conducted to some hideous dungeon as a prisoner of state'. In her time, the basement hall was not improved by serving as a dump for rubbish, which was 'piled confusedly' behind the pillars; such objects as the fire engine and the Government House printing press took on a sinister aspect in the gloom and put Miss Roberts in mind of instruments of torture; while the palanquin bearers of the other guests, sleeping peacefully on the floor wrapped in their cloths, were transformed by her imagination into 'the dead bodies of the victims to a tyrannical Government'.

On either side of this dim underworld lay the offices of the Military Secretary, the Comptroller of the Household and the ADCs, who between them looked after a household of nearly a thousand, assisted by a regiment of *babus* to whom fell such tasks as writing out invitations. Also in the basement was the room where those wishing to be presented to the Governor-General or Viceroy handed their names to the ADC-in-waiting, according to the procedure laid down by Wellesley, out of whose regulations grew the traditional etiquette of the Viceregal Court as well as of the provincial Government Houses.

Together with the protocol, Wellesley instituted much of the pageantry of Government House. He believed it necessary for the Governor-General to 'entrench' himself 'within forms and ceremonies' as a protection against what he called the 'stupidity and ill-bred familiarity' of Calcutta society; while at the same time he was friendly and unbending towards those whom he invited to his table. He would give young officers an open invitation to come to whatever meals they pleased; but when he held a Levee or Ball he would make his entry to the sound of trumpets and process to the Throne attended by his Staff and Bodyguard in their glittering uniforms, together with servants bearing the traditional Indian emblems of royalty: the gold and silver sticks and maces, the peacock fans, the *chowri* or whisk made of a yak's tail.

The great ball which Wellesley gave in January 1803 to celebrate the Peace of Amiens – the first and perhaps the most magnificent entertainment ever held at Government House – opened in this manner. Eight hundred Europeans were invited, as well as a number of distinguished Indians. The dancing was followed by a sit-down supper in the Marble Hall, and then by fireworks, with transparencies and huge set-pieces including a battle of pyrotechnic elephants. The whole surrounding city was illuminated, and the side of the Fort facing Government House became, in the words of Lord Valentia, who was present, 'a blaze of light'. But though the fireworks and illuminations cost over £3,000, they were not an unqualified success, largely because the rush-lights had been robbed of oil by the populace. Lord Amherst was to achieve a more spectacular effect at his ball in April 1828 in honour of the heroes of the First Burma War, when George IV, the two victorious generals and the cities of Bhurtpore and Ava were portrayed in thousands of lights on the front of Government House.

There was little need to improve on Wellesley's ceremonial when, in 1858, the Crown took over the remaining prerogatives of the East India Company and the then Governor-General, Lord Canning, became the first Viceroy. Lady Canning, at the time, envisaged little change, while recording her husband's dismay at the prospect of 'Drawing Rooms and *kissing*'. If anything, the Viceregal court became less formal, and, though the Viceroy had henceforth to receive the curtsies of the ladies, he did not, in the manner of his brother-Viceroy in Dublin, have to kiss them. The *chobdars* with the gold and silver sticks and maces disappeared except on state occasions, having previously attended the Governor-General at all times, as well as his wife: thus when Lady Amherst visited the Calcutta Botanic Gardens with Bishop Heber in 1823, she was accompanied not only by mace-bearers, but also by two men with gilt spears, and two with swords and bucklers. But if the Vicereine of later years was deprived of all these trappings, she was at least able to enter the Ballroom with her husband, whereas until the time of Lady Canning, who insisted on the rule being changed, the Governor-General made his state entry by himself, leaving his wife to come in afterwards through a side door.

From the time of the Cannings until the end of the Raj, the state kept up at the Viceregal court remained more or less constant; except during the reign of John Lawrence, the only Indian Civilian ever to become Viceroy, who brought to Government House something of the simplicity of his earlier life in the Punjab. But in the first half of the century, splendour and simplicity tended to alternate. The veteran Lord Cornwallis, who became Governor-General for a second time after Wellesley, carried out a deliberate policy of retrenchment. His economies were, however, cut short by his death, and his successor, Lord Minto, reverted to something of Wellesley's state, while personally finding it irksome. Lord Moira, afterwards Marquess of Hastings, and his wife, who was the first Lady Sahib at Government House – Wellesley and Minto having left their wives in Europe and Cornwallis having been a widower – outdid even Wellesley and behaved in an exceedingly royal manner. Calcutta society regarded them as too formal; the ladies were expected to appear at Government House in Court plumes, which meant that many of them had to stay at home owing to the shortage of ostrich feathers.

Ten years later, everybody was grumbling because Lord and Lady William Bentinck went to the opposite extreme: 'Lord William Bentinck on the throne of the Great Mogul thinks and acts like a Pennsylvanian Quaker,' wrote the French naturalist, Victor Jacquemont. 'You may easily imagine that there are people who talk loudly of the dissolution of the Empire and of the world's end, when they behold their temporary ruler riding on horseback, plainly dressed and without escort, or on his way into the country with his umbrella under his arm.'

When the fireworks at one of the Bentincks' entertainments were ruined by the damp and smoked everybody out of Government House, it caused much mirth; for Calcutta society was affronted by the way in which they extended their invitations to all and sundry – according to Emma Roberts they even invited ships' stewards and 'persons in the pilot service, very respectable men, no doubt, but from their habits, education and manners, scarcely fitting guests for the circle of a court'. They also asked 'less elevated' Indians, while forbidding them from entering Government House with their shoes on; which caused many of them to stay away, until the relaxation of this rule by the next Governor-General brought them in flocks, complete with new and squeaky European footwear. If the Bentincks drew the line at Indians in shoes, they were also somewhat chary about inviting Eurasians. The latter had, at various times in the past, been excluded from Government House alto-gether; but in the words of Miss Roberts, 'the charm of the dark-eyed beauties prevailed', so that eventually even half-caste illegitimate daughters managed to infiltrate themselves.

Government House regained most of its splendour under that other-wise ineffective Governor-General, Lord Auckland, the one-time suitor of Lady Byron; only to be virtually deserted by the next two rulers, Lord Ellenborough and Lord Hardinge, who spent most of their time up country. Ellenborough certainly liked show, but he had no use for Calcutta society, preferring to impress the potentates of India with performances like his parade at Ferozepore, when the army was ar-ranged in the form of a star with a throne for himself at the centre; 'He ought to sit upon it in a strait-waistcoat' was the old Duke of Welling-ton's comment when told of this conceit. No doubt his tastes were in-fluenced by the fact that he had long been divorced from his wife, the celebrated 'Aurora, Light of Day', who after being the mistress of the King of Bavaria was now married to an Arab sheikh, having dyed her golden hair black.

It was doubtless the neglect of the Ellenborough and Hardinge re-gimes which made the furnishings of Government House seem so down-at-heel to Lord Dalhousie when he arrived in 1848. Though he was much more concerned with increasing the territory of British India and reforming its government than with ceremonies and entertain-ments, he nevertheless felt constrained to live up to his position and not only refurbished Government House but replaced the existing state *howdah*, which he described as being 'of wood painted like a street cab', with a new one of silver, causing himself to be pilloried in the English newspapers for his extravagance, whereas, as he pointed out, his new *howdah* was no finer than that of the average Indian noble. When the Governor-General possessed a *hatikhana* of 146 elephants, it may seem surprising that there was not a better *howdah* than the one which Lord Dalhousie condemned; but it must be remembered that the elephants were intended for transport rather than for state. When Viceroys could tour the country by rail, the *hatikhana* was reduced, being finally given up in 1895. Lord Curzon, who was depicted by the Radical English Press as riding habitually on elephants when in India, did not in fact possess a single one, as he himself rather plaintively pointed out: for his Coronation Durbar of 1903 he was obliged to borrow elephants from the Indian Princes.

It was thus exceptional for the Governor-General or Viceroy to ride in state on an elephant. On normal state occasions he rode in an open carriage with postillions and a mounted escort of the Bodyguard, an Indian force originally constituted by Warren Hastings. This force, usually numbering 130 but increasing at times to over 400, played a leading part in the pageantry of Government House. The magnificent troopers, tall as Life Guards, with their scarlet and gold jackets, high boots and zebra-striped puggarees, mounted guard on the stairs and in the corridors – occasionally being seen surreptitiously fanning themselves when the weather was at its hottest. During Durbars, they stood immobile between the pillars of the Marble Hall; and at Drawing Rooms they formed a semi-circular *cheval de frise* facing the Throne. There was also a Governor-General's Band, some thirty strong, half European and half Indian; but Lady Canning thought it inferior to the bands of the Governors of Bombay and Madras.

As well as the Bodyguard and the Band, all the upper servants of Government House were dressed in scarlet and gold. To a new Vice-regal family, the first impression of the house was of hosts of red and gold servants making low salaams. Lord Auckland and his sisters arrived for the first time by moonlight, when 'all the halls were lighted up' and the great steps 'covered with all the turbaned attendants'; it seemed to Fanny Eden 'more like a real palace, a palace in the Arabian Nights, than anything I have been able to dream on the subject'.

Her sister, Emily, was surprised to find how many servants were attached to her personally. She had 'an astonishingly agreeable *khitmagar*' as her particular attendant: 'he and four others glide behind me whenever I move from one room to another; besides these, there are two bearers with a sedan at the bottom of the stairs, in case I am too idle to walk, but I have not trusted my precious person to their care yet. There is a sentry at my dressing room door, who presents arms when I go to fetch my pocket handkerchief, or find my keys. There is a tailor, with a magnificent long beard, mending up some of my old habit-shirts before they go to the wash, putting strings to my petticoats, etc., and there is an *ayah* to assist Wright and a very old woman called a *matrani*, who is the lowest servant of all, a sort of under housemaid.' She had soon increased her retinue by a second tailor and two Dacca embroiderers, who worked away in the passage outside her room while the sentry, 'in an ecstasy of admiration', mounted guard over them. At that particular moment, her passage was also inhabited by the *punkah-wallah* standing upright and pulling away at his *punkah* 'in a sweet sleep'; by the servant of Chance, her dog; by her *jemadar* sketching a bird (having taken up drawing as a compliment to her); by the *ayah*, chopping up betel-nut; by five other servants, sitting in a circle learning English; and by a Chinese pedlar waiting with rolls of silk.

Fanny, being the younger sister, was only followed by three servants; but brother George, the Governor-General, never stirred without 'a tail of fifteen joints', as Emily called it. She found it amusing when the three of them accidentally met, 'all with our tails on', but complained of how, in their brother's presence, she and her sister could no longer be fanned and have the mosquitoes driven away from them by their attendants, this privilege being afforded to the Lord Sahib alone. She forgot that the peacock fan and the yak's tail were emblems of royalty, and that their purpose was to drive away depression and evil spirits from the august personage rather than to keep him cool and free of mosquitoes. It fell to the beautiful and masterful Lady Canning to assert the rights of her sex, and to insist on having a yak's tail waved over her as well as over her husband.

A lady straight from England took some time to get used to having bearded Indians constantly in and out of her bedroom and boudoir. One sultry afternoon, when Emily Eden had let 'all the hooks and eyes loose' and gone to sleep, an army of servants rushed in to announce the Lord Sahib, who had with him the Bishop and two other ecclesiastics. She managed to do herself up, but was unable to retrieve her sash, which was under the Bishop's chair. Lady Canning felt 'shy about playing on a rather bad pianoforte, and singing to the sentry, the *jemadars*, six bearers, two *bheesties*, three *punkah-wallahs*, etc, and a great many more people than that', while Lady Dufferin was frequently surprised by 'a creature very lightly clad in a dingy white cotton rag' who turned out to be one of the gardeners come to present her with a posy, according to the charming custom of Indian gardeners.

Emily Eden was impressed by the efficiency of the servants. When they went up country, or migrated to the Governor-General's country house at Barrackpore, the entire staff of Government House went with them, together with most of their personal belongings; yet within ten minutes of their return everything was in its usual place and there was a hot breakfast – 'more like a dinner' – for eighteen people ready on the table. All the while, the servants remained 'as quiet and composed as ever'; she could just imagine the noise which the same number of

English servants would make, with their creaking shoes. But good as were the Indian servants, the Viceregal family generally brought English valets and ladies' maids with them. Lady Canning had two English maids, who would go off grandly for their evening drive in one of the Government House carriages. Almost invariably, too, there was a European chef at Government House. The austere Lawrence did without a chef altogether; while the chef of the Auckland regime seems, from his colour, to have been more Creole than French, despite his impressive name of St Cloup. He could produce an excellent dinner for eighty, and a sit-down ball supper for five hundred, with 'wonderful *plats*' – no easy task when aspics quickly melted in the heat – but he was, in the words of Emily, 'eccentric, not to say mad'. Whenever he came to see her about the bill of fare, which sometimes ran into four sides of foolscap, he would be 'dressed in the very pink of the mode, and with a new pair of primrose gloves'.

The Cannings' French chef, M. Crepin, died of cholera soon after their arrival. Apart from their sorrow on his account, there would have been the fear of infection through the food – much worse than it was for Fanny Eden to lose her tailor by the same dread disease. Yet Lady Canning remarked, after M. Crepin's death (which followed quickly on the death, also from cholera, of the 'very pretty' young wife of a Lieutenant in the Bodyguard): 'Somehow one never thinks much about cholera here.' Her generation was well used to cholera in England.

And for all the germs going around Calcutta, none of the Viceregal occupants of Government House or their wives contracted a fatal illness there; which is more than can be said of the Government Houses at Madras and Bombay. The only one among them, from Wellesley's time until 1912, who died at Government House was Lady Canning herself; her death was caused by jungle fever caught in the swamps of Purnea through which she had travelled on her way back from a sketching trip to Darjeeling. By then, she had been nearly six years in India and was thoroughly run down; whereas after her first hot weather she remarked on how well she felt.

But while Government House may not have been particularly unhealthy, the Indian climate and the long hours of work took their toll of more than one Governor-General, including Lord Canning and his immediate predecessor, Lord Dalhousie, both of whom died prematurely after returning to Britain. Each was speeded to the grave by the loss of his wife, Lady Dalhousie having died of seasickness aboard the ship in which she was travelling home to recover her health. After 1864, when Simla became the official summer headquarters of the Government of India, the Viceroy was away from Calcutta from April to November, so escaped the worst months; but the earlier Lord Sahibs and Lady Sahibs had their fair share of the Bengal hot weather, even though they sometimes went to Simla, usually in conjunction with touring the Upper Provinces.

'We are beginning to feel the real heat,' wrote Lady Canning, within a month of their first arrival. 'The *punkah* on one's – usually damp – skin tells with great effect . . . Our dear old doctor goes about arranging our shutters and thermometers, and doing all he can to make us comfortable.' With the shutters shut, and the *punkahs* going the whole time, the great high rooms of Government House were kept reasonably cool. But as Lord Canning remarked, 'Any attempt to go out, even in a carriage, makes one gasp, and dissolve immediately, and an open window or door lets in a flood of hot air, as though one were passing the mouth of a foundry.' Even at breakfast-time the heat could be unbearable: Emily Eden depicts herself and the rest of the party surveying in 'bilious despondency' a table laden with tea, chocolate, eggs, meat, fish, pineapples, mangoes and mango fool, and then calling for iced water. The nights, too, were muggy and oppressive, so that it was customary to have a *punkah* suspended beneath the canopy of one's bed. Lady Canning, who disliked *punkahs* and also felt sorry for the *punkah-wallah*, was at first reluctant to have hers pulled; but she eventually gave in, 'shocked at being hardened now to the feeling of giving work and trouble, that at first I minded so much'.

Then came the monsoon. Lady Canning gives a vivid account of a hurricane during her first May in Calcutta. 'The house shook, windows crashed and smashed, *gilnils* (Venetian shutters) were blown in here and there. In my bedroom the windows had been left open, and though the shutters were shut, the rain came in horizontally and drenched everything, even on the far side of the room, and left it ankle-deep in water, which rushed down the stairs in a cataract.'

As the rains grew more prolonged, the air felt, in Lady Canning's words, 'like an orchideous-plant hothouse'. Her shoes turned 'furry with mildew in a day'; her husband's dispatch-boxes assumed 'the appearance of a bottle of curious old port – white and fungus-y'. With the rains came the insects, 'all sorts of crickets and grasshoppers perpetually creeping up under one's scarf, and black beetles an inch long, cockroaches at least two inches'. The dinner-table was 'covered with creatures as thickly as a drawer of them in a museum, and in enormous variety'; it was necessary to have lids, 'like little pagoda roofs', on all the glasses.

The fauna of Government House was not limited to the insect kingdom. In June, according to Fanny Eden, the snakes altogether took possession of the place. In the following month, a monkey invaded her dressing room, breaking her china and carrying off her French servant's parrot. Lady Canning spoke of lizards running about her bedroom floor, and she was particularly troubled by bats: 'One evening I had five in the room flying about and squeaking, and worse in the night: I was glad of my mosquito net for protection.' As late as Lord Curzon's time, jackals would emerge from the drains towards midnight, and howl in the shrubberies, while stinking civet cats would clamber up the pillars and pipes to the roof of the house, sometimes entering the bedrooms on the southern side. By this time, however, the creatures most generally associated with Government House were a thing of the past. These were the six-foot tall adjutant cranes which formerly perched on the parapet, as can be seen in most early views of the house, providing an exotic substitute for the urns which one would have expected to find there, and which Lord Curzon, in fact, added. Fanny Eden counted 150 of these great birds on the parapet at the same time, and noticed that if one of them took the rightful place of another, it would be kicked off. She heard a story of how one of these cranes swallowed a baby whole, for they lived by scavenging, in the days when all refuse was thrown into open drains and there were human corpses floating in the Hughli; their disappearance coinciding with the advent of modern sewerage.

Being British, the inhabitants of Government House were not content to watch the wild animals and birds, but filled their rooms and the adjoining verandahs with pets. Fanny Eden, who at the time was not a girl but a maiden lady in her fifties, kept a goat, a lemur, a gazelle and a small lory; the last three lived in her dressing room, where the lory narrowly escaped being carried off by the invading monkey, along with the servant's parrot. Lady Canning at first drew the line at keeping tame parrots, when there were so many wild ones screaming outside the window; but her husband could not resist buying a pair from a pedlar at the gate, one of them having 'a scarlet head and shoulders and sky-blue epaulettes and a chocolate back', the other with 'a *veste* and *culottes* of *gros bleu* and crimson, like velvet'. Lady Dufferin, not content with the crows and parakeets flying in and out of the pillars, had an aviary constructed in her verandah. The lonely Lord Dalhousie, after his wife's death, made friends with a mouse, to which he would throw crumbs, saying that it was his only confidant.

It goes without saying that Government House had its dogs. The Eden sisters' dog, Chance, was known as 'the young prince', since all the servants made such a fuss of him, and his special attendant wore a coat of Chinese brocade and a gold breastplate. There was a terrible occasion when, as Fanny rode out of the Government House gate with him 'frolicking' in front of her, he was attacked by a couple of bull-dogs. He was rescued just in time by his servant, who knocked down the owner of the bull-dogs and threatened to kill him. When, a year or two later, poor Chance fell gravely ill and had to be shot, everybody in Government House could be heard sobbing.

Chance's adventure with the bull-dogs was witnessed by many, for there was always a crowd of petitioners at the gate of Government House. One of them would often throw himself in front of Lord Auck-land's horses as he drove out; but the postillions were clever at avoid-ing him. On another occasion, a man threw his baby under the Lord Sahib's horses' feet, but it somehow escaped injury. Still more frighten-ing for Lord Auckland and his sisters was when, during a big dinner, one of the sepoys on guard went mad and rushed into the Marble Hall, brandishing his bayonet.

The Eden sisters found Calcutta society dull. The guests at Govern-ment House did not quite come up to the brilliance of the entertain-ments. According to Emily, whole families would plod round and round the Marble Hall, as though they were 'a regiment marching round'. The élite of Calcutta do not seem to have much improved by the time of Lady Canning, who described them as 'much duller than I could have con-ceived possible'; though she noticed a 'quite extraordinary difference' between the 'Indian families', who were 'more insipid than words can express', and the people of 'good English county' stock. By 'Indian families' she meant families long connected with India, rather than of Indian blood.

When she gave a 'drum', she was dismayed to see 'rows of women seated, and men standing like waiters behind'; while at one of her dinner parties, six couples who were all paired together turned out to be not on speaking terms. She realized that the main trouble with her guests was their formality and shyness; this was brought home to her when she first wore her pearls: 'I thought how my English friends would exclaim, but here none of course would think an observation respectful, so it fell flat'. She realized, too, that most of the wives were very young. She herself was one of the oldest women in Calcutta, though still beautiful and in her early forties; the octogenarian Mrs Ellerton, who could remember the days of Warren Hastings, being wholly unique.

'It is quite a mistake to suppose that the society here is *bad*', she wrote to her mother at the end of 1856. 'Even flirting is very rare and of the mildest description, and I really believe hardly any woman but *me* goes out riding without her husband.' Lady Canning's rides took her into the lanes behind Alipore, and continued after dark by the light of the fireflies. She much preferred them to 'dowagery' drives in a carriage and four with postillions and runners. When she got on her horse she would go at a hand-gallop until she was too hot to bear it any longer. It was a way of working off her frustration at being idle and 'utterly useless' while her husband led the life of ceaseless toil that was the lot of every Governor-General and Viceroy; tied to the great room in the south-west wing of Government House from the moment breakfast was over until the small hours of the following morning; leaving his desk only for meals and a little exercise.

But like a true Victorian lady, she did not allow herself to be bored, even though Calcutta was at times 'absolutely monotonous'. She collected insects to send to the Queen's children, but they became 'so unsavoury' that they had to be buried. More rewarding, she began a series of drawings of Indian trees and flowers, frequently visiting the Botanic Gardens for this purpose. She had plenty of the talent which made her sister, Louisa, Lady Waterford, into a painter of professional standing.

Her ability to see the world around her with an artist's eye meant that, however inactive she may have been, she was constantly being delighted by the beautiful and the exciting. She never tired of the sunset, as seen from the western windows of the house; it was, to her, 'like the most brilliant Claude, the river being quite still, and great ships, anchored, waiting for the tide to turn'. She saw an infinite variety in the monsoon lightning: 'First it was white, as if strings of silver were thrown through the air quite horizontally; then in other places like lightning from the hand of Jupiter; in others like trees – sometimes blue, sometimes pink . . . On the grass, near one of our arched gates, I saw five Mohammedans at their prayers in a row on one small mat, and two others on another in front of them, all turned to the west (for remember, Mecca is west from here). These people and the arch near them were every instant lighted up quite blue with lightning.'

Lady Canning's artistic contemplations were interrupted by the outbreak of the Mutiny. Her first reference to the stirring events of 1857 is a laconic journal entry for 11 February: 'The General at Barrackpore made a good little speech to the sepoys of the regiment, who are supposed to be rather disaffected on account of the new Minié cartridges, of which they complain on the ground that the grease used in making them up is beef-suet.' On 22 April she was able to write: 'All our sepoy troubles are over.' But when she returned to Calcutta from Barrackpore on 12 May, she learnt of the arrival of a 'telegraph' – she avoided saying 'telegram', regarding it as 'a new Yankee word' – telling of a violent outbreak at Meerut. On the following Sunday, after a succession of still more alarming 'telegraphs', she and her husband joined in the prayer 'In time of war and tumults'. To suit their mood, a storm burst, 'out of clouds like ink and sepia', just as they were entering the church.

Throughout the Mutiny, life at Government House went on as usual. In the prevailing atmosphere of panic, the Governor-General and his lady were determined to set an example of calm, keeping up the morale of the British community with a succession of dinners, parties and entertainments. 'Many people wish us to put off the ball on the Queen's Birthday,' wrote Lady Canning towards the end of May. 'I would not for an instant suggest such a thing. It may not be a cheerful ball in this time of anxiety, but we ought not to appear in a state of mourning for this temporary outbreak.' In the event, the ball was, as she recorded, 'a very fair one . . . the respectable and serious made a point of coming, and a number of natives'. Most of the 'Armenians and half-castes' stayed away: she heard that they were 'thoroughly frightened'. The European guard of honour who, by custom, presented arms at the entry of the Governor-General, offered to remain in the basement until the ball was over; but to the Cannings, this was 'not to be thought of'. So the guard of honour was dismissed as usual, leaving the house and the guests under the sole protection of the Indian troopers of the Bodyguard.

There were many rumours to support the popular belief that the Cannings were careless over security. According to one newspaper, the venerable Indian major-domo of Government House had plotted and then absconded; Lady Canning was amused to read this story just as the functionary in question was handing her a cup of tea. The fact that Government House was still guarded by Indian troopers aroused much criticism, until, in August, Lord Canning agreed very reluctantly to the Bodyguard being disarmed. They continued to be posted on the stairs and in the corridors, only without their weapons; and they were replaced by European pickets at night.

Instead of drawing pictures of flowers, Lady Canning now set to work making clothes for the refugees who were pouring into Calcutta, helped by her two English maids, her own three tailors and four extra tailors brought in specially. She also gave away most of her own 'large trousseau', while desiring that her things should go 'to officers' wives and others who are ladies' – she was not being snobbish but sensibly assumed that women with a position to keep up needed to wear some-thing better than the ordinary hand-out. These more favoured refugees were invited to dine at Government House, together with 'crowds of officers', some back from the fighting, others just off the great troop-ships lying in the Hughli. One evening, a lady whose nerves were 'very shaky' startled the assembled company by saying, as she sat down at table: 'I hope we shall rise safely from dinner'. Another lady guest was made of sterner stuff, and was 'boiling over with indignation at not being allowed to go up-country with her husband', declaring that 'she was not a common woman, but had a revolver, and knew how to use it'. During these months, Lord Canning was 'fearfully overworked', writing dispatches until his eyesight failed and he 'sank from exhaustion'.

The atmosphere of Government House in the eighteen-eighties under Lord and Lady Dufferin seems almost trivial after the intensity of the Cannings' life; though behind Lord Dufferin's suave, charming and dilletantish exterior lay a tremendous capacity for hard work – and unlike his predecessors earlier in the century, he found time to visit the Calcutta slums. By now, the Viceregal family only stayed in Calcutta during the winter months, when the weather was mostly delightful and there was a constant round of gaieties. Lady Dufferin did not have to spend long hours in a darkened room beneath the *punkah* as Lady Canning did; and unlike the childless Lady Canning, she was never lonely, her three debutante daughters being with her most of the time and her sons coming on visits.

The balls were now larger than ever: at one of them there were 1,200 guests. So were the official dinners, which were usually for over 100. As an innovation, Lady Dufferin and her daughters were present at one such dinner which was otherwise all men, and 'made it appear less of a public dinner and more of a private entertainment'; while at a dinner on New Year's Eve, a Hungarian violinist played as a change from the Viceroy's band. There were levees, garden parties and a reception for *purdah* ladies at which no men, not even servants, were allowed to be present; it was meant to be in the afternoon, but the guests were late and darkness fell with nobody to light the chandeliers.

As well as inviting Indian ladies to Government House, Lady Dufferin occasionally paid them return visits. She once attended an Indian ladies' dinner party, sitting cross-legged on the floor wearing a beautiful sari given to her by her hostess and eating with her fingers out of many little silver bowls. It was not normally the custom for the Viceroy to dine out – except in the houses of the Commander-in-Chief, the Chief Justice, the Bishop and the Lieutenant-Governor of Bengal, and at official banquets and functions like the Eton dinner and the Scotch dinner on St Andrew's Day – but Lord Dufferin went with Lady Dufferin to an Indian entertainment given by Rai Juggodanund Mookerjee. There was a theatrical performance, in which the actors, in their *dhotis*, appeared to the Vicereine as 'ordinary men in cotton sheets', whereas her more romantically-minded husband saw them as 'ancient Romans in their togas'. There was also a *nautch*, followed by 'a thoroughly European meal' and a visit to the *zenana* – to which not only the Viceroy but some of the lesser men of the party were admitted – where the lady of the house presented her Viceregal guests with bouquets and betel-nut, hung them with garlands and saturated their handkerchiefs with rosewater.

Improvements in transport brought a stream of visitors from Europe to Government House; so that by the Dufferins' time there was a side to Viceregal entertaining unknown to the Cannings. Already, during the previous decade, there had been the visit of Albert Edward, Prince of Wales, whose engagements in Calcutta ranged from receiving India's only woman potentate, the veiled Begum of Bhopal, to hearing an Indian poet sing of Queen Victoria's 'astonishing beauty' and attending a state performance at the theatre of a farce called *My Awful Dad*. Now, the guests staying at Government House included the Duke and Duchess of Connaught and various European royalties; as well as the Duke and Duchess of Manchester, Lord and Lady Rosebery, and Lord Randolph Churchill – whose son Winston was to spend some weeks in the house fourteen years later, writing *The River War*.

Even if they were not already well acquainted with them, the Viceroy and Vicereine could be on much easier terms with guests of this sort than with most of the inhabitants of British India; so that their presence provided an excuse for many smaller and gayer parties interspersed with the more formal functions, as well as for early morning hunts with the hounds kept by a rich ADC, Lord Herbrand Russell, and afternoons of tent-pegging. Lord Rosebery was treated to a more unusual diversion, a trip to the tiny French colony of Chandernagore, twenty miles up river from Calcutta, where the French officials, who suffered intense boredom in their little enclave, made many bows to the Viceregal party and plied them with 'votre plat national, le kek'. At Christmas, the Dufferins' house-guests all helped to decorate the tree; it was 'a regular Christmas' and not the somewhat hybrid festival experienced by Lady Canning, when the *khansama* showed his knowledge of English customs by serving hot cross buns.

Christmas in Calcutta was marked by the chief sporting event of the year, the Viceroy's Cup, when the Viceroy and Vicereine would drive, Ascot-fashion, up the course. In the Dufferins' time, racing loomed large at Government House, for the Military Secretary, Lord William Beresford, was a leading figure of the Indian Turf: his horse, Myall King, won the Viceroy's Cup in 1887, and was to win it twice more. 'Lord Bill' was the beau-ideal of Viceregal courtiers; he served five successive Viceroys, taking time off to fight in the Zulu War, where he won the VC. A son of the fourth Marquess of Waterford – and, incidentally, a nephew of Lady Canning's brother-in-law, the third Marquess – he was one of four celebrated brothers who included the future Admiral, Lord Charles Beresford; and like his brothers, he combined a rollicking, devil-may-care Irish gaiety with a talent for handling people and getting things done. 'From the highest military affairs in the land to a mosquito inside my Excellency's curtain or a bolt on my door, all is the business of this invaluable person, and he does all equally well', Lady Dufferin wrote of him, while admitting that she found driving to and from the races on his coach something of an ordeal, particularly when he had just dislocated his shoulder in a steeplechase. It was, however, nothing like as frightening as being driven back from a paperchase by one of her Royal guests, Prince Bernard of Saxe-Weimar, who knocked up against bullock-carts and weaved in and out of the statues on the Maidan, saying calmly, in response to the ladies' shrieks, 'Sat is nosing, my life is not expensive.'

Under the cheerful but dignified rule of the Dufferins, Government House may be said to have reached its heyday. There is a latent sadness about the yet grander Viceroyalty of Lord Curzon, not only on account of his quarrels with the Indian Civil Service, the Home Government and Lord Kitchener, but also because of the ill-health of his beautiful and charming wife, the only American ever to become Vicereine, who died soon after his final return to England. But while he may have been a difficult character, Curzon had a greater appreciation of the fabric and traditions of Government House than any other Viceroy, and he brought the running of the Viceregal court to perfection.

Knowing how hard he worked on more serious matters, one wonders how he can have found time not only to attend but also to plan so many and such vast entertainments. During each of the winters when he was in residence at Government House, there were two Levees, a Drawing Room, a State Ball, a State Evening Party, a Garden Party, several lesser balls and a number of official dinners; together with an informal dance and two or three smaller dinners every week. Calcutta society was still growing. There were now 1,600 guests at the State Ball, 600 at each of the lesser balls, 120 at the large dinners and 1,500 at the State Evening Party, which was given mainly for Indians. In one month, the number of meals served at Government House to guests and residents amounted to 3,500.

For all the trouble he took over such occasions as the Fancy Dress Ball of January 1903 – at which the costumes were meant to recreate Wellesley's famous ball of exactly a hundred years before – Curzon did not really enjoy them. He much preferred the simple and imposing ritual of a Durbar, when an Indian chief came to Government House to pay him his respects; and when nobody else was present apart from the retinues of himself and his visitor and a few personal guests watching from behind a screen. The Viceroy would await the arriving potentate the on steps of the Throne, attended by his Staff and by servants bearing the emblems of royalty. From here, in Curzon's own words, 'he looked down the long vista of the Marble Hall with its gleaming white pillars, absolutely empty save for the Bodyguard in their magnificent uniforms, standing like statues on either side. In the distance could be heard the music of the band playing upon the great exterior staircase. An intense silence prevailed, broken at length by the crunch of wheels on the gravel and the horse-hooves of the Bodyguard, as they escorted the carriage containing the Prince to the foot of the steps. At that moment thundered out the guns from the distant Fort, giving to the Chief his due salute. One – two – three – up to the total of seventeen, nineteen, or twenty-one, the reverberations rang out. Not until the total – carefully counted by the Chief himself – was completed, did the procession, which was being formed on the terrace at the top of the staircase, attempt to move forward. Then he would be seen to advance along the crimson carpet laid outside and to enter the Marble Hall in all his panoply of brocades and jewels, the Foreign Secretary leading him by the hand. As they approached at a slow pace along the polished floor, not a sound was heard but the clank clank of the scabbards on the marble.'

Followed by his *sirdars* or nobles, the Chief came through the great doorway into the Throne Room and gave the stipulated bows. According to his visitor's rank, the Viceroy either descended from the steps of the Throne to greet him, or else awaited him on the dais. The Chief tendered the *nazar*, a token offering of one or two gold *mohurs*, which the Viceroy touched and remitted; he also presented his *sirdars*. Everybody sat down, the Chief and his retinue to the right of the throne, the Viceroy's Staff on the left; and a short conversation ensued. The Viceroy then gave his guest the traditional hospitality of rose-water and *pan* or betel-nut – what Lady Dufferin irreverently called 'sticky leaves wrapped up in silver and gold paper' – and after a few more minutes of conversation, the potentate retired, walking backwards as far as the doorway to the Marble Hall, where he made a final bow.

The ceremony lasted not much more than a quarter of an hour, and was little different from an occasion witnessed by Emily and Fanny Eden, except that, in those days, the visiting potentate brought real presents. From behind a pillar, Emily and Fanny watched wistfully as gold stuffs, bracelets, shawls 'that made one's mouth water', and a necklace of pearls and emeralds were laid at their brother's feet; they knew that, according to the rules, all this largesse had to be sold for the benefit of the East India Company.

As well as doing so much to perfect the ceremonial of Government House, Curzon also restored and modernized the building itself, improved the furnishings and filled the gaps in the collection of portraits, continuing to take an interest in the house after he had returned to England. Great was his indignation when, with the removal of the seat of Government to Delhi in 1912, it ceased to be the palace of the Viceroy and was denuded of most of its original contents. Before this happened, the house enjoyed a magnificent swansong when the reigning King-Emperor and Queen-Empress came to stay. They had stayed here before, as Prince and Princess of Wales, and Curzon should have been their host, but his final dispute with Whitehall, which led to his resignation, robbed him of this honour. On that earlier occasion, the Royal visitors witnessed a unique spectacle. The Tashi Lama came on a State visit to the Prince, accompanied by a retinue of Tibetan warriors on shaggy hill ponies, who, when they saw the great ceremonial steps of Government House, could not resist urging their steeds to gallop up and down them over and over again. None of the awaiting dignitaries was able to keep a straight face; the Prince of Wales himself had to slip away into an adjoining room where he laughed until the tears ran down his cheeks.

George V was not the only reigning British Monarch to stay at Government House; the present Queen stayed here in 1960, as the guest of the Governor of West Bengal. In the India of today, Wellesley's palace continues to serve the purpose for which it was built. There are still sentries at the gates, starched *khitmagars* in the halls and corridors. The rooms look bare with no portraits, and they seem rather too large and too many for the present scale of entertaining – the great apartments on the second floor are mostly under dust-sheets – yet there is little of the air of past glory which pervades so many of the buildings of the British Raj. Perhaps it is because the change from splendour to simplicity has been gradual; with a transitional period in the years from 1912 to 1947, when the house was occupied by the Governors of Bengal – including those two least conventional of Governors, the Australian, Richard Casey, and the former railwayman, Sir Frederick Burrows – who though they naturally kept up far more state than their Indian successors, nevertheless did not quite make use of the house in the way that the Viceroys did.

A writer who dined at Government House in the nineteen-thirties gives us a vignette which is wonderfully evocative of this period, showing that the house did not lose all its magic with the departure of the Viceregal court.[1] After dinner, he and a fellow-guest, an elderly Colonel, walked out onto the verandah. It was a glorious night with a full moon and the shadows of the pillars 'like strips of black velvet on the white marble'. Suddenly there was a movement and two figures appeared out of the shadows: a young man in scarlet and gold, and a

[1] Philip Steegman, *Indian Ink* (London, 1939)

66

girl in white with golden hair. They stood still, not realizing they were being watched, and he kissed her. Then, impulsively and at the same moment, 'as if Heaven had suddenly called them', they both looked up and blew a kiss with their fingers to the moon. It was, thought the writer, a moment of unforgettable beauty; but the Colonel was not impressed. 'Damned young fool,' he muttered, 'he had better go back to his regiment.'

3

BARRACKPORE, CALCUTTA

HE mongrel name of Barrackpore carries in it the whole romance
of British India; it could be the title of a story by Kipling. This
mixture of English and Indian makes it a particularly apt name
for the old Viceregal country house some fifteen miles from Calcutta.
In its green and shady park beside the Hughli river, Barrackpore was as
close to an English country house as any dwelling east of Suez – it reminded Lady Canning of Syon and Lady Dufferin of Cliveden – yet it
had all the magic of India. There are other contrasts in its story, contrasts so typical of the Raj: grandeur and shabbiness; for the house,
with its imposing stucco façades, seems to have been frequently rather
dilapidated; luxury and discomfort; gaiety and heartbreak. Historically
speaking, Barrackpore is the equal of Government House, Calcutta,
having been the scene of as many crucial meetings and far-reaching
decisions; and to a greater degree than the somewhat impersonal palace
could ever do, it captured the affections of its illustrious tenants.

The military cantonment which gave Barrackpore its name was first
established in 1775, and ten years later the Government acquired a
property adjoining it of seventy acres with two bungalows. This was
originally used by the Commander-in-Chief, but in 1801 Lord Wellesley appropriated it as a country residence for himself and his successors. According to Wellesley's own account, the house here was 'an
old cottage in a state of considerable decay' when he took it over, which
was probably an exaggeration, for in a drawing done in 1803 by Henry
Salt, the artist who accompanied Lord Valentia, it appears as a commodious building by the water's edge with a very English type of portico.
This, however, was after Captain Charles Wyatt, the architect of Government House, Calcutta, had carried out various repairs and improvements. Salt's view also shows the group of thatched bungalows,

described by Lord Minto a few years later as 'neat Swiss cottages scattered about the lawn', which were used by the Governor-General's staff and guests. Lord Valentia, though he only came for the day, had one put at his disposal, retiring there after breakfast while his host was busy with dispatches, and returning to the main house for dinner.

A year after Valentia's visit, the house was found to be unsafe, so Wellesley ordered it to be pulled down and rebuilt. Having barely finished his palace in Calcutta, he now decreed that the new house at Barrackpore should be on a no less palatial scale; he even contemplated joining the two Government Houses by a straight avenue. Wellesley's second palace had only reached plinth height when the Directors recalled him as a punishment for his extravagance in building the first. They were still angrier when they heard of the Barrackpore project, which was to cost a further £50,000; and though there was nothing more they could do to punish the 'Magnificent Marquess', since he was no longer in their employ, they made sure that all work on the new house should cease. It stood for some years like a ruin; Mrs Maria Graham, who saw its 'unfinished arches' by moonlight, thought it 'completed the beauty of the scenery'. Lord Hastings contemplated finishing it in a more modest way, but having decided instead to enlarge the temporary house which Wellesley had built a short distance upstream, he pulled it down, and his wife erected a greenhouse on the site.

Wellesley's 'makeshift' was, in the words of the first Lord Minto, 'a very considerable building compared with the European scale', with three large rooms opening onto a verandah. As enlarged by Hastings, it became an imposing mansion with a deep entrance portico of eight Tuscan columns on the north front, and colonnaded verandahs on the other three sides. It may have incorporated features from the design of the ill-fated palace, since both were almost certainly by the same architect, Captain Thomas Anbury, who succeeded Wyatt as Superintendent of Public Works. Perhaps for this reason, it looked larger than it actually was, consisting only of one very lofty main storey on a handsomely arcaded and rusticated basement. A staircase led up from the north entrance to an immense drawing room occupying most of the centre of the house, with the dining room and billiard room on one side of it. The rest of the main floor was taken up by the private apartments of the Governor-General and his family, while the basement was occupied by servants. Guests and staff still had to sleep in bungalows in the grounds. No doubt on account of its shortage of accommodation, the house continued to be regarded as temporary for the next forty years. This may explain why it was allowed to become so ramshackle and why, as late as 1840, the basement lacked glass and there were no interior doors.

Lord Auckland and his two sisters, Emily and Fanny Eden, found the furnishings of the house 'in a wretched state' on their arrival in 1836. 'M—'s armchair, which I intended for my own room, I have actually been obliged to lend to the drawing room, where everybody makes a rush for it, it is so soft,' Emily wrote. 'Indeed, the sofas are so wretchedly hard . . . the furniture here is worse than that of any London hotel, but everything in India is so perishable that one year of neglect may reduce a house to the worst state.'

More than ten years later, when Lord Dalhousie became Governor-General, there was still no proper dining-room table. A set of camp tables was used, which accompanied the Governor-General on all his tours, and consequently became very knocked about. Dalhousie adorned the dining room with red damask and a thick carpet, but this did not prevent the wife of his successor, Lady Canning, complaining that the house was 'exceedingly ill *monté*'. But she was able to improve things 'marvellously', in her own words, with '450 yards of rose-chintz, a great many armchairs, small round tables, framed drawings etc, and flower-pots in numbers'. In spite of these and subsequent alterations, the house kept many of its original furnishings from the time of Lord Hastings, which must have added greatly to its charm: long mirrors, marble tables, lustres and the old-fashioned wall lights with glass shades such as one sees in pictures of Calcutta houses in the eighteenth century. There was also a series of portraits of the Mysore Royal Family painted about 1800 by Thomas Hickey.

Whatever people may have thought of the house, they invariably fell in love with the surroundings: the garden, the park, the broad river with its thickly wooded banks. Wellesley enlarged the park to nearly 350 acres, clearing jungle and swamp; he had the naturally flat ground shaped into hillocks and hollows. The landscape was particularly Arcadian to the north of the house, where a watercourse, spanned by a graceful Classical bridge, had been drained to form a valley, beyond which was a Corinthian temple known as the Temple of Fame, built by the first Lord Minto in memory of the officers who fell during his conquests of Mauritius and Java in 1810 and 1811. As the years went on, the number of buildings adorning the garden and park increased: a charming little Georgian church, guard bungalows with rusticated and pedimented doorways, domed lodges, a Gothic artificial ruin and a monument to Lord William Beresford's famous racehorse, Myall King. The guest and staff bungalows, originally of thatch, were rebuilt in a more elegant style in 1863. One of them was known as Honeymoon Hall, from being constantly lent for that purpose.

Apart from buildings, almost every Lord Sahib or his lady added something to the garden and grounds. Lord Ellenborough made a terrace walk along the river. Lady Canning made an Italian garden surrounded by a balustrade, as well as a raised walk bordered with poinsettias, leading straight down from the south front of the house to the landing-stage. Lady Ripon covered this walk with a green and shady tunnel of bamboo, and also laid out a rose garden. Only that part of the garden which lay between the house and the river was private to the Governor-General and his family; the rest of the grounds were open to the public. 'I do not mind that,' wrote Lady Canning, 'for it looks cheerful to see people, and the regiments send their bands to play in the evenings, and it has quite a gay effect.'

Like other homesick Britons, the Eden sisters were particularly delighted by the Englishness of the park at Barrackpore. The more romantic Lady Canning found it 'too English for me to appreciate properly . . . short grass well-mown and smelling of hay, and not a coconut in sight'. She remedied the latter deficiency, so that, after a few years, there were palms and tropical plants in plenty. The lushness of the growth, the flowers, flaming bougainvilleas, pink lotus on the ponds, blue convolvulus running riot over everything, must always have given an exotic flavour to the grounds, English though they may have seemed. And India made its presence felt in other ways. At the end of the park was a *ghat* where Hindus burnt their dead. There were barges on the river, with turned-up prows and sterns and stubby sails, from which came the sound of tom-toms and Indian pipes. The sky was full of brilliant green parakeets, and at night there were clouds of fire-flies and huge bats.

When Bishop Heber stayed at Barrackpore in 1823, he met lynxes and other strange animals being taken for an airing in the park. They came from the menagerie, which had its origin in Wellesley's abortive natural history institute. The animals were housed in a charming group of cages, some Gothic, others Classical, and included, at various times, tigers, leopards, monkeys, bears, rhinoceroses and a giraffe, as well as many rare and colourful birds. At the time of Lord Auckland, a rhinoceros took to straying in the park and chased a neighbour, who was still more annoyed when the Governor-General laughed. Lady Dalhousie made a pet of one of the bears and kept it in her room; her daughter, Lady Susan Ramsay, became very attached to it after her death. 'It was Lady Susan's sole recommendation to me for kindness,' Lady Canning remarked sadly, on her first visit to Barrackpore, 'and I am rather at a loss how to show it: I suppose a lump of cake now and then will do.'

In addition to the animals of the menagerie, eight or a dozen elephants were kept at Barrackpore, part of the Governor-General's or Viceroy's *hatikhana*, and were used for riding about in the park, and in the surrounding country. When they carried the Lord Sahib or his family they were decked in scarlet and gold, and followed by some of the Bodyguard on horseback. Emily Eden felt the dreaminess of an evening elephant ride by the river, 'a red copper-coloured sky bent over all'. Lady Canning used to go out sketching on an elephant, and she also noted how 'a ride upon the elephants has a wonderfully reassuring effect upon people who arrive very much alarmed at us'.

In the Cannings' day, before India was much frequented by important and aristocratic visitors from Europe, the people who came to stay at Barrackpore included many quite humble civilians, officers and clergy, who, together with their respective families, were invited here for a rest-cure. As they lodged in the bungalows in the park, being carried over to meals in the main house in *tonjons* or hooded chairs unless they were energetic enough to walk, their Viceregal hostess did not have them much on her hands. Yet even with her unlimited resources, Lady Canning was bothered by their 'strange ways of bringing uninvited children, and puzzling one's arrangements dreadfully . . . imagine one lady bringing with her two women, who brought three babies!' These guests had other ways of being tiresome. Going in to Sunday breakfast, a clergyman accosted Emily Eden and said: 'Pray, Miss Eden, are you aware that your *malis* are at work this morning?' Fortunately the officer in charge of the Barrackpore establishment was at hand, and was able to tell the clergyman that of course they worked on Sunday as they were absent for more than half the week with their own religious festivals.

The Indian Princes, who stayed so often with the Viceroys of later years, were rarely seen at Barrackpore in its heyday before the Mutiny. There was, however, the exiled Amir of Afghanistan, Dost Mohammed, who came to stay with Lord Auckland and his sisters, and was put up in the best of the bungalows. He made himself very agreeable, sat to Emily for his picture and was very much taken with the giraffe in the menagerie. A ball given in his honour was a great success. It was customary to give frequent balls at Barrackpore during the hot weather, when the Governor-General and his family were in residence here for several months. Any number of guests could dance in the great drawing room and have supper in the dining room, which was larger than 'Willis's Room at Almack's', according to Emily Eden. In her day, the sort of gentlemen who now 'prop the bar' would retire to the bungalows and smoke hookahs, which had not yet been abandoned by the British in India.

There was, however, the problem of whether to invite only the military from the neighbouring cantonment, and risk offending Calcutta society, or whether to extend the invitations to ladies and gentlemen who had to come all the way from Calcutta, in which case, if it was a bad night, more than half the guests would be sure not to turn up. Emma Roberts describes how a ball at Barrackpore in the time of Lord and Lady William Bentinck was spoilt by a south-westerly gale. 'A very large proportion of the guests determined to go up by water, anticipating a delightful excursion by starlight; but the horrors of the storm burst upon them ere they could reach their destination; the Hughli ran mountains high, washing over the decks of the frail little summer-vessels, and driving many on shore, to the consternation of the passengers and the utter ruin of their ball-dresses. The travellers by land were not better off: the horses took fright at the lightning; the road was rendered impassable by trees torn up by the roots; ladies, terrified out of their senses, made an attempt to walk, and the party, when collected at last, presented a most lugubrious spectacle, a concourse of wet, weary, miserable guests, eagerly impatient to return to their homes, yet compelled to await more favourable weather.'

Provided there was no storm, the river afforded a most convenient way of travelling between Barrackpore and Calcutta. Emily Eden was delighted with her first trip to Barrackpore in the *Sonamukhi*, the Governor-General's State Yacht, which was in fact a very luxurious houseboat, originally pulled by men walking along the bank, but now towed by a steamer. They were accompanied by a flotilla of *feelchehras*, or

State Barges, carrying rather more than 400 servants: 'such a simple way of going to pass two nights in the country,' she observed ironically. Other servants had already gone ahead, for there was no permanent domestic staff at Barrackpore. 'All the establishment that is left at Calcutta is established here before we arrive,' Emily wrote during this first visit. 'There is even the tailor squatting at the door with his spectacles on, just as I left him squatting there.' On their arrival at Barrackpore, Lord Auckland and his sisters were still more amazed to find all their personal possessions, even their pianoforte, awaiting them, as if by magic. Two days later, everything was back at Government House.

The *Sonamukhi* or 'golden face' – an allusion to her gilded prow – was built for Lord Hastings, and contained a drawing room, a bedroom and two dressing rooms, all decorated in white and gold, and with 'very showy' white and gold furniture covered in green morocco. Dost Mohammed was particularly impressed with the furniture, and with the oilcloth on the floor, which he thought 'beautiful'. The *Sonamukhi* even boasted of marble baths; whereas in the actual house at Barrackpore, which, as late as the nineteen-thirties, was without any form of plumbing, there were only tubs.

The trips between Calcutta and Barrackpore were only a secondary function of the State Yacht, which was primarily intended for journeys of several weeks up the Ganges and the other great rivers, when the Governor-General went on tour. The rest of the Boat Establishment was maintained for this same purpose. Having been greatly increased by Wellesley, and again by Lord Hastings, it amounted, in its heyday, to more than two hundred craft. As well as the *Sonamukhi* and the *feel-chehras*, there were fast skiffs called *baulias*, tow-boats, cook-boats and a Band-boat. This fleet was normally kept at Barrackpore; the boats made a brave show along the river opposite the house, all of them painted green and gold, which contrasted with the scarlet liveries of the boatmen.

For all its glory of State Barges and elephants, breakfasts under the banyan tree, luncheons on the creeper-hung verandah overlooking the river and evenings on the terrace by moonlight, life at Barrackpore had its discomforts. There were often snakes in the basement of the main house as well as in the bungalows, and according to Emily Eden one was even liable to meet jackals in the passages. She also describes an invasion by giant ants, which covered the whole dining room floor with their millions and made the white marble tables seem brown.

Then there were storms such as that which caused havoc among the Bentincks' guests. One moment, all was calm; a moment later, with a crash of thunder, the wind began to roar, and the servants were rushing about catching at the blinds and shutters and trying to prevent everything from being blown off the dinner-table.

Far more dramatic than any storm was the mutiny of sepoys at Barrackpore in 1824. Lord and Lady Amherst were in residence at the time, and refused to leave. For twenty-four hours they were at the mercy of the mutineers, since even the sentries on the house belonged to one of the mutinous regiments; but they came to no harm. Then the British troops arrived and the mutiny was quelled; though not without what Lady Amherst described as 'a frightful scene – English soldiers firing on British uniforms, pursuing them in all directions; some of our servants were wounded . . . many shots entered the cook-house, and many fell into the water under our windows'. She saw great numbers trying to swim the river, but few reached the opposite shore; later there were dead bodies floating past. For the Amhersts themselves, Barrackpore was the scene of an even greater tragedy two years later, when their eldest son, Jeff, a young officer of great promise, died here of fever.

Barrackpore was certainly unkind to the Amhersts; but for most of the other people who lived here, it had pleasanter memories. 'Barrackpore is delicious and takes the sting out of India,' wrote the first Lord Minto. Lord Dalhousie and his wife so loved Barrackpore that after she died he could not bear to go near it for two years. Lady Canning also loved the place, and when she died in 1861 she was buried in the garden, within sight of the river. Every night when he was here during his remaining months in India, her broken-hearted husband would slip silently from the house and visit her grave, on which a light was always kept burning. He survived her less than a year, dying soon after his return to England. Those months left an undertone of sadness at Barrackpore, beneath all the gaiety.

Lady Canning's death really marks the end of the great days at Barrackpore. From 1864 onwards the Viceroys spent the hot weather at Simla, so that Barrackpore became just a weekend retreat, having formerly been lived in for several months of the year. For this reason, and owing to the reduction of the Barrackpore garrison after the Mutiny, the big parties and balls became a thing of the past. The Boat Establishment, made obsolete by railways, was replaced by a couple of steam launches. The menagerie, having declined, was done away with in the late eighteen-seventies by Lord Lytton, and the Viceroy ceased to keep elephants in 1895. After the Government of India moved to Delhi, Barrackpore was handed over to the Governor of Bengal.

Today, the Governor of West Bengal still uses one of the bungalows at week-ends, but the main house is a police hospital. It was in a sorry state when I visited Barrackpore in 1967, and the garden had a neglected and melancholy air; the park could hardly be seen for new and unsightly buildings. Yet the place was still romantic. Trees were in flower near the bridge and the Temple of Fame, including one of a fantastic beauty, like an ash but of a delicate mauve colour. Slim, elegant monkeys, perhaps the descendants of those in the menagerie, walked about the grass and climbed the branches. I felt most strongly what the place must have been like when I walked towards the river, which was unchanged, its banks thickly wooded and the same craft, with their turned-up prows and sterns, passing slowly by. It was easy to imagine Lord Curzon, who loved Barrackpore as much as any of his predecessors, landing here on one of those Saturday evenings which, years later, he was to remember with such pleasure: the peaceful twilight journey up river in his steam launch, the walk from the landing-place to the house, 'hand-borne lanterns twinkling in the darkness ahead'. Close by was Lady Canning's grave, with its rather Celtic monument designed by her sister, Louisa, Lady Waterford. The little consecrated plot was beautifully kept; and what was most remarkable, there was a sentry standing guard over it. Perhaps he was merely there to guard the inner gate which lay just beyond, and had come nearer the grave so as to be out of the sun; but I prefer to think that it was a tribute from the India of today to the wife of the man who, from his policy of forgiveness after the Mutiny, was known as Clemency Canning.

4

PARELL, BOMBAY

FOR the last three generations of the British in India, Government
House, Bombay, meant the comfortable but unassuming cluster
of bungalows on Malabar Point. It was only those of an earlier
generation again who could remember the departed glories of Parell,
the spacious old house which was the principal residence of the Governors of Bombay from 1829 to 1885, having been their country retreat
from as far back as 1719. More than the other Government Houses,
Parell evokes that combination of magnificence and misery which was
the keynote of the Raj in its younger days; for along with memories of
vast reception rooms hung with crystal chandeliers, a noble staircase
and a park full of exotic trees goes the sinister knowledge that the house
was abandoned after a Governor's wife had died there of cholera.

This tragedy, which had its counterpart in the history of most old
Indian houses, would hardly have caused Parell to be given up if the
house had not already long been regarded as unhealthy. One would be
tempted to believe that its inhabitants suffered a curse as usurpers of
sacred property, for it was originally a Fransciscan friary, and then a
college of the Jesuits, who were expelled by the English in 1690 – the
long and lofty banquetting hall being in fact a desecrated church. Or
the curse may have come from an angry Hindu, the house having been
built on the site of a temple of Parali Vaijnath, whence its name. More
likely it was unhealthy on account of its situation in the middle of the
so-called Island of Bombay, six miles north of the city, close to a swamp
and with coconut groves shutting out the sea breeze.

In earlier days, when the settlement was concentrated on the eastern
or landward side of the island, rather than on the western shore facing
the open sea, Parell cannot have been much more unhealthy than the
rest of Bombay. Having both the heat of Madras and the humidity of

Calcutta, and with the air made foul by the local practice – afterwards prohibited – of manuring the coconut trees with rotten fish, Bombay was, in the first half of the eighteenth century, the least favoured of the three main English settlements. The proverb 'two monsoons are the life of a man' originated here; and as well as pestilence, it had suffered war and other disasters, losing much of its trade. Ships sailed direct from the Cape of Good Hope to Madras, so that Bombay was a backwater, 'the unfortunate island', where the inhabitants had a name for being parochial and inhospitable. That Governor Charles Boone should, in 1719, have acquired so large a country house as Parell is a sign of his self-confidence; for under his vigorous rule the settlement first began to recover.

Forty years later, thanks largely to the growth of the Parsi ship-building industry, Bombay was reasonably prosperous. But its society was still rather dull, and there was far less money about than there was in Calcutta or even Madras. So it came as a surprise to visitors, particularly to those familiar with the other two settlements, when they were entertained by the Governor at Parell and saw his splendid Banquetting Hall, eighty feet in length, and the Ballroom of the same size which had been built above it; a traveller of 1763 declared that nothing in India could compare with them. Despite the simpler habits of the Bombayers, the Governor kept up as much state as his colleagues of Madras and Calcutta, being surrounded by the same retinue of guards and mace-bearers; though owing to the scarcity of horses on the island, his carriage was pulled, in the Bombay fashion, by a team of white oxen; which, swinging their tails as they trotted, were liable to bespatter the occupants with dung.

From the time of William Hornby, who was Governor in the seventeen-seventies, the Governors lived increasingly at Parell, preferring it to the airless Government House in the Fort, though the latter remained their official residence until 1829. We have a glimpse of Parell at the end of the eighteenth century – about the time when Colonel Arthur Wellesley, the future Duke of Wellington, stayed here – in a letter from the valet of Major Harris, an ADC, to his master's wife in England. 'I am sorry to see the gentlemen live so fast' he wrote, while tactfully adding that the Major's wine was always three parts water.

It seems likely that Hornby made various improvements to the house, which Mountstuart Elphinstone enlarged fifty years later by adding two side wings. Having thus grown piecemeal, Parell lacked the architectural distinction of the Government Houses at Calcutta and Madras.

With its massive walls, relieved only by occasional verandahs and windows set rather far apart, its castellated parapets and high, red-tiled roof, it kept an air of the original convent; it also might have been an old Middle Eastern *serai*. Nevertheless, it looked impressive when approached from the main gate of the park, along an avenue of magnificent trees nearly a mile in length.

And if the house was plain outside, it became very much of a palace within, after being redecorated and refurnished by Mountstuart Elphinstone when he took over as Governor in 1819. One of the greatest figures of early nineteenth-century India, a scholar and philosopher who preferred reading to the pleasures of society, a bachelor who was happier living under canvas than in the luxury of a Government House, Elphinstone nevertheless knew what a fine room should look like; for as the younger son of a peer, he had grown up in elegant surroundings. And although he had served in India without a break for the past twenty-three years, he was conversant with the latest European fashions, including the 'Egyptian Taste' of the French Empire. Writing to a friend in Calcutta of what was required in the way of furnishings for Parell, he spoke of relieving the walls of the Banquetting Hall and the Ballroom above it with neo-Classical ornament in panels, alternating with panels containing paintings of various subjects; and he specified 'Cleopatra couches' for the two drawing rooms beyond the Ballroom.

All these rooms, together with the staircase and the first-floor verandah – which was so large that Elphinstone used to walk in it for an hour every morning during the rains – were to be lit by chandeliers: four 'very handsome' ones in the Banquetting Hall, three 'superb' ones in the Ballroom; while that in the larger drawing room was to be 'very superb'. With the chandeliers he needed vast quantities of glass shades, to protect the candles from the sudden storms of Bombay, which, he feared, would blow out the new-fangled 'patent lamps'. He also ordered side-boards and 'a handsome set of dining tables', observing how, at present, these articles had to be borrowed when there was a large party. In the same way, he complained of how, when there were many for dinner, they had to make do with cheap cutlery; so he asked for twenty or thirty dozen of silver forks and spoons, together with a complete service of plate and 'a large handsome set of glassware'. He ended by enjoining his correspondent not to buy carriage horses for him 'unless elegant ones'; it was a far cry from the days when the Governor's carriage was pulled by oxen.

While doing so much to improve the house, Elphinstone derived more pleasure from the park and the surrounding country. 'The views here are really delightful', he wrote. 'I go out to them of an evening with a sort of avidity and complaisance, and quit them with regret. Among all my gloomy forebodings, it is a comfort to me that I have not lost my love of nature, nor for poetry.' Although the main front of the house merely looked out over 'the flats' – a burnt-up plain in the dry season which turned to paddy-fields in the monsoon – towards the coconuts and deciduous trees of the Mahim woods, there were hills at the back of the park, where Elphinstone would love to walk. The park itself was a paradise of tropical trees and plants. There was the teak tree and the sacred Asoka, with its rich crimson blossom; there were tamarinds, pepul-trees and all manner of palms, including the traveller's palm and the lofty *caryota* with its pendulous clusters of dark red berries. The botanically-minded Lady Canning was in raptures when she stayed here on her first arrival in India, and particularly admired the ancient cypresses, 'entirely covered with flame-coloured bignonia, like pillars of fire'.

Close to the house was an old garden, said to date from the time of the Jesuits, with walks and flower-beds watered by stone channels; ending with a terrace that ran between a mango-grove and a lake. To Bishop Heber, who was a guest of Mountstuart Elphinstone, the most interesting thing in the garden was 'a slip of the willow which grows on Buonaparte's grave', brought here by someone whose ship had called at St Helena. He was also impressed by the collection of wild animals kept in an adjoining paddock, which included various sorts of deer, a tiger and an ostrich, 'a noble wild ass from Cutch' and 'a very singular ape from Sumatra'. Heber devoted much space in his journal to the latter, which the Indian servants called 'junglee admee' or 'wild man': 'They evidently regard it as a great curiosity, and, I apprehend, it owes something of its corpulency to their presents of fruit.'

When they tired of the park, the inhabitants of Parell could ride or drive in the Mahim woods, which to Lady Canning seemed like the hot-house at Kew combined with *Swiss Family Robinson* and *Paul et Virginie*. Beneath the shade of the huge old trees were tanks covered with pink and white lotus, and clusters of native huts thatched with palm leaves; in summer all was ablaze with the *palas* or flame of the forest. The woods extended westwards to the shore, and along the coast as far as the ferry to the neighbouring island of Salsette, where the

9　Parell, a nineteenth century view.

10　Parell, a reception for Chiefs held by Albert Edward, Prince of Wales, in one of the upstairs drawing rooms in November, 1875. The Prince is seen conversing with the twelve-year-old Gaekwar of Baroda.

11   Hyderabad Residency, the south front in 1813.

12   Hyderabad Residency, view from the north-east, showing the look-
      out on the roof.

Governor's guests would be taken to see the cave-temples. Heber and his wife and daughter had an alarming experience when returning from one of these expeditions after dark. They were in the last of the procession of five carriages conveying the Governor's party, and as they waited at the end of the causeway for the raft to ferry them across, they were cut off by the tide which rose as high as the doors of their carriage. They escaped in a canoe, blaming their discomforture on 'the perfect apathy and helplessness of the natives', who in the end had the laugh, for while the Bishop and his family crossed in their flimsy craft, the carriage followed them 'in perfect safety' on the ferry, so that they need never have abandoned it.

The learned Recorder of Bombay, Sir James Mackintosh, who was lent Parell from 1804 to 1812, would go for a dawn canter in the Mahim woods, riding an Arab called 'Sir Charles Grey' while his companion's mount was named 'Bobberywallah'. As he rode, he would talk of his home in Scotland, and of salmon-fishing on the Don. But while much of his heart was in the Highlands, a fair portion of it was here at Parell, where he and his family spent eight happy years, even though the place gave them intermittent fever. 'Poor Parell!' he wrote sadly, when leaving it for good. During his time here, the house abounded with books – there was always the latest novel of Scott, and the most recent volume of the *Edinburgh Review* to have reached India. Nor did it ever lack stimulating company, though the talk was not allowed to go on into the night. Having dined at four, and taken tea at seven, Sir James would read for a while to his wife and children and then retire to bed.

Though Mackintosh, as a mere judge, was in the nature of an interloper at Parell, he had so much in common with his fellow Scot, Mountstuart Elphinstone, that it is not he but Elphinstone's predecessor, Sir Evan Nepean, the first English politician to come to Bombay as Governor, who seems the odd man out during this period. For all the retinue, and the extra servants, life at Parell under Elphinstone cannot have been much different from what it was in Mackintosh's time. There was the same wit and learning, the same love of books – while working incredibly hard as Governor, Elphinstone found time to read Milton, Pepys, Ben Johnson, Chateaubriand and Scott, as well as the Greek and Latin classics and works in Italian and Persian.

Elphinstone, however, differed from Mackintosh, the family man, in that he suffered periodically from melancholy and craved solitude. He particularly enjoyed Parell when the house was empty: sitting in the room of a friend who had just left, he found the quiet 'delightful'; though he admitted that the room was 'not so pleasant as it was formerly'. There was a mystical side to his nature which must have taken pleasure in Mrs Heber's account of the adventure at the ferry, if she described it to him in the terms in which she recorded it in her journal: 'The scene was beautiful and wild . . . the glorious moon and stars shining overhead, and reflected with brilliancy in the still waters, in the middle of which we appeared to stand, without any visible means of escape.'

Yet Elphinstone was far from being a romantic recluse among Governors. He did his duty as a host – though he was himself virtually a teetotaller – kept the conversation going at public breakfasts, and frequently took his guests and his staff pig-sticking. He would speak of being 'plagued with the prospect of large parties'; but when they took place, he often enjoyed them. 'Very hot and very crowded but on the whole very pleasant' was his verdict on the King's Birthday Ball at Parell in 1826; a dinner for 110 in 1822 'went off well notwithstanding the heat'. When the King of Johanna, an island of some importance in the sea route to and from the Cape, visited Bombay in 1827, Elphinstone gave a dinner for him at Parell with dancing and jugglers and a troupe of Indian actors in 'ancient Hindu costume' whom he described as 'wild and fanciful figures not ill dressed nor ill supported'. There was not infrequently a breath of Africa or Arabia at Parell in Elphinstone's time: thus, the Hebers' fellow-guests included the Arab captain of a brig belonging to the Imam of Muscat, and a French officer named Le Chevalier Rienzi – a descendant of Petrarch's friend – who had been travelling in Egypt and Abyssinia.

While managing to save an average of £3,000 a year out of his annual salary of £10,000, Elphinstone entertained on a more lavish scale than his successor, Sir John Malcolm – yet another Scot – who limited himself to one dinner and one ball a month, and for the rest of the time did the honours of Parell with 'endless decoctions of tea and coffee'. It was at a ball at Parell in Malcolm's time that an envoy of the Shah of Persia, seeing the ladies dance a quadrille, thought they were performing a *nautch* in his honour, and begged the Governor not to let them trouble themselves any further on his account.

The Persian gentleman may have felt by instinct what Mrs Maria Graham observed in 1812, namely that the men of the Bombay British community were 'of a higher caste than the women'. She was, however, notoriously critical. Speaking of Bombay society in general, she compared it to the society of 'a country town at home', which was her way of calling it provincial. Forty years later, Lady Canning described it more charitably as being of 'a homely sort of country-neighbour style'; though, like Mrs Graham, she felt that the ladies' manners left much to be desired: 'they sit *clouées* to their chairs until one has them quite dragged up by force to come to be introduced.' But she admitted – as Mrs Graham did before her – that they were well dressed.

Lady Falkland, a no less qualified judge, being the daughter of William IV and Mrs Jordan, went further, and wrote of her first reception at Parell after becoming Lady Sahib in 1848: 'The ladies were dressed in the newest fashions from Europe, and their toilettes were quite *en règle*.' The talk, however, did not match the clothes. 'Our topics were dusty roads, cool houses, the reviving climate of the Deccan (which seemed, from all accounts, to be a kind of paradise), healthy and unhealthy stations, and the coming monsoon.' Lady Falkland felt that this was only to be expected, for it was May, perhaps the hottest month in the year, and the reception was held at midday, according to a barbarous custome which she resolved to change.

Yet at evening parties in the cooler season, she did not find any great improvement in the conversation, which was confined to local topics. It became clear to her that people who had been in India for twenty or thirty years were no longer interested in the 'courts, camps or cabinets of Europe'. A Governor like Malcolm, who was himself an 'old Indian', would have had plenty of common ground with these people; but the Falklands came of the new breed of aristocratic Lord Sahibs and Lady Sahibs fresh from England. When Lady Falkland mentioned a major European event to an old officer, he stared blankly at her and said: 'I know nothing at all about it.' When she spoke of a well-known English politician, he replied: 'I know nothing at all about him.' When she tried to draw him out on some other subject, he cut her short by saying: 'I take no interest at all in it.'

This officer was typical of the ancient military gentlemen who found employment in the less important Indian commands. Since the end of the Third Maratha War, Bombay had been far from the fighting. Unlike Calcutta or Madras, it did not possess a large cantonment, the headquarters of the Bombay army being at Poona. So its society lacked the military flavour of so many Indian stations, which, particularly in the stirring times of the eighteen-forties and fifties, did much to relieve the monotony of life. One seldom encountered a Havelock or a Nicholson at the Parell dinner table; neither was the ballroom much graced by brave young officers on leave from the Punjab.

Nor were there many Indian princes to add glitter to the scene; though there were plenty of rich Parsis, the ugliness of their chimney-pot head-dresses covered in 'shining chintz like oil-cloth' being made up for by the charming presence of their wives, who, unlike Hindu or Muslim women were seldom left at home. The Parsis and the British had always freely associated, so that the social life of Bombay, while it may have been more parochial than in other parts of India, was at the same time more cosmopolitan. Bombayers remained immune to the prejudices which, as the century progressed, caused the British elsewhere in the country to become segregated from their Indian neighbours. Society was also less rigid, for there was a growing and increasingly prosperous community of merchants that cut across the civilian hierarchy. Yet surprisingly – or perhaps understandably – the ladies of Bombay were no less exact in matters of precedence than their sisters of the north and east. Lady Falkland, at one of her dinner parties, saw a lady who was feeling ill and longed to go home. She urged her to do so, but the lady insisted on staying until the more senior guests had departed.

Although the Governor of Bombay lived in grand enough style, with a posse of ADCs, a magnificent bodyguard, a band and an army of servants – including the inevitable French chef – Parell was less formal than Government House, Madras, and very much less so than Calcutta. Things seem to have been run more casually. Once, when visiting the mainland near Bassein, Mountstuart Elphinstone was accidentally separated from his staff. For some hours he wandered alone in 'neglected lanes', not knowing where he was but admiring the beauty of the countryside; at length he came to a house where the servants were away and he was not expected, but where he managed to get 'a hard egg and some native bread'.

When the Falklands landed from their ship in 1848, there was nobody to meet them, owing to a misunderstanding; so they drove to Parell in a 'hackbuggy'. The sepoys at the gate refused, at first, to let them in, but as Lady Falkland proudly recalled, 'I soon showed them the way!' Despite this inauspicious start, Lady Falkland entered with zest into her duties, and has left a charming account of her day-to-day life at Parell. In the early morning she would sit, 'wondering at everything', on a verandah overlooking the garden. 'There was nothing in the scene to remind me of Europe, except perhaps, at very rare intervals, an English servant determined to wear a black beaver hat and doing all he could to have a sunstroke. Despite the early hour, it was always overpoweringly hot. There were no clouds rising in the deep blue sky, and the sun would pour down its heat on the burnt-up grass and trees and drooping shrubs.'

'A very tall, portly Parsi, who is the *maître d'hôtel*, would walk forth to begin his day's occupations, and then appeared sundry Parsi and Muslim servants carrying tea or coffee to their different masters' rooms. These would be followed by the *durzis* or tailors going to their work. Everybody has a private tailor in India . . . Then the *dhobi* passed by, with a red turban and a long white dress, carrying a basket full of linen, which he meant to wash by beating and slapping it on a stone in the tank at the back of the garden. Then at a quick pace came the gardeners, having on their heads red cloth skullcaps and very little other apparel, carrying on their shoulders a long bamboo stick, at each end of which hangs a large copper *chattie* full of water, with which they were going to refresh the drooping plants. Such was the scene from my verandah looking outwards.'

'If I turned round, in a room immediately adjacent was an individual (wearing moustaches, like all the natives) clothed in white drapery (twisted round his body and descending to the knees), a white jacket, and a blue and white turban – his black, shining legs and feet being uncovered; over his shoulder hung his badge of office – a duster – with which he occasionally rubbed a chair or table; he represents the housemaid . . . Near him was another Hindu in a similar dress, except that he wore a blue turban and held a tray of small glasses full of coconut oil to place in the lamps suspended round the room.'

With this motley crowd always coming and going, it was no wonder that the Commissioner of Police, when testing the security arrangements of Parell during the Mutiny, succeeded in appearing by the Governor's bedside at six one morning disguised as a sweeper. The diversity of the Parell servants extended to those waiting at table. Lady Falkland recalled how the diminutive Goanese, in their tight white jackets and trousers, were not seen to advantage by the side of the Muslims and Parsis, whose ample and well-starched white dresses rustled like ladies' petticoats. But the Muslims and Parsis were themselves divergent in their headgear; for while the former wore red or green turbans, the latter sported their peculiar chintz-covered caps.

As the morning grew hotter, Lady Falkland moved from the verandah into a lofty inner room and sat beneath the swinging *punkah*. Except when the weather was unusually cool, it was not customary for European ladies to go out until late afternoon, so the long hours had somehow to be whiled away; reading, working up some sketches made on a visit to a Hindu temple, going through the arrangements for next week's ball with the ADC. After tiffin came the most trying part of the day, at any rate during the hotter months. From three to five it was 'too hot to take a siesta – too hot to do anything in comfort'. But at five the sea breeze, usually so elusive at Parell, made its presence felt, ruffling the tops of the palm trees, causing the lustres to tremble and produce 'a pleasing harmonious carillon'.

Now was the time to go out. There may have been a visit to a school – perhaps to the Byculla orphanage, two miles from Parell, in which Governors and their wives always took a particular interest, it being attached to the church where they worshipped. There was an embarrassing scene during one of these visits when 'a very little child, an inmate of the institution, with large black eyes, a flattish nose, and a complexion shading off from bistre into yellow ochre' suddenly clung to the legs of a gentleman in Lord and Lady Falkland's party and, 'looking up most imploringly into his face, cried out, "Pa-pa! Pa-pa!"' Lady Falkland hastened to point out that the gentleman in question had only just arrived from England, and had never been in India before.

When there was nothing else to do, the Governor and his wife would join the fashionable crowd on the Esplanade, the fine open space by the waterfront at the southern end of the city. To get there from Parell meant a drive through five miles of bazaars. The narrow streets, overhung by tier upon tier of crazy wooden balconies, were so packed with humanity that the 'gorah-wallahs' or syces who ran beside the Governor's carriage were 'constantly calling out to the pedestrians to get out of the way . . . On all sides, jostling and passing each other, are seen Persian dyers, Bannian shop-keepers, Chinese with long tails, Arab horse-dealers, Abyssinian youths, servants of the latter, pedlars, toddy drawers, carrying large vessels on their heads, Armenian priests, with flowing robes and beards, Jews in long tunics and mantles, their dress half Persian, half Moorish'.

It was dusk when they reached the Esplanade, and the band had just struck up. 'As there is scarcely any twilight in the tropics, we sat for half an hour in the dark, with our faces turned to the western breeze. The only lights were those for the musicians, who were playing from notes, and the lamps of the numerous carriages. The ladies remained in their *britzkas*, and the gentlemen flitted about from carriage to carriage, paying their *devoirs* to the fair occupants . . . The children were led by their attendants round and round the bandstand, which I thought would give the little things a decided taste, or dislike, for music in future years.'

'We returned home by the native town again; it was still animated – marriage festivities were going on, many of the houses were gaily lighted, discordant musical instruments were heard in all directions; some shops were still open, and from their ceilings hung heavy brass lamps, throwing a dim light on dusky Hindus, enveloped in large white cloths, their heads just peering over baskets piled up with rice and all kinds of grain; while over our heads passed the flying-foxes with their lazy and mysterious flight.'

Back in the quiet spaciousness of Parell, the lights in the chandeliers flickered as the *punkahs* swung slowly back and forth. Even if there were no guests expected for dinner, it was likely that the Governor and his wife would be staying in for the rest of the evening; though they dined out more often than the Governor-General did in Calcutta. There was seldom a play, or a concert; as Lady Falkland lamented, 'poor Bombay is out of the beat of artists.'

Dinner was served in the huge upstairs verandah. One night, when the Falklands were peacefully enjoying their meal here, the monsoon broke. 'Vivid flashes of lightning dazzled the sight, and tremendous peals of thunder shook the building. We had barely time to have the table removed ere the rain came down in torrents, and in a few minutes what had been our dining room was converted into a tank or pond.' Lady Falkland admitted that she 'almost wished to go into the flooded verandah and enjoy the monster shower bath'.

The air became cooler while the rain was falling, but the storm had passed and the temperature had risen again by the time the Governor and his wife retired to bed. As on most nights at this time of the year, it was, in the words of Lady Falkland, 'impossible to sleep with closed windows, and nearly as impossible to do so with open ones . . . The beasts, the birds, the insects, the reptiles appear to join in one universal tumult, and even human beings seem to take very little repose. In a temple not far off a priest is beating a drum and I conclude, invoking the help of some god or goddess. When the drumming ceases I sink into a doze, but to be again roused by howling jackals tearing over the flats in pursuit of prey, by the hooting of the "night hawk" . . . then by the deep-toned note of an enormous frog, mingled with the "chip, chip" of many a grasshopper, and about daylight a lively bird, anxious to be "up and doing", begins a merry chirp, or a crow with his very vulgar "caw, caw" destroys all hopes of rest. At last, as day dawns, I see, outside the bed, those little greedy mosquitoes clinging to the curtains, and staring at me, thinking how good I should be! And I rise, weary and but little refreshed, to go to the launch of a ship at the dockyard in the fort.'

Shortly before their departure in 1853, the Falklands took part in a more momentous public function – the opening of the first twenty miles of the Great Indian Peninsular Railway from Bombay to Tannah. Railways, steamships, the Suez Canal and its precursor, the overland route across Egypt, gave Bombay a new importance as the Gateway of India. Everybody who came to India landed at Bombay, and the more distinguished arrivals were entertained at Parell. It was here that a new Viceroy and Vicereine had their first taste of Government House life, and gathered the first impressions of the sub-continent that was to be their kingdom. Having stepped ashore at the Apollo Bunder in the late afternoon, and driven in the dusk through the bazaars which were decked with coloured lamps and banners of welcome, and lined with cheering crowds and bands playing God Save the Queen, they reached Parell after dark. 'With all its arches and verandahs lighted up, and rows of servants in scarlet and gold dresses or in white,' it looked, to Lady Canning, 'like an opera scene.' She was even more impressed by the dinner that followed: 'in a verandah entirely draped with white muslin, and with those beautifully dressed servants to wait, and strange fruits on the table, and strange flowers, and a very good band of music outside.' Yet it seemed to her that the heat made people 'very quiet, and gentle, and low, for I had rather a feeling as if I was brusque and noisy, so very piano is the tone'.

The Cannings stayed a week at Parell, and Lady Canning was delighted and fascinated with everything, though she found it hard to grow accustomed to such Indian habits as getting into a cold tub '*after* exercise, doing exactly what we should think the most dangerous thing possible', and she took an instant dislike to *punkahs*, when she first encountered their 'mesmerising effect' in Byculla church. There was an expedition to Salsette, and a picnic in the cave-temples there, which had been specially furnished for the occasion with carpets, chairs and tables, looking-glasses and even 'an enormous bath'. Lady Canning was impressed by how spotless and highly-polished everything was, and learnt with interest that the cleaning material used was cow-dung.

The more celebrated cave-temple on Elephanta Island, across the harbour, was the scene of an even grander picnic which seems to have been an obligatory entertainment for exalted visitors. By a perverse custom – doubtless in the hope that it would be cooler – it was held at night, which not only precluded the guests from enjoying the views across the Bay and the natural beauties of the island, but doomed the cave-banquet to take place in an atmosphere made unpleasant by the heat and smell of countless oil-lamps. Lady Canning, however, was enchanted with the spectacle, which put her in mind of Belshazzar's Feast: the 'strange colonnades and illuminations', the gigantic, calm faces of the sculptured deities, the flaming torches and the 'crowds of really naked coolies fluttering about at a distance'. She was no less enthusiastic about the great ball given in her husband's and her honour, when every tree in the garden of Parell was illuminated with rush-lights. The Governor, Lord Elphinstone, a nephew of Mountstuart Elphinstone – not the only instance of an Indian Government House being occupied by more than one generation of the same family – was 'charmed' when she declared it to be 'the prettiest fête, I really think, I ever was at'. 'Elphy's establishment' at Parell was henceforth to be Lady Canning's ideal as a Viceregal hostess.

Parell's most illustrious guest, Albert Edward, Prince of Wales, arrived in the evening of 8 November, 1875, having driven through more than usually crowded streets adorned with triumphial arches bearing inscriptions of welcome – including one which said: 'Tell Mamma we're happy.' There was only room in the house for the Prince himself, together with his host, Sir Philip Wodehouse, and one or two of the most important members of his suite, most of the party being accommodated in 'a fair camp' along the avenue, which stretched away on either side to provide quarters for the troops, servants and hangers-on. Owing to the swampiness of the ground, the tents were pitched on wooden platforms, which, according to the war correspondent, William Howard Russell, who accompanied the Prince on his India tour, 'did not afford very equable support, and as one walked, the planks went up and down, giving a general impression of an earthquake about the premises'. There were, moreover, 'horrible suspicions of snakes'.

Nevertheless, after the rigours of the day, which ended with a State banquet, the gentlemen of the suite – except for the unfortunate whose turn it was to sit up all night outside the Prince's room with a pair of pistols – forgot their misgivings and walked gratefully along the avenue to bed, beneath a sky aglow with the fires of the camp-followers.

Those of the Royal party who, like Russell, had been in India before, felt very much at home as they awoke to 'the cry of the great wood-pecker, and the chattering of the familiar mynah', and were greeted by the *bheestie* with his water-skin and the *khitmagar* with a cup of tea. Outside the tent waited the humble sweeper, the syce with a horse ready for the morning ride, and the red-turbaned barber, 'a handsome, smooth-faced fellow who makes his English go a long way, and who is a master in his art, though his fingers are deadly cold, and he is for his trade overfond of garlic'. Each of the gentlemen had five or six such stalwarts to attend on him, as well as a personal servant engaged for the duration of the tour out of a crowd of aspirants who had confronted him on the previous evening. Each, in addition, had brought his own European servant – the Duke of Sutherland had also brought his piper.

That day, and the three days that followed, were packed with events, ranging from another State banquet to a performance by con-jurers and snake charmers, when the Prince's physician, Dr Joseph Fayrer – a Mutiny veteran who had attended the dying Henry Law-rence in the Lucknow Residency – rather unsportingly demonstrated that the snakes had no fangs. The most impressive occasion was when the Prince received each of the numerous Chiefs who had come to Bombay for the Royal visit. He sat on a silver throne in front of a por-trait of the Queen in one of the great upstairs rooms at Parell, attended by servants bearing the emblems of royalty, and flanked by his suite all wearing magnificent uniforms – including the journalist, Russell, who had been required by the Prince to provide himself with one, and had designed his own, 'with so generous a gold stripe to his kersey breeches' that he was chaffed by his fellow-Irishman, Lord Charles Beresford, for having 'gold trousers with a white stripe inside'.

The Chiefs drove up to the house one by one, each being saluted with his requisite number of guns by a battery of Royal Artillery sta-tioned in the park. As each potentate, followed by his *sirdars*, was brought into the Presence, the Prince rose and advanced down the crimson and gold heraldic carpet to meet him. Russell called this carpet the 'kudometer', for the distance which the Prince advanced along it denoted the precise rank of his visitor. The greatest impression was made by the little Gaekwar of Baroda, aged twelve and so covered with jewels that he was likened to 'a crystallised rainbow'. There were some smiles among the gentlemen of the suite when the no less bejewelled Maharaja of Mysore made his entry, for the band outside decreed at that moment to strike up the duet of the Brave Gendarmes, 'We'll run him in'.

Ten years after being *en fête* for the Prince, Parell stood empty and abandoned. Even before Lady Fergusson, wife of the then Governor, Sir James Fergusson, died here of cholera in 1882, there was a period from 1877 to 1880 when the house was unoccupied. This was during the reign of that high-powered administrator, Sir Richard Temple, whose brief sojourns in Bombay between whirlwind tours of the remoter parts of his province were spent at Malabar Point, the marine residence which the Governors had possessed since the time of Sir Evan Nepean. When Temple first became Governor it was May, and he was told that Parell was excessively hot, and that the resident bandsmen were going down with fever; but he also avoided coming here in the cooler months. And indeed, it was not an ideal cold-weather house either, not even in Bombay, its huge rooms being open to the corridors with rows of arches. Lady Dufferin, who stayed here in December, was so troubled by draughts that she derived little pleasure from the novel experience of seeing the garden lit by electricity.

By the eighteen-eighties, Parell had lost its former attraction as a country house, its park being caught up in the spread of the over-crowded city. The neighbourhood had been deserted by the fashionable in favour of the wooded slopes of Malabar Hill, facing the open sea. So the Governors followed suit and Malabar Point became their sole Bombay residence. For some years the future of Parell was in doubt, and there was talk of selling it. Then, after Bombay had suffered a fearful visitation of plague in 1896 – believed, by some of the more loyal Indians, to have been a Divine punishment for the besmearing of a statue of Queen Victoria – the house was turned into a plague research laboratory, which it remains to this day. 'No *punkahs* cooled the big bare rooms at Parell,' wrote a tourist of 1907. 'The floors are not swept but washed, and everything possible is done to keep the dust from flying about.' Gone was the crimson carpet which the King-Emperor had trod as Prince of Wales; gone, too, was the silver throne on which he had sat, along with the portraits and the chandeliers; and in their place were rows of flasks containing the 'pampered plague germs'. The Goddess of Contagion, that uninvited guest at Parell in years gone by, was now being propitiated by having the house as her exclusive domain.

5

HYDERABAD RESIDENCY

YDERABAD, in the Deccan, the capital of the Nizam's dominions, was one of the largest and most fascinating of Indian cities.
It lay among trees and artificial lakes, surrounded by bare
granite hills and weird-shaped rocks, reminding the Victorian writer
and traveller, Wilfrid Scawen Blunt, of a town in Arabia. To add to this
impression, the gaily-clad crowds in the streets included people in
Arab dress; descendants of the chieftains and soldiers from Muscat and
the Hadramaut who, until the custom was forbidden by Lord Dalhousie, entered the service of successive Nizams. The prevailing atmosphere, however, was not so much Arabian, or South Indian, as Persian,
for Hyderabad was the last surviving fragment of the Mogul Empire.
The Nizam's forebear, Asaf Jah, was Viceroy of the Deccan under the
Emperor; when, after Aurungzeb's death, the Empire started to break
up, he became to all intents and purposes an independent sovereign. His
successors, unlike the successors of the other Mogul Viceroys in Bengal
and Oudh, maintained the independence of their vast kingdom by
entering into treaties of friendship with the British. The British Resident was thus in Hyderabad not as the agent of a conquering power,
but as the ambassador of an ally. Nevertheless, as the representative of
the might of British India, which completely encircled the Nizam's
dominions, he wielded a very considerable authority. He was, moreover, the actual ruler of certain territories ceded by the Nizam; and he
had control of a substantial British force stationed at Secunderabad,
immediately north of the capital, and officially intended for the Nizam's
use.

The Resident at Hyderabad was thus the most important of all the
Residents and Agents in the Political Department. Yet even taking into
account his high position, the Hyderabad Residency was unexpectedly

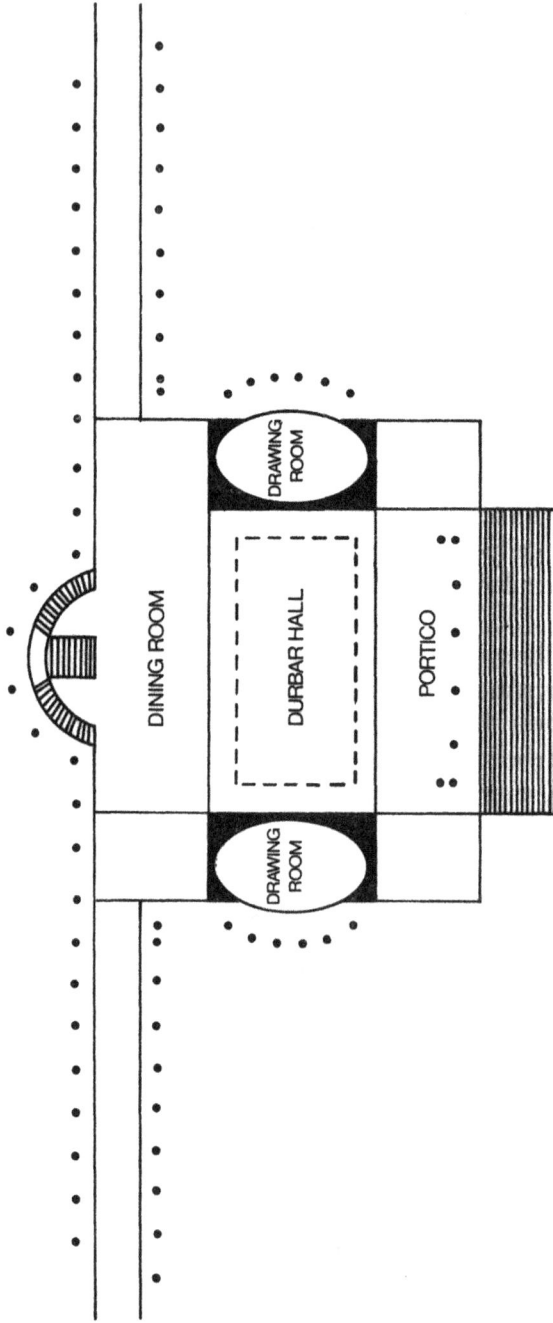

HYDERABAD RESIDENCY main (lower) floor
The corridor on the left leads to the Residents private wing and that on the right
to the State suite.

grand. With its vast Corinthian portico, its Durbar Hall lined with Ionic columns, its oval drawing rooms and its magnificent staircase, it was more palatial than any Indian Government House apart from those in Calcutta and New Delhi, and would probably not have been on this scale but for the two loves of Major James Achilles Kirkpatrick, who was Resident from 1797 to 1805 and negotiated the most important treaties with the Nizam, prevailing upon him to get rid of his French troops and to replace them with the British Contingent.

Kirkpatrick's first love was splendour. He found the old Residency, which consisted of a group of bungalows and an open-sided Indian building used as a dining hall, 'uncomfortable and inconvenient'. As a preliminary to building a fine new house, he obtained a grant from the Nizam of sixty acres on the opposite side of the Musi river to the city. According to a story, Kirkpatrick showed the Nizam a large plan of the proposed Residency compound when applying for this land, and to his chagrin, his request was turned down. Afterwards, however, the Nizam's Minister explained that his master, who did not understand scale, had been frightened by the size of Kirkpatrick's plan which was 'almost as large as any of the maps of his kingdom he had yet seen'. So Kirkpatrick had the same plan drawn on a tiny card, and when he presented this to the Nizam, he immediately obtained his grant.

The new house was commenced in 1803 to the design of Lieutenant Samuel Russell of the Madras Engineers, son of the Academician, John Russell. It consisted of a large and imposing main block, of two storeys on a high basement, with a pair of flanking wings. The main feature of the exterior was the portico on the north front, its pediment carried by six giant Corinthian columns. The south front had a central bow and an Ionic colonnade running through both storeys, rather like at Government House, Calcutta; it faced the main approach from the direction of the city, which was by way of a triumphal arch and a forecourt bounded on either side by the stables, the *hatikhana* and other outbuildings in an impressive row. This side of the house was designed for Oriental pomp; through the arch and into the forecourt would come the Nizam, complete with elephants and an army of horsemen and foot followers; through it, in an elephant, horse and foot procession that was hardly less splendid, the Resident would sally forth when paying a return visit. The north front, facing the park, was more English, reminiscent of one of the great Palladian mansions built by the Whig aristocracy fifty years earlier.

Unlike Government House, Madras, the house did not appear to be surrounded by verandahs, although the colonnades and porches were deep enough to be used as such, and the main portico was virtually an open-sided hall, sixty feet long and fifty feet high, at the top of the great flight of steps. The Durbar Hall was of the same length and height as the portico, and lay immediately behind it, with a large oval room on either side, from which one entered four other reception rooms. A grand staircase in the bow of the south front, dividing into two gracefully curving flights, led up to the gallery of the Durbar Hall, off which opened a series of rooms similar in size and style to those below. The staircase also led down to the south entrance, and to the underworld of offices, which included the treasury, guarded night and day by a party of sepoys.

For an Indian house, the new Residency was unusually well appointed; there were delicately moulded friezes and doorcases; the staircase had an elegant wrought-iron balustrade; the portico and some of the rooms were paved with black and white marble, while other floors were of parquet. Before the house was built, Kirkpatrick ordered a Wilton carpet fifty feet by thirty for the Durbar Hall, which was originally intended to be this size. He then decided to increase the length of the room by ten feet, so wrote to England for a second carpet that would cover the larger expanse of floor.

While his superior, the 'Magnificent Marquess' Wellesley, and his neighbour at Madras, Lord Clive, had to answer to the East India Company Directors for their costly building schemes, Kirkpatrick indulged in all this princely extravagance knowing that the Nizam would foot the bill. One might have expected the Nizam to have ingratiated himself with his British ally by paying for the new Residency; but there was more to it than that. Kirkpatrick was his adopted son, a consequence of the Resident's other love, which was for the beautiful Muslim girl, Khair-un-Nissa.

It was natural that the ladies of the Nizam's court should have heard of the Resident's good looks and his gallant military career – he was known to the Indians as Hushmat Jung, or 'Glorious in Battle'. Among them was Khair-un-Nissa – the name means 'Excellent among Women' – the daughter of a noble family of Persian descent, who managed to catch a glimpse of Kirkpatrick and immediately fell in love with him. According to one version of the story, she took to sleeping on the verandah of a house where he was in the habit of spending his nights

13   Hyderabad Residency, Kirkpatrick's model of the house in the Begum's garden.

14   Hyderabad Residency, the Guard of Honour for the visit of the Viceroy, Lord Elgin, in November, 1895.

15 Hyderabad Residency, Sir Stuart Fraser and his daughter Violet, with their trophies under the main portico.

16 Lucknow Residency.

with a low-caste mistress, and was eventually seduced by him; but Kirkpatrick's own account is more romantic. Writing to his brother, William, he told of how, after he had turned away an old woman sent by her to press her suit, Khair-un-Nissa herself entered his house as he sat alone one evening. There followed 'a long nocturnal interview', when he had 'a full and close survey of her lovely person', while being strong enough, as he put it, to 'safely pass the fiery ordeal. . . . I, who was but ill qualified for the task, attempted to argue the romantic young creature out of a passion which I could not, I confess, help feeling myself something more than pity for. She declared to me again and again that her affections had been irrevocably fixed on me for a series of time, that her fate was linked to mine, and that she should be content to pass her days with me as the humblest of handmaids.' By the time she took her leave, Kirkpatrick was thoroughly smitten; and shortly afterwards, he agreed to go to her house, where Khair-un-Nissa's grandmother added her pleadings to those of the girl herself. They told him that she was being forced into marriage with a cousin, a prospect so repugnant to her that she had attempted to end her life by poison, and that he alone could rescue her from this fate by responding favourably to her advances. This was too much for Kirkpatrick's chivalrous soul; as he told his brother, 'I must have been something more or less than man to have held out any longer.'

After a son had been born of the union, Kirkpatrick resolved to make Khair-un-Nissa his lawful wife, and to give her a home in the Residency. The Nizam approved of the marriage, and to forestall the opposition of some of Khair-un-Nissa's family, he made Kirkpatrick his adopted son. This did not prevent Kirkpatrick from getting into serious trouble with Wellesley; for not only did the East India Company disapprove of its servants marrying Indian women of rank, for fear that they would thus fall under the influence of the local potentates, but Kirkpatrick's enemies at the Nizam's court made matters worse by writing a libellous account of the affair to Calcutta. Wellesley accordingly sent John Malcolm, the future Governor of Bombay, with a commission to conduct an inquiry on the spot, and to supersede Kirkpatrick if he thought fit. When, however, Malcolm landed at Masulipatam, before travelling overland to Hyderabad, he was met by the commandant of Kirkpatrick's cavalry escort, who managed to convince the sensible Scot that if he appeared at the Nizam's capital it would lower the Resident's prestige even though the charges against him were proved false. So Malcolm returned to Calcutta, and Kirkpatrick was able to justify himself to Wellesley, with the help of brother William, who had preceded him as Resident at Hyderabad and was now the Governor-General's secretary.

Secure once again in his post, and with the resources of his father by adoption, the Nizam, on which to draw, Kirkpatrick was able to devote himself to the building and furnishing of his new Residency. He wrote to England for a reflecting telescope, some 14 feet long and costing £500, with which to adorn his terrace; he hoped to be instructed in its use by one of his staff, who was the son of a Professor of Astronomy at Edinburgh. He also sent for chemical and electrical apparatus of large dimensions, to amuse his younger guests. To illuminate the new building on festive occasions, he asked for a hundred of the largest Chinese lamps available and several thousand smaller ones. He laid out the Residency compound in suitable style; with a flower garden, a lake, an orchard planted with all the fruits of India and Europe, including orange trees sent specially from Portugal; and a park stocked with deer. Elsewhere in the grounds were separate houses for his staff, and quarters for his guards, his cavalry escort and his band.

Within the Residency compound, a short distance from the west wing of the house, Kirkpatrick built a *zenana* for his wife. It was decorated with paintings of birds, flowers and beasts; it had fountains to cool the air and was surrounded by an enclosed garden. A hundred years later, the 'Begum's Garden', as it came to be known, was little changed from what it was in Khair-un-Nissa's time; a secluded and rather haunted place. Kirkpatrick's staff would frequently see him walking in the direction of his *zenana*, but they never set eyes on Khair-un-Nissa, who lived in strict *purdah*, not even emerging to admire the new Residency when it was finished. Instead, her husband built her a model of it at one end of her garden, so that she could see what it was like. This miniature palace, complete with portico and balustrade, remained a feature of the Begum's Garden, a delight to future generations of Residency children who were, however, discouraged from playing in it since it harboured snakes and insects. It must surely have delighted the little son of Kirkpatrick and Khair-un-Nissa, and his sister, who was born a year after him; but they did not enjoy it for long. When they were hardly more than four or five years old, Kirkpatrick sent them to be brought up by his family in England, where their Indian names, which meant 'Lord of the World' and 'Our little Princess and English Lady' were exchanged for William George and Catherine Aurora. They never saw India or their parents again. Soon after their departure, in October 1805, Kirkpatrick died while on a visit to Calcutta. It is not certain how long Khair-un-Nissa survived him; presumably she died soon afterwards, for while we know that the children frequently corresponded with their Indian grandmother, who lived to a great age, there is no evidence of their having written to Khair-un-Nissa herself.

Under Kirkpatrick's successor, the charming and cultured Captain Thomas Sydenham, the atmosphere of the Residency became less Oriental and more redolent of fashionable London society, with the elegant Mrs Sydenham, who had been Maid of Honour to the Duchess of York, as hostess. Both Sydenham and Henry Russell, who came after him, embellished the house, furnishing it in a style that was more than worthy of the rooms. The staircase was adorned with sculpture: the Apollo Belvedere, Leda and the Swan, Venus rising from the Sea. Mirrors, in neo-Classical frames, reflected the columns of the Durbar Hall to infinity. Sir John Malcolm, who had known the old Residency, was amazed at what he found when he re-visited Hyderabad in 1817. He waxed eloquent on the chairs and couches, 'all covered with crimson velvet, with massive gilt arms and backs', the girandoles and the lustres: 'the central one, which was made by Blade, and is considered the finest ever seen, cost £950 in England.' The best pieces came from Carlton House. With an eye to obtaining certain political concessions for the Company, the Directors bought them from the Prince Regent at the price he asked; and then made the Nizam pay for them.

All this extravagance did not please Sir Charles Metcalfe, who became Resident in 1820. He regarded the Residency as 'a magnificent and uncomfortable pile, on which immense sums have been unconscionably spent by my predecessors, at the expense of the Nizam's government' and thought of building himself a 'cottage' thirty miles away where he would find the solitude his melancholy nature craved. 'As long as the billiard table stands,' he lamented, 'the Residency will be a tavern. I wish that I could introduce a nest of white ants secretly . . . and cause it to disappear.'

Although Metcalfe did his duty with occasional dinners, balls and suppers, the Residency was considered dull under his regime. Local European society preferred to frequent the house of Sir William Rumbold, grandson of the notorious 'Nabob' Sir Thomas Rumbold and a partner in the firm of William Palmer and Company, bankers to the Nizam. Not only were Rumbold's entertainments far more lavish, with music and song instead of official conversation. There was also the charming presence of Lady Rumbold, and of her friend Miss Ross Lewin, the belle of Calcutta; whereas Metcalfe's establishment was austerely male – he is believed to have married his Indian mistress, but she was not at Hyderabad, not even in the *zenana*.

Metcalfe may have been a man of simple tastes, but he had a sense of his own importance. That people should have preferred the banker's house to the Residency became an obsession with him; and he was mortified to hear that Rumbold, and his Eurasian senior partner, William Palmer – who kept an even better table – received more salutes than he did when they went about in their palanquins. He thus had a personal motive for his celebrated attack on William Palmer and Company, which was his prime concern during his years at Hyderabad. Palmer and Rumbold certainly charged the Nizam unsurious rates of interest; but they may not have been quite the 'plunderers' Metcalfe made them out to be.

Having been Metcalfe's stronghold in his war against William Palmer and Company, the Residency was the scene of some real fighting during the Mutiny. Although the Nizam remained true to his role as the faithful ally of Britain, many of his subjects sympathised with the revolt of their fellow-Muslims in the North. A massacre of Europeans was planned; had that happened, there might have been a rising throughout southern India, for Hyderabad was a key position. The Resident, Colonel Cuthbert Davidson, had only recently assumed charge; he was a kindly man with a hearth-rug beard, and the conspirators mistook his benevolence for weakness. Attempts were made to scare him into abandoning his post, to which he replied that he had taken a fancy to be buried in the Residency garden. While cheerfully sending away most of his troops to where he considered they were more urgently needed, he moved some of the remainder into the Residency compound, to re-inforce his escort and guards. One evening in July, 1857, an immense mob of insurgents, led by 500 fierce Rohilla warriors, poured out of the city and across the bridge to attack the Residency. Davidson had been warned by the Minister, Salar Jang, and was well prepared; every gate was closed and bristled with bayonets. The insurgents began to fire down into the compound from houses overlooking the wall; for while in Kirkpatrick's and even in Metcalfe's time the Residency had been surrounded by open country, it was now hemmed in on three sides with bazaars. The guns of the Madras Horse Artillery thundered in reply, and some of the houses held by the insurgents quickly collapsed. Firing continued for most of the night, but shortly before dawn the insurgents fled, thirty-two of them having been killed or wounded.

As a consequence of this attack, the Resident's escort was strengthened, and the wall of the Residency compound fortified with bastions. Iron doors were fitted to bar the way from the centre of the house to the wings, and these were henceforth closed every night. A look-out was erected on the roof, for signalling to the cantonment of Secunderabad.

But for Davidson's sangfroid, the house might have ended as a battle-scarred ruin, like the Residency at Lucknow. It had another narrow escape in 1908 when the Musi river, which ran immediately outside the wall of the compound, flooded, causing havoc in the city, inundating the Residency grounds and outbuildings and depositing an ox and cart up a tree in the park. Disaster in a different form threatened in 1861, when the Nizam offered to refurnish the house at his own expense; but his misplaced generosity was fortunately resisted.

In fact the character of the house changed remarkably little during the century and a half after it was built. Sydenham reduced the height of the Durbar Hall to one storey, forming a great drawing room in its upper half; but the hall was subsequently restored to its original height. So long as Sydenham's drawing room existed, the two upper oval rooms were also used for entertaining; after it was done away with, they reverted to being bedrooms, and the reception rooms were confined to the lower storey. This meant that, in later years, the house could accommodate an unusually large number of guests; for by then the Resident and his family no longer slept in the main block, as they formerly did, but in the east wing, which afforded them a self-contained private apartment, the corresponding rooms in the west wing serving as a suite for the Viceroy, or other guests of particular eminence. Corridors and colonnades had been added to join the wings to the main block; originally, the only connection was at basement level, beneath the platform on which the house stood.

The Residency grounds, first laid out by Kirkpatrick, were improved by his successors. The north front, with its great portico, faced over a formal garden, where, in the eighteen-sixties, there was a particularly fine display of zinnias. Sir Richard Temple, who was then Resident, sent the first bouquet of them to the Nizam, under an Oriental canopy and accompanied by a brief but deferential letter in Persian. As early as Temple's time, the garden boasted of a swimming bath; but the water was contaminated and gave him dysentery.

Beyond the garden was the park, where the trees grew to an enormous height and girth; in particular the mahogany trees and tamarinds. In one vast banyan was a rookery of flying foxes, of which Wilfrid Scawen Blunt has left a vivid description. 'All day long they hang, many hundreds of them together, head downwards from the branches . . . as the sun goes down and it begins to darken, they one by one awaken and stretch and scratch themselves, and at last one lets down a wing and a leg, and drops from his perch, and flaps away just like a great crow, and is followed by another and another, till there are thousands in the air.' The flying foxes long remained a feature of the Residency grounds; in the nineteen-thirties, the Resident's wife, Lady Mackenzie, used to hold battues of them. As well as various sorts of deer, and a flock of Gujarat cranes, the park contained a herd of buffaloes, which provided milk for the house. The health-conscious Mrs Russell, on becoming the chatelaine of the Residency in 1919, went to see if they were being milked hygienically. The buffaloes, not used to white faces, charged at her, and she was obliged to take refuge in the kitchen quarters.

West of the house, close to the Begum's Garden, was the Residency graveyard, dominated by the mausoleum of Mrs Sydenham, who died before her husband left Hyderabad. By the end of the Raj, four Residents had been buried here. The funeral service of the last of them, Sir Alexander Pinhey, who died in 1916, was held beneath the portico. When the harmonium started to play, a swarm of bees which had its nest in the capital of one of the columns descended in anger; everybody fled and the horses harnessed to the waiting gun-carriage bolted.

The portico was usually the scene of more cheerful gatherings. Here, the young Nizam was ceremonially received when he came to a Durbar held by Lord Dufferin; an English guard of honour faced the great flight of steps and the avenue up to the house was lined with cavalry. On this occasion, he came in a yellow coach and four, with yellow postillions and yellow syces. At other times he was more traditional and rode on an elephant; he would send a procession of three elephants with a message of welcome to the newly-arrived Resident, who would afterwards set out on an elephant of his own, accompanied by other elephants and a cavalry escort, to present his credentials to the Nizam. The ride was unforgettable. For an Indian city, Hyderabad had unusually wide and long streets; they abounded in mosques and palaces. Every window and balcony was full of spectators; the streets were lined with the Nizam's troops keeping back the multitude, which was gayer and more picturesque than most Indian crowds since the men nearly all carried arms and accoutrements.

Processions were a great feature of Hyderabad life. All the nobles had long retinues and private troops – as late as 1923, the then Nizam's aunt kept a bodyguard of Amazons. When Temple gave a ball for the Queen's Birthday, he stood spellbound on an upstairs balcony, watching his Indian guests approaching from the city, each with a torchlight procession of retainers. It was always customary to invite the nobles of Hyderabad to balls and dinners at the Residency. Being mostly Muslims, they were not prevented by their religion from eating with Europeans. Their womenfolk would come to *purdah* parties in the Durbar Hall. They would sit on the floor, surrounded by their babies, and by their rather untidy female servants who joined in the conversation. Even the Nizam would come to dinner, and to see the Resident and his wife at other times. The Nizam for whom Lord Dufferin held his Durbar came to the Residency on a much more informal visit in 1909, to say good-bye to the Acting Resident, Michael O'Dwyer. He brought his *satar*, a musical instrument like a mandolin, and played Persian melodies, accompanied by two court musicians in gorgeous costume. At the end of the performance, Mrs O'Dwyer presented him with an illustrated edition of Omar Khayyam.

The Nizam had clearly taken no offence when O'Dwyer, a few months earlier, rebuked him indirectly for dangerous driving. The recent acquisition of a fleet of thirty motor cars had given him a taste for speed, which his English chauffeur was only too pleased to gratify. When his car killed an old woman, it distressed the Nizam and he sent a generous gift to the bereaved family; but he would not learn the lesson. The Residency was showered with complaints, particularly from the military authorities; for the Nizam drove as fast through the cantonments as he did in his own territory. After dropping one or two hints to the Nizam without success, O'Dwyer tackled the English chauffeur. 'It's no affair of mine,' he said, 'whether you kill people in the Nizam's territory. But if you kill anyone in my jurisdiction, by Heavens! I'll hang you.' From then on, all complaints ceased.

O'Dwyer also recalled how when an English lady, the wife of a State official of no great importance, was looking in vain for a seat in the crowded grandstand at a polo tournament, the Nizam, seeing her, bowed, and invited her to the seat next to his own. Sport made for good fellowship between the Nizam and his nobles and the Europeans. There were frequent race meetings, with events for elephants, camels and ponies as well as for horses. Sometimes they were enlivened by the appearance of what was known as the 'Chivalry of the Deccan', when, in the words of Temple, 'clouds of horsemen in every variety of costume would be careering over the plain'. At a race meeting in 1883, Wilfrid Scawen Blunt watched a certain Mohammed Ali Bey cut a sheep in half with a single sword stroke. The nobles often entertained the Resident and other important Europeans to fêtes and picnics on a sumptuous scale, usually accompanied by firework displays arranged by French pyrotechnic artists who had been in the Nizam's service for generations, and held near a lake, so that the fountains of fire and the writhing serpents were reflected in the water.

The Residency served as a link between the Indian world of Hyderabad, where sport and pageantry were combined with a culture and refinement comparable, in one Resident's opinion, only with Peking, and a European society which, from numbering 130 in Metcalfe's time, had increased many times over by the end of the century. As well as the many Europeans in the State service, and in business, there were the officers from the great cantonments at Secunderabad, five miles to the north, and at Bolarum, six miles further north again, where the Resident had his country retreat.

It was cooler here than at the Residency; though in April and May the Resident tended to leave Hyderabad altogether and retire to Ootacamund, in the Nilgiris. But while those two months could certainly be very hot, the climate of Hyderabad was regarded as one of the best in India. The winter months were delightful; while in late summer there were what Temple spoke of as 'those surpassingly lovely days which occur during the intervals between bursts of rain at that season in the Deccan', when the usually arid landscapes turned a brilliant green. The inhabitants of the Residency suffered less from the heat than they did from the mosquitoes, which were particularly bad; sometimes, when there were dinner parties, a light was put under the table to decoy them there, the gentlemen being issued with gumboots and the ladies with pillow-cases, to protect their legs. Another source of discomfort in hot weather, when the Resident and his family slept out of doors, was the all-night noise of singing and musical instruments from the nearby bazaars. Even after the forceful O'Dwyer had found a regulation empowering the police to enforce silence from eleven onwards in the Residency quarter, there was the noise from the city; in particular from the palace of one of the nobles, whose bard would, every two hours of the night, proclaim *urbi et orbi* and with full musical accompaniment his titles and honours and the great deeds of himself and his ancestors. However, at a hint from O'Dwyer, the nobleman courteously agreed to sacrifice 'the strident recital of his greatness'.

Mosquitoes and nocturnal chantings were nothing to the attractions of being Resident at Hyderabad; in Temple's words, 'the pleasantest appointment that could be found'. The Resident lived in as grand a style as any Governor, but his work, though calling for skill and finesse, was nothing like as arduous as ruling a large province. Temple had plenty of time for sketching. Once, when he was out with his brushes, a Muslim gentleman asked him why he painted with his own hand, when he could easily have found a professional artist to do it for him. By way of rejoinder, Temple asked the Muslim why he killed wild beasts with his own gun and spear, when he could have had it done for him by a trained hunter.

Sketching, however, could not absorb a tithe of Temple's surplus energy, and he would frequently set out on what he described as 'rapid rides from one end of the Deccan to another', collecting data on the country and its inhabitants, examining deserted mosques, exploring cave temples, savouring the well-being engendered by vast spaces, a peach-coloured Indian sunrise and a nip in the air. On one of these rides, he covered three hundred miles in five days. Every mile was made easy by the Nizam; tracks were marked, camps awaited him all along the route. Arriving back at Hyderabad, he stopped outside the cantonment for a 'full brush-up', and then cantered straight onto the race-course, just as the bell was ringing for the second race.

Temple's flair for putting on a show like this met with a certain amount of disapproval, particularly among Indian Civilians of the quieter sort. Of the latter school was John Graham Cordery, Resident during the eighteen-eighties, who employed his leisure in translating the Iliad. When Temple was Resident he had Cordery as First Assistant; the Second Assistant, Major Tweedie, spent *his* spare time translating Hafiz, so there were daily discussions on Greek and Persian poetry. The two Assistants, the Military Secretary, the Surgeon and the Commandant of the Escort formed a close little circle within the Residency, each living in his own house in the grounds. In the eighteen-nineties, Sir Trevor Chichele Plowden had an Assistant who was young and gay and held late-night jollifications in his house, which was close to the east wing of the main building. The Resident's daughter, the beautiful Pamela Plowden – Winston Churchill's early flame – took part in these junketings unbeknown to her parents, having used a ladder to get down from the terrace outside her room at the end of the wing, where she was thought to be safely asleep.

Having originally been very inaccessible – Temple made his first journey here, in Davidson's time, 'jolting tediously over stony roads in a van drawn by bullocks' – Hyderabad became much frequented by visitors after the opening of the railway. They ranged from the balloonist, Professor Wells, complete with balloon, to Winston Churchill's brilliant but erratic uncle, Moreton Frewen. In 1883 Cordery was obliged to entertain Wilfrid Scawen Blunt, an early example of a type of visitor very prevalent during the latter years of the Raj: the convinced anti-Imperialist with powerful friends at home.

Blunt reckoned that he was invited to the Residency to keep him 'out of mischief'. He and his wife, the intrepid Lady Anne, grand-daughter of Byron, were lodged in great comfort, with one of the wings to themselves. After going round the city on an elephant, he declared it to be 'after Cairo, the most gay and busy in the Mohammedan East. Compared with Madras, it is as Paris to a decayed watering place'. With his knowledge of the Arab world, he felt very much at home in the society of the Hyderabad nobles, and persuaded himself that all his new friends lived in constant terror of the Residency. 'I notice that Ik Balet Dowlah trembled before the little red-faced Cordery like a boy,' he recorded in his diary.

Very soon, Blunt sensed that he and Lady Anne were out of favour with their host. 'Cordery is alarmed at our independent visits to the city,' he wrote, noting that it was usually customary for English visitors to be 'bear-led' by someone from the Residency. The last straw was when Blunt took it on himself to be the unofficial adviser of the Viceroy, his friend Lord Ripon, who came to Hyderabad during his stay. Cordery's protest took the form of trying to prevent the Blunts from driving in procession behind the Viceroy's carriage; but drive they did, for Lady Anne had been specially invited to do so by the Nizam.

It must have been a relief to Cordery to go back to entertaining globe-trotting German princelings, like the young Mecklenburg, who flocked to Hyderabad in search of big game. The abundance of game in Hyderabad State was not least among the advantages enjoyed by the Resident, who could have all the sport he wanted, with everything arranged by the Nizam's servants and officials. Sir Stuart Fraser, Resident from 1916 to 1919, would go on *shikar* with his young daughter, Violet, a slender beauty who was a deadly shot. Father and daughter were eventually photographed beneath the Residency portico with their trophies covering almost the whole of the great steps. The photograph shows their preference for shooting tigers and panthers, which were the scourge of the villagers, rather than wild animals of the more harmless sort. Ten of the tigers were shot by Miss Fraser, who was able to enjoy the pleasures of *shikar* once again when she returned to India on a visit in 1935. Having had a shooting camp arranged for her by the Maharaja of Mysore, she came to Hyderabad, hoping the Nizam would do likewise. The Resident, with whom she stayed, was less sanguine: the Nizam was known to be not over-lavish with his hospitality. And sure enough, when Miss Fraser in due course received an invitation from His Exalted Highness, it was only to have tea with him. However, she made the most of the occasion, and told the Nizam all about the Maharaja of Mysore's shooting camp. 'Very dangerous, very dangerous,' he remarked gruffly; but he was not going to be outdone by Mysore. A day or two later a *farman* arrived at the Residency, announcing that His Exalted Highness had ordered a shooting camp for Miss Fraser. Unfortunately, it was arranged at too short notice for there to be any tigers, but the food was excellent and so was the champagne.

If the late Nizam lived frugally for one reputed to be the richest man in the world, the legend of his parsimony has nevertheless been grossly exaggerated. He may not have set much store on playing the bountiful host like some Indian Princes, but he was second to none of them in spending money on schools, hospitals and other projects that would benefit his people. Sir Arthur Lothian, Resident during the Second World War, found him sensible, tolerant and courteous.

As is well known, the Nizam considered that the granting of independence to the rest of India did not affect the treaty of alliance between his country and Britain. Had Britain remained faithful to that treaty, Hyderabad might now have been an independent state within the Commonwealth, with a British Representative still living at the Residency. The Attlee Government, however, preferred to abandon Hyderabad to its fate; and Nehru lost no time in forcing it to join his new India. The Nizam's dynasty no longer reigns and the Residency has become a women's college.

6

LUCKNOW

LUCKNOW in the first half of last century, when it was the capital of the Kings of Oudh, has been described as Stamboul in lath and plaster. It was a city where seedy magnificence rubbed shoulders with intense squalour; a city of intrigue, corruption and vice; a city to which flocked adventurers from all over Asia, as well as from Europe and even America; a city dedicated to pleasure, a city renowned for producing the best roses in India and also the best nautch-girls. Most of it was a warren of mud huts and narrow streets, deep in filth and packed with all kinds of humanity and beasts, including tethered tigers; but to the northwards, along the lush green banks of the Gumti River, there was a fringe of palaces and tombs, built in a style that was so indiscriminate a mixture of Oriental and European that Bishop Heber, on seeing the Great Imambara and the neighbouring Rumi Darwaza, could not decide whether they reminded him more of the Kremlin, or of Earl Grosvenor's Gothic mansion at Eaton in Cheshire.

Ever since Lucknow became their capital in 1775, successive Nawabs of Oudh – who assumed the title of King in 1819 at the instigation of the British – vied with each other in adding to this confusion of gimcrack architectural fantasies. Building was not, however, their only extravagance; with the exception of Sa'adat Ali, who reigned from 1798 to 1814, they were as dissipated as they were incompetent. As their misrule grew more flagrant, the Calcutta government tightened its grip on Oudh, so that the real power lay not in the Farhat Bakhsh or 'Delight-giving' Palace, where the King, resplendent in crown and robes that were meant to look like those of the King of England, drank champagne surrounded by a vast multitude of concubines, favourites and hangers-on, but in the Residency, half a mile away to the west.

Compared with the royal pleasure domes on either side, the Residency buildings, which stood aloof on rising ground screened by a belt of trees, looked suitably British. There was no confusion of East and West here; apart from the little Gothic Residency Church, the buildings were Classical. The actual house of the Resident, however, for all its Classical detail, was irregular; a tall, three-storeyed block, with turrets and other projections, and with a long, low wing stretching from one side. It looked like a castle which had been given large fanlighted windows and generally civilized in the eighteenth century; or else it might have been one of those irregular Classical villas of the Romantic Revival. In fact it was started in 1780 and grew piecemeal over the following three or four decades, successive Residents adding a room here and a verandah there. It was a house intended to be practical rather than grandiose, while being on a fairly large scale. The main rooms were on the top floor, so that they were airy and enjoyed splendid views of the city and the river, where floated the fish-shaped royal barge and the King's steam yacht. In hot weather, the Resident and his family retreated down the stone spiral staircase into the *tykhanas* or underground chambers beneath the entrance hall. These subterranean rooms were a feature of old houses in Upper India; they stayed cool, though their atmosphere usually became oppressive with the smell of candles and oil lamps.

The house contained little furniture. A prominent object was the billiard table in a corner room upstairs, which for half a century was handed on from one Resident to the next. There was nothing to compare with the magnificent furnishings of the Residency at Hyderabad, although the Lucknow Residency was built and equipped at the Nawab's expense, just as that at Hyderabad was paid for by the Nizam; but at Lucknow, there was no question of any Resident becoming the adopted son of the Nawab, as had Kirkpatrick, nor of one liking splendour quite as much as he had done.

Nevertheless, there was one Lucknow Resident who regarded the house as unsuitable for doing the honours of Britain at what was then, for all its shortcomings, the most brilliant court in India. So he built a detached Banquetting Hall just inside the main entrance to the compound, facing the Residency proper across the flower garden. It was on the same principle as the Banquetting Hall at Government House, Madras, only far less monumental, resembling one of the more impressive Calcutta merchants' houses, with verandahs of coupled columns, raised on an arcaded and rusticated basement. Unlike the building at Madras, it was not just a single great hall, for its main storey, approached up a staircase lit by Venetian windows, was divided into two State apartments, with fluted columns and friezes of plasterwork, and a suite of rooms for guests. Below, in the basement, there was an early form of swimming bath.

These two main buildings were surrounded by stables and out-offices, by houses for the Staff and barracks for the Resident's escort; all within a comparatively small area, described by Bishop Heber as a 'close', which was entered through an archway with a guard-house, built by Major John Baillie, who was Resident from 1811 to 1815. When Heber came to Lucknow in 1824, the doctor's house, near the Baillie Guard, was put at his disposal, the doctor himself being away. At breakfast with the Resident, Mordaunt Ricketts, he found 'so large a party as completely to give the idea of a watering-place'. During his stay here, Heber was lent an elephant so that he could visit such sights as the royal menagerie, the King's country retreat known as the Dilkusha or 'Heart's Delight', and Constantia, the eccentric palace of the eighteenth century French military adventurer, General Claude Martin. He also officiated at the Resident's marriage, which was attended by the King, the Prime Minister and other dignitaries; afterwards, he and the King talked about literature and steam-engines. Heber had already met the King at a breakfast in the Banquetting Hall, when he presented him with the Bible in Arabic and the Prayer Book in Hindustani; and he had also been invited to breakfast with him at the Palace. The meal on this last occasion was very English: tea, coffee, eggs, fish, butter and hot rolls, which the King had given to the Resident and the Bishop with his own hands. The table was set with French and English china, and the gallery in which the breakfast took place contained exclusively English furniture, European lustres and a portrait of Lord Hastings, the Governor-General who had raised the Nawab to being, as a cynic put it, 'King by the Grace of the East India Company'.

Oudh was very much a centre of political interest in the first half of last century; and it lay on the route to Delhi and the Punjab, which were no less important politically. There were thus many more distinguished guests at the Lucknow Residency during these years than there were at the Residency at Hyderabad. A visit by the Governor-General and his entourage was a regular occurrence. Lord Auckland and his two sisters came at the end of 1837, their party including the young Prince Henry of Orange, the first European Royalty to go on a pleasure trip to India. His presence was a source of ecstasy to Lord Auckland's chef, St Cloup, who had known him as a child when he was cook in the Royal Palace at the Hague.

The King entertained the Governor-General and his party to breakfast, and there was the usual exchange of presents. Prince Henry, much to his delight, was allowed to keep the presents which the King gave him not being bound by the East India Company's rules; but all the others had to surrender theirs to the Company, Emily Eden being very loth to part with a pair of emerald drops. Some of these presents were sold for the Company's benefit; others eventually found their way back to the King, having been stored at the Residency and then issued to future distinguished visitors to give to him when he received them in audience. The King was the gainer in this circulation of jewels and shawls, for the Company deemed it expedient that whatever was given him should be worth 500 rupees more than what he gave in return.

Among the entertainments held in honour of Lord Auckland, there was a wild beast fight, elephants versus rhinoceroses, from which the ladies, for fear of accidents, excused themselves. There was also a fireworks display on the river, with a procession of boats full of nautch-girls. 'The Prince of Orange was charmed with his evening,' wrote Emily, who noticed how the illuminations on the far bank spelt out in huge letters, 'God Save George Lord Auckland, Governor-General of India', 'God Save the King of Oudh' and then, after a full stop, 'Colonel Low, Resident of Lucknow', with no mention as to 'whether he was to be *saved* or not'.

The King, Muhammad Ali, should certainly have prayed for the preservation of Colonel John Low, who had put him on the throne when his nephew, Nasir-ud-din, died in the previous July leaving a young son of doubtful paternity. The boy's mother attempted a coup in his favour, and there was fierce fighting in the palace, parts of which were set alight. Low hastened to the scene, having ordered 1,000 East India Company troops to march on the palace at the same time. The troops were late in arriving, so he had to force his way unprotected through a hostile mob to the throne room, where the youthful pretender was installed. Not only did the Resident come to no harm, but when he entered the throne room, which was full of armed men shrieking excitedly, the band struck up *God Save the King*.

17 Lucknow Residency after the Siege.

18 Lucknow Residency, the billiard room after the Siege.

19   Government House, Lucknow.

20   Ganesh Khind, Poona.

Opinion was divided as to whether Nasir-ud-din drank himself to death, or whether he was poisoned following the dismissal of his English barber and favourite, who had kept a strict watch over his food. This personage, with the unlikely name of de Russett, wielded great power, and was looked on askance by the Residency; though his ascendancy was actually due to a former Resident, who, being impressed by his hairdressing skill, introduced him to the King. If William Knighton's account of him in *The Private Life of an Eastern King* is at all true, Nasir-ud-din must have been easily the worst of his line. Yet the ever-curious Mrs Fanny Parkes, who came to Lucknow twice during his reign, does not appear to have heard anything unduly scandalous about him. He came to a dinner at the Residency, where she was staying; the dinner was followed by a dance, which did not start until after he had left; for the English ladies were not allowed to dance in his presence. They had done so on a previous occasion and he had said: 'That will do, let them leave off', thinking they were quadrilling for his own amusement. On her second visit to Lucknow, Fanny watched a meeting on elephants between Nasir-ud-din and the Governor-General, Lord William Bentinck. As the Resident drove up to the scene in his four-horsed barouche, men ran alongside with baskets of live birds which they released as a compliment to the great man – like releasing prisoners from gaol.

Twenty years later, another woman visitor, Honoria Lawrence, saw a Lucknow that was still unchanged: the royal processions, richly caparisoned elephants, jingling camels, kettledrums and running footmen in scarlet, the Residency party in a smart English carriage with outriders, ladies dressed in the latest fashion and officers in gay uniforms riding alongside. But the days of the Kingdom of Oudh were numbered. When Honoria's husband, Henry Lawrence, came to live at the Residency in March 1857, it was not as Resident but as Chief Commissioner, administering Oudh on behalf of the Governor-General. For in the previous year, Oudh had been annexed by the East India Company, at the instigation of Lord Dalhousie; the last King, Wajid Ali, had been deposed, and banished to Calcutta. The court, with all its colour and extravagance, was a thing of the past. Its abolition had reduced half the city to beggary, for not only did the actual court functionaries, servants, musicians and entertainers rely on it for their livelihood, but also the craftsmen and tradespeople.

Lawrence did his best to cool the smouldering populace. He tried to restore the morale of the traders by receiving them at the Residency; he also kept open house for the nobles and gentry, many of whom were no less impoverished. He gave other entertainments to keep up the spirit of the British, who knew as well as he did that Oudh was a powder-keg. Doing hostess for him was the wife of a military friend, Honoria having died three years before.

In the midst of all the comings and goings, Lawrence's life was lonely, with no intimate companionship beyond that of his nephew George. It was not, however, destined to last much longer. His statesmanship, energy and tact had worked wonders in the Punjab after it was annexed, but the present situation was beyond his control. Resentment at the annexation of Oudh was not confined to the province itself, but was widespread among the thousands of former subjects of the deposed King who were sepoys in the Bengal Army. While putting on a brave face, Lawrence prepared for the worst. He surrounded the hitherto quite unprotected Residency compound with entrenchments; he quietly laid in supplies. The swimming bath beneath the Banquetting Hall came in useful for storing grain.

Early in May, the Mutiny broke out at Delhi and Meerut; it spread to Lucknow before the end of the month. During the stifling June days that followed, an army of coolies and prisoners in irons worked overtime to complete the Residency defences. The compound was thronged with soldiers, sepoys, scared Indians in carriages, elephants, horses and camels; the patrician quiet of the house and the Banquetting Hall was shattered by the noise of children, for most of the European population had already brought their wives and families here for safety. Every room was packed, and as the situation deteriorated, the servants began to desert, leaving the women to sweep and cook and draw their own water in what was the hottest month of the year.

When Lawrence and his troops – who included 700 Indians – finally withdrew into the Residency on 30 June, there were nearly 5,000 souls within the cramped and exposed area of the compound. The insurgents kept up a ceaseless cannonade and fired muskets at the defenders from the houses which hemmed in the compound on more than one side. Two days after the siege commenced, Lawrence was mortally wounded by a shell which burst in his room on the first floor of the main house. He was taken to the house of the Residency physician, Dr. Joseph Fayrer, where he died on 4 July. The Commissioner of Lucknow, John Sherbrooke Banks, succeeded Lawrence as Chief Commissioner, but was himself killed after little more than a fortnight. So fierce was the enemy fire that the Residency buildings afforded little protection, even with all the windows barred. The women and children were crowded into the subterranean *tykhanas* of the main house, and the men inhabited the floor above. The upper storeys were untenable, though as the ground floor began to fill with sick and wounded, the overflow from the hospital in the Banquetting Hall, officers moved upstairs, braving the shot and shell which came plunging through their rooms. Of all the top floor rooms, that which was most exposed to fire was the billiard room. The billiard table, however, survived the siege, albeit in a battered state and without its cloth, which was cut up and made into a suit for one of the defenders.

On 11 August part of the house fell in; four men were buried alive beneath the rubble. The main structure withstood another six weeks of shelling, just as the defenders – or rather, those of them who survived – were able to endure six more weeks of heat, flies, sickness, privation and enemy fire, until the relieving force under Sir Henry Havelock and Sir James Outram arrived on 25 September. The final relief did not take place until November, following the arrival of a second force under Sir Colin Campbell.

By the end of the siege, most of the verandahs of the main house had been shot away, and the windows blown out. The walls gaped and were pitted with bullet holes; the stucco facing had fallen off in many places, revealing the solid brick core. But, like the Banquetting Hall, the house was not so badly damaged that it could not have been repaired, in which case it would have been the most historic and also the most haunted Government House in India. Instead, the Residency buildings were left as ruins, with the Union Jack flying above them by night as well as by day and the compound turned into a garden. This memorial to British valour and to Lawrence and the other men, women and children, numbering nearly 2,000, who died during the siege and lie buried in the cemetery adjoining the ruined Residency Church, is still scrupulously maintained, although the India of today tends to regard the Mutiny in a different light from that in which it was regarded before the end of the Raj.

After the Mutiny, the Chief Commissioner took up residence in a house to the south-east of the city, not far from Constantia. It was built in the reign of Sa'adat Ali, and was known as the Hayat Bakhsh Kothi, or 'Life-giving House', a somewhat ironical name since it is said to

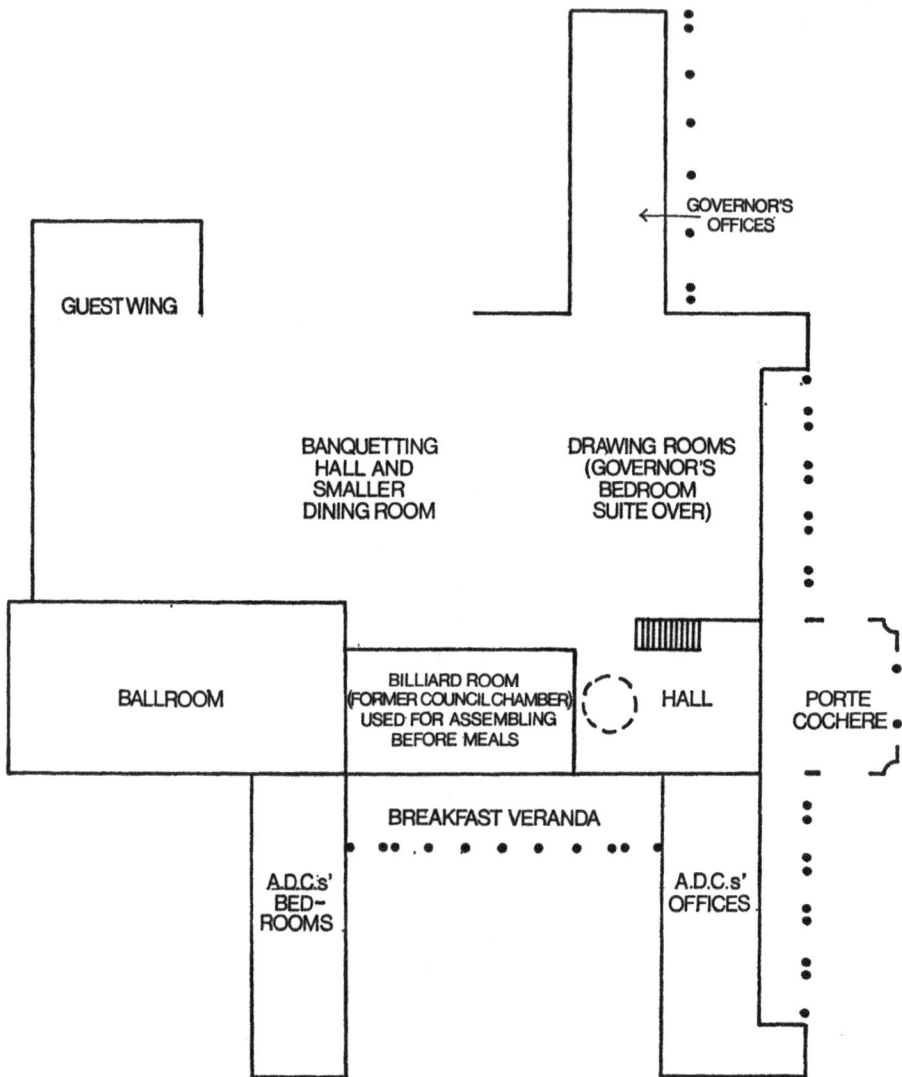

GUEST WING

GOVERNOR'S
OFFICES

BANQUETTING
HALL AND
SMALLER
DINING ROOM

DRAWING ROOMS
(GOVERNOR'S
BEDROOM
SUITE OVER)

BALLROOM

BILLIARD ROOM
(FORMER COUNCIL CHAMBER)
USED FOR ASSEMBLING
BEFORE MEALS

HALL

PORTE
COCHERE

BREAKFAST VERANDA

A.D.C.s'
BED-
ROOMS

A.D.C.s'
OFFICES

GOVERNMENT HOUSE, LUCKNOW ground floor

have been originally used as a powder-magazine by General Claude Martin. To the British at the time of the Mutiny, it was known more simply as 'Banks' Bungalow', having been occupied until the beginning of the siege by John Sherbrooke Banks, Lawrence's short-lived successor. In the fighting that followed the relief of the Residency, it was one of the chief rebel strongholds, standing as it did in a very conspicuous position. It was captured by the British in November, 1837, abandoned when Campbell withdrew his force from Lucknow later in the month, and finally recaptured on 10 March, 1858 by Sir Edward Lugard's division. On 11 March the gallant Major William Hodson of Hodson's Horse was carried into the house mortally wounded; he died in a downstairs room early next morning. The khaki-clad figure of Major Hodson was supposed in later years to visit the house and to walk through the rooms.

It is surprising that Banks' Bungalow should have survived the Mutiny more or less intact, particularly as it was roofed with thatch. It would have been on account of the thatched roofs that the house was called a bungalow, thatch being the traditional roof-covering for this type of dwelling in Upper India; for in fact it had a two-storeyed centre, rising above the outer rooms and verandahs, which were of one storey only. The effect was that of a comfortable planter's house, quite unlike the palaces and mansions of Lucknow's gaudy past, a sign of how the place was in eclipse following the Mutiny. It was a far cry from the splendid entertainments in the Residency Banquetting Hall, and a still further cry from all the lavishness of the Farhat Bakhsh and the Dilkusha, when John Strachey wrote, on becoming Chief Commissioner in 1866: 'There is no doubt that Lucknow has a large capacity for champagne and other liquors, and although I intend (DV) to be mean to the last degree, this craving of the military and other stomach will have to a certain extent to be gratified.'

During the long reign of Sir George Couper, who held the office of Chief Commissioner from 1871 to 1882, first by itself and then in conjunction with the Lieutenant-Governorship of the North-Western Provinces, with which it was amalgamated in 1876, the house and its surroundings were considerably improved. Work began on the house in 1873, and was completed within a few months. The thatched roofs were done away with, and the upper storey extended, so that the house lost its air of a planter's bungalow and became more like one of the old 'Garden Houses' of Madras or Calcutta, with upstairs verandahs of coupled columns. The ground floor verandah still projected out from the two-storeyed building behind it, and was lengthened at one corner to form the inevitable porte-cochère.

When the Prince of Wales came to Lucknow in 1876, the several Mutiny veterans in his suite – notably Dr Fayrer – were just about able to recognize Banks' Bungalow; but in the words of one of them, the war-correspondent, William Howard Russell, 'the approaches to it baffled all attempts of memory . . . swarded parks, vistas, rides and drives, far prettier than those of the Bois de Boulogne, spread out where once were streets, bazaars, palaces'. These improvements, resulting from Mutiny damage and clearances for the sake of security, included the laying out by Couper of spacious gardens and grounds around what the old-timers still persisted in calling 'the Bungalow'.

For Russell, Fayrer and the others, the visit awakened many memories, particularly as their host, Couper, was himself a Residency veteran, and had been Lawrence's secretary at the time of his death. The Prince unveiled a monument to the Indians who fell in the defence of the Residency, and the surviving Indian defenders, collected from all over the country and dressed in their old uniforms, were presented to him. It was a touching scene, particularly when the Prince took one of them by the hand, causing him to burst into tears with emotion. But another old soldier could not resist putting in a word about his pension, murmuring: 'Fourteen rupees a month, Shahzadah! It is not much, is it?'

A splendid entertainment given in the Prince's honour by the Taluqdars, the great landowners of Oudh, could not disguise the fact that the Mutiny and the subsequent reprisals had left a legacy of bitterness. Ten years later, when Lord and Lady Dufferin came to Lucknow, the atmosphere was much easier and the place seemed to have recovered something of its former gaiety. Banks' Bungalow was now well and truly Government House; the scene of an evening party, with little lamps of many colours hanging on the trees, great candelabra placed about the lawn, two bands and a brilliant gathering of Taluqdars and descendants of Kings of Oudh in diamond headdresses.

On the day after he arrived in Lucknow for his first State visit, Lord Dufferin went down with fever, which not only prevented him from attending the functions arranged in his honour, but kept him here much longer than had been planned. For ten days he lay ill in bed at Government House, while downstairs his host and hostess, Sir Alfred and Lady Lyall, made desperate efforts to entertain his large retinue, not to mention Lady Dufferin and her daughter and her daughter's friend. 'Everybody is bored and rubbed up by it, so that the party becomes sad, not to say sultry,' Lyall reported to his sister. 'Lady Dufferin nervous and much vexed by her husband's illness in a strange house – the two girls glum and subdued.' The only jovial member of the party was Lord William Beresford, 'accustomed to all the vicissitudes that can possibly happen to Viceroys'; apart from the august patient himself, who bravely attempted to be pleasant and gay.

It was with some relief that the Lyalls watched the convalescent Lord Dufferin being carried into the Viceregal train, though he was normally such a delightful person. The more prosaic Lord Ripon had proved an easier guest, though a family bereavement had prevented him from attending the ball which the Lyalls gave in his honour; it had also caused Lady Ripon to be 'shrouded like a native Rani in her carriage'. The Ripons came during the Lyalls' first period at Government House, Lucknow, which they used less than their other two Government Houses at Allahabad and Naini Tal. Lyall was pleased with the house, and more so with the weather, for Lucknow was renowned for having the best winter climate of any station in the plains of India. He was less enamoured by the society: 'Nothing could be more wearisome than the dinner parties here, for there really *is* nothing to talk about except army and civil service shop; no pictures, no music and no refinements of civilization. A lady sang, not so very badly, *Ruby* and *When Sparrows Build* – even her singing carried me away into an entirely different world.'

He was carried away to a different world again when the 'wonderfully amusing' German-born Duchess of Manchester turned up in Lucknow. As would be expected, Lucknow attracted many tourists; so that when the Lyalls were here, they generally had a full house, thereby providing themselves with more congenial company than the place itself afforded. By Lyall confessed to being 'a little bored by eating *all* my meals with so many'. Yet he was happy at Lucknow, where, for all the surfeit of 'chaff and fun', he could still lead 'the old familiar up-country life'; rising early, taking long rides in the 'soft, hazy harvest landscape' and 'seeing all sorts and conditions of natives'.

Forty years later, there was a Governor to whom Lucknow meant even more. 'I shall never like any place as much as Lucknow,' declared Sir Harcourt Butler. 'After all, I have lived the best part of my life here.' His ambition was to restore to it something of its former glory as the capital of the Kingdom of Oudh. One way in which he achieved this was by greatly enlarging Government House, thus ensuring that Lucknow would be the principal cold-weather residence of future Governors, even though Allahabad remained the administrative headquarters of what were now known as the United Provinces. The house had already been enlarged in 1907, when a ballroom, like a massive church, was built out at the back; as well as a wing for guests; but the impending visit of the Prince of Wales was an excuse for embarking on further additions and improvements after little more than ten years.

Butler added a new banquetting hall, new kitchens and other accommodation. He filled in the corners of the old house and recast the main front in a style of architecture that had, as he admitted, a 'strong infusion of Public Works Department', extending it so that the entrance became central, having been formerly to one side. The effect was still lopsided in that whereas the centre – which now had a more impressive porte-cochère, and a very Baroque pediment containing the Royal Arms – was of two storeys, as was the rest of the house to the right of it, the new left-hand wing was of one storey only. Butler hoped his successor would add the extra storey required to make the front symmetrical, but this was never done.

Most of the building took place during the hot weather of 1920, so that when Butler returned from Naini Tal in October of that year, the house was already transformed. 'The banquetting hall and the kitchens are a dream', he wrote to his mother. 'They would delight your heart.' Needless to say, the work was by no means finished; even with all the resources of the United Provinces at his disposal, Butler was not spared the delays, disappointments and vexations that are the lot of everyone who builds. 'The workmen are still in the house, and the dirt and confusion and the stupidity of the PWD are beyond all belief,' he lamented to his mother after Christmas. 'They promised the house complete by 1 December, then 1 January, now it is February, having all the marble to be polished (three weeks job at least) and all the woodwork to be sandpapered.'

It was particularly frustrating in that 3 January was the day on which Butler was to be ceremonially installed as His Excellency the Governor, having been elevated from being His Honour the Lieutenant-Governor by the 1919 Government of India Act. 'I went to bed on the 2 January as HH and woke up on 3 as HE, with seventeen instead of fifteen guns,' he told a former colleague. 'As all the other heads of provinces are treated in the same way, I do not feel what an Indian friend of mine calls "duly inflated".' Nevertheless, and despite the presence of the workmen, the installation ceremony was quite impressive. The guests were grouped on either side of the ballroom, with the Chief Justice and other dignitaries at one end and the band of the Royal Welch Fusiliers in the gallery. His Excellency entered to a fanfare of trumpets and took his seat on a gold chair of state; then, when the ceremony was over and the seventeen guns had thundered forth outside, he processed down the red carpet to the strains of the *Star of India March*, leading the assembled company into an adjoining room where there was champagne and Christmas cake.

The workmen eventually departed, leaving Butler in sole possession of what was now one of the most spacious and comfortable of Indian Government Houses, even though it may have lacked the distinctive character of some of the others. The general effect was cool and simple: large, lofty rooms with white or panelled walls and marble floors. There was not much decoration; one of the drawing rooms had an attractive pair of stone chimney-pieces, of Oriental design, carved with chrysanthemums, mermaids and the fish which was the emblem of Oudh. The two drawing rooms were to the right of the hall, where stood a large silver model of the Himalayan foot-hills, made by melting down all the silver caskets which had been presented to Butler. From the inner end of the hall one reached the ballroom, the banquetting hall, the smaller dining room and the room where the party assembled before luncheon or dinner. Such was the formality of the United Provinces that it was customary for the ADC to introduce everybody in the room to the Governor and his wife when they entered, even people staying in the house who might have been their relatives or close friends. Breakfast was usually eaten in a verandah off this room, overlooking a wide expanse of lawn. In a vain attempt to reduce the mosquitoes, which in Lucknow were notoriously virulent, Butler cleared the trees and bushes from the immediate surroundings of the house, which were consequently rather bare, but there were eucalyptus and other trees in the further parts of the compound, providing shade for the buffaloes and Indian cattle that grazed beneath them.

It was the fate of Viceroys and Governors to build for their successors. Butler was at least able to entertain in his palace for the best part of two winters, with, for full measure, a visit from the Prince of Wales.

His other guests ranged from the Edwardian hostess, Mrs Ronnie Greville, to Baden-Powell. Then there was Lutyens, making the jokes for which he was notorious: when a fellow guest complained of colic, he offered to build him a New Belhi.

After dinner at Government House, Butler liked to sing a few songs. He had his favourites, which included the latest hits of the Co-Optimists, as well as such pre-war numbers as *Gilbert the Filbert* and many older ditties, printed and bound into elegant little volumes known to the contemporary Indian *beau-monde* as 'Harkie's Hymn-Books'; these were handed out to his guests, all of whom were expected to join in. And join in they did, Indians as well as British. 'I'm tickled to death, I'm single, I'm tickled to death, I'm free,' chanted Maharajas and Nawabs with countless wives. High-caste Hindus, who at dinner had refused every course for fear that it contained part of the cow, sang heartily of the Roast Beef of Old England. *Coal Black Mammy* made none of them feel colour-conscious; not even a delightful Taluqdar of such duskiness that he would always come to Government House in a grey dinner jacket, saying that if he wore a black one, nobody would be able to see him.

It must not, however, be imagined that Butler spent all his time entertaining Taluqdars, Princes and fashionable tourists. He was unsparing of himself in the business of being Governor; once, he stood for five hours shaking hands, and at the end of it his feet were so swollen that he could hardly walk to his car. He was able to sit through a Council meeting from eleven till six-thirty, never stirring from the Chair and doing without either food or drink. He would leave the cool of Naini Tal and return to Lucknow for a spell of hard work in July, which was, as he said, like being 'in a prolonged Turkish bath,' with Government House full of the mammoth Lucknow mosquitoes and empty of guests.

Butler was followed, after an interval of six years, by the even more eminent Malcolm Hailey. With Lady Hailey as chatelaine, Government House became as informal as protocol permitted. During breakfast on the verandah, which often lasted for two hours with high officials dropping in to see the Governor, a donkey would come up the steps to be patted and fed. Dogs reigned supreme; an ADC who trod inadvertantly on the tail of one of Lady Hailey's favourites while trying to avoid her train as he followed her ceremonially down the stairs had his face slapped.

To show off her skill with a rifle, Lady Hailey would ask her guests, while entertaining them in the red and gold Chinese boudoir above the hall, 'Would you like me to pick you a bunch of flowers?' She would then take her .22 on to the balcony and shoot down the cannas growing in a bed across the sweep, leaving each of them with just enough stalk. Her sporting propensities and love of animals had something slightly exotic about them, for she was Italian, and never lost her accent.

As a foil to the ebullient personality of his wife, there was Hailey himself, with his splendid physique and his scholar's mind, his dry humour and his humility. The artist, Philip Steegman, who came one winter to paint his portrait, gives us a rather better picture of him in words. He recalls a ride with the great man in the country around Lucknow. 'As we galloped through the crisp air, with the pink glow of the evening sunlight playing preposterous tricks with his long whisks of white hair, he would pull up and talk with the peasants coming home from the fields, listening to their troubles and sorting out their problems.' Then, as the Governor and his guest walked their horses home through drifts of sweet-smelling dung smoke, 'he would suddenly jerk the talk back to Rome or London or Paris'.

This was the 'old familiar up-country life' of Lucknow which Lyall had known and liked so well. In many ways, things had changed very little in the half century since he was here. Yet the days of the Raj were numbered. Steegman shows us the Governor riding among his people, and gives us a glimpse of him later in the same evening, when he had bathed and changed and was going into dinner, throwing back his white whisks in 'a gesture of approval' at the sight of the double line of saluting *khitmagars*, in white, scarlet and gold. But in order to get the full picture of a Governor's life in the late nineteen-twenties and early nineteen-thirties, we would also have to see Hailey trying to come to terms with the forces of Indian nationalism, which were nowhere stronger than within his own United Provinces. As a sign of things to come, he actually handed over for a time to an Indian, albeit an Indian who was a staunch friend of the Raj, the Nawab of Chhatari.

Between the brief period when Government House was tenanted by the Nawab – he cannot have been the first Indian to live here, for there must have been others before the time of Banks – and the advent of the new India, when the house became the residence of the Governor of Utar Pradesh, there were a few more years of the old order, including the reign of yet another great Governor, Sir Maurice Hallett. Compared with Hailey, with the no less resplendent figure of the Nawab, and even with the portly Harcourt Butler, Hallett was unimpressive to look at: short, stocky, bespectacled, not caring about his clothes and happiest in an old Trilby hat, but he had a brilliant mind and a loveable personality. He was here during the Second World War, and his simple ways suited the atmosphere of the times: he was able to appear mostly in a bush shirt, and he helped food production by tilling the Government House grounds, using bullocks to tread his wheat in the traditional way. Yet Government House kept its grandeur, though wartime austerity greatly reduced the scale of entertaining. There was still the array of *khitmagars* under the command of Francis, the butler, who had been here many years and was actually of Portuguese descent, rather than Goanese. Lady Hailey, had she been still alive, would have been glad to know that one of the ADCs kept a grey monkey in the verandah outside his bedroom.

When the time came for Hallett's departure, it was the eve of Independence. India was in a ferment; the police feared there might be an attempt to blow up the white and gold Royal train – made for the King-Emperor and Queen-Empress in 1911, and inherited by the Governor of the United Provinces – in which he would be travelling. But on the lawn of Government House there were five hundred Indians who had come to say goodbye, and every one of them was in tears. They wept to see the last of a Governor whom they loved and who had loved them in return, but it seemed to those present that they were also weeping at the passing of the Raj.

7

POONA

OONA looms large in the British-Indian myth, though more for
those who have not been to India than for those who have. In
fact, this city and cantonment on the high table-land of the Deccan
a hundred miles east of Bombay was something of a backwater after it
became British in 1817. Before that, it was of great political importance
as the capital of the Marathas. During the second half of the seventeenth
century, this once-peaceful people turned into a race of fierce warriors,
and for a hundred years and more they were the chief Indian power.
They set up a confederacy of kingdoms with the Peshwa of Poona at its
head; they plundered as far afield as Bengal; they speeded the downfall
of the Moguls and threatened the rise of the British. It took three major
wars before the British were finally able to defeat them, Poona falling
into British hands during the third and last of these conflicts, after a
decisive battle at Kirkee, a couple of miles north-west of the city.
Before the battle, Mountstuart Elphinstone, the British representative at
the Peshwa's court, stayed calmly in his Residency until the last possible moment, only managing to escape with the clothes on his back.
The Residency was thereupon burnt by the Peshwa's people, and all
Elphinstone's books and manuscripts were lost in the blaze.

It was typical of the India of those days that the Peshwa's army
should have included a regiment raised and trained by a British soldier
of fortune named Major Ford. When war seemed imminent between the
British and the Marathas, Ford told the Peshwa that he could not fight
against his countrymen. Despite the Peshwa's attempts to keep their
allegiance by threats and promises, Ford and his troops went over to the
British side at the Battle of Kirkee, contributing in no small way to the
British victory.

When the battle commenced, Ford's regiment was stationed at

Dapuri, a few miles north of the battlefield, where he had his house. In 1829, after his death, the house was bought by the then Governor of Bombay, Sir John Malcolm. Poona had been incorporated into the Bombay Presidency following the Maratha defeat, and when Mountstuart Elphinstone was Governor, he started the custom of coming here for part of the hot weather. Being 2,000 feet above sea-level, it was much healthier than Bombay, though by no means cool. The surrounding country was bare and treeless, but there were fine distant views of the Ghats, those mountains rising from the plain of the Deccan close to its western edge and there were scattered hills nearer at hand.

Even after subsequent Governors had taken to spending the earlier months of the summer at the hill station of Mahabaleshwar, they still came to Poona during the monsoon, when Mahabaleshwar was unsafe owing to torrential rains. The Governor also needed to spend some time at Poona since it was the headquarters of the Bombay Army. Having been a military camp in Maratha days, it continued to be an important garrison under the British, with one cantonment to the east of the old city, and another at Kirkee. It was, however, a garrison far from the front line. After the Third Maratha War southern India enjoyed an unbroken Pax Britannica; henceforth, all the fighting was in the northwest. Even the Mutiny was a long way off though, of course, many units of the Bombay Army were sent on active service against the insurgents. The legendary Poona Colonel was thus something of an armchair soldier; one suspects that the more battle-scarred officers of Meerut, Rawalpindi and Peshawar did much to further the legend of his crustiness.

Malcolm took a great liking to Ford's old house at Dapuri, which was enlarged and improved by his successors so that it grew into a sizeable Government House. Its tower looked picturesque among the foliage of the garden, which became daily more beautiful during the rainy season when the Governor was in residence, the trees being festooned with brilliantly coloured creepers, and the air filled with the scent of acacia flowers. The grounds were bounded by the Pauna river, a tributary of the Mula, which in turn joined the larger Mutha just north of the city.

Sir Robert Grant, Governor from 1834 to 1838, used to walk up and down a particular path in the garden after sunset. He died while in residence here; and after sunset on the day of his death, a sentry saw a cat leave the house by the front door, and walk up and down the path which he used to frequent. The sentry mentioned this to the rest of the guard, who were Hindus, as he was; and they, from the *subadar* down-wards, were convinced that the soul of the deceased Governor had entered into the cat – an ironical fate for so staunch a Christian as Grant, who wrote *O Worship the King* and other well-known hymns. The cat had therefore to be treated with due respect and proper honours, and as the sentry did not know which of the Government House pets it had been, the *subadar* ruled that, in future, every cat seen leaving the front door after dark was to be regarded as His late Excellency. This became an unwritten addition to the standing orders of the guard, being passed on as a matter of routine when one guard was relieved by another. So for the next twenty-five years, whenever a cat slipped out through the front door of Government House, Dapuri, after dark, the sentry pre-sented arms.

None of Grant's successors during that period had any idea that his transmigrated soul was being thus honoured. If they had, they might have thought him fortunate to have been reincarnated as a cat, rather than as one of the multitudinous other creatures that infested Govern-ment House during the monsoon months when it was occupied. Lady Falkland, whose husband was Governor some ten years after Grant, was frequently woken up at night by the noise of the servants killing a snake in her verandah. When this happened by day, all the party hurried onto the verandah to assist in the killing. The Falklands' French chef killed a cobra in the kitchen. He proceeded to rush about the garden, holding the snake in one hand and covering up his head with the other, for he had forgotten his cap. As well as snakes, there were all kinds of insects, particularly those which flew in through the dining room windows during dinner; myriads of moths, white ants which covered the table cloth with their shed wings, large armoured beetles, eye-flies, which hovered over people's eyelids, green mantises and blister flies. The latter were highly unpleasant: if one of them was crushed on the face or neck, it caused a painful blister.

Lady Falkland remembered one occasion at Dapuri as 'The Blister Fly Ball' – as distinct from the *Butterfly's Ball*, a poem of her childhood – and described it in detail. The evening started with torrential rain, roads were flooded and the guests were late. After a very long time a cadet appeared, and greeted his hostess with: 'It's a very rainy night.' 'Very!' she replied, and the young gentleman then followed up his greeting with the remark: 'It is a very long way from Poona here.' 'It is indeed, a very long way,' said Lady Falkland. 'I don't think anyone will come,' said the cadet, to which Lady Falkland could only reply: 'I fear, indeed, no one will.'

This conversation was interrupted by the butler, who made the cadet go and have his boots brushed, as he was dirtying the beautiful white cloth on the ballroom floor. By now, the rain had ceased, and carriages began to arrive, but their occupants were all middle-aged: Colonels and Collectors who did not dance. Then came a troop of young Hussars. 'I always knew by the expression of the aide-de-camp's face who was about to enter,' Lady Falkland recalled. 'He was all smiles when flounces, feathers and fans were at hand, while his face lengthened at the sight of swords, spurs and sabretaches.'

At long last, to the hostess's great relief, there was an influx of women and it was possible for the dancing to start. But no sooner had the band struck up than a swarm of blister flies came in through the ballroom windows. They climbed into the folds and trimmings of the ladies' dresses, and up the gentlemens' sleeves; into whiskers and even on to bald heads. Those of the guests who were not engrossed in re-moving blister flies from their partners waltzed and 'polked' over the millions of insects attracted to the white cloth on the floor; which by the end of the evening was black with the insects' squashed remains.

The only people appearing to enjoy the evening were two Amirs of Sind who lived in Poona and who, like other Indians, were glad of an invitation to a 'European nautch'. They sat together on a sofa; the older white-bearded one with his feet tucked under him; the younger, whose beard was black, with his knees drawn up to his nose. Behind them stood a couple of servants, fanning them.

The Falklands found very little 'Eastern magnificence' at Poona. The *sirdars* and the other Indian gentlemen of the district for whom the Governor would sometimes hold Durbars, were mostly very poor. One or two insisted on keeping their elephants, but had been obliged to sell everthing else in order to be able to do so. Others kept their jewels, but came in broken-down, one-horse carriages. Others again came on foot, with attendants holding not swords but umbrellas.

They must have been very much put in the shade by the Governor and his ADCs; even more so ten years later, when the Governor was the elegant Sir Bartle Frere. It became customary for the Governor not to appear in uniform when he made his annual inspection of the troops at Poona; but Frere in his white hat and perfect frock coat, a single star on his breast, outshone all the top brass as he rode down the lines

21 The Lord Sahib and Lady Sahib of Bombay, with their staff, Bodyguard and servants. (Lord and Lady Brabourne, 1937.)

22 Simla, Viceregal Lodge.

23   Simla, Viceregal Lodge, the hall, decorated for Lady Reading's Feast of Lantern 1924.

24   Government House, Allahabad.

splendidly mounted, and with an easy and graceful seat. 'I thought these civilians always put on uniform on such occasions,' growled one old officer who was present. 'I daresay they *did*,' replied an admirer of Frere. 'I suppose in former times they never had any decent mufti, only bazaar-made clothes, you know.'

Frere was no mere elegant figurehead, but one of the greatest of nineteenth-century Indian Civilians, who, like Sir Richard Temple after him, had the distinction of rising to the Governorship of Bombay, which by then was usually the preserve of politicians from home. He was as successful in dealing with the tribes along the Baluchistan border as he was in making Bombay the most up-to-date and sanitary city of the East, so that in his time it had a lower death-rate than London. To help him in his improvements, there was the great cotton boom, a result of the American Civil War, which prevented American cotton from reaching Europe. Frere took advantage of this wave of prosperity to adorn Bombay with many impressive public buildings in the Gothic style, while at Poona he set about building a new Government House, closer to the city than Dapuri, which was eight miles out. The old house, for which Malcolm had paid less than £1,000, was sold at the height of the boom for something like £30,000. The fate of the former Government House was sad; it became a brewery, and was later used as a *godown*, or store, by the Public Works Department. By the nineteen-thirties, it was a ruin; Governors and their wives, out riding in the country, would look at its crumbling tower as they passed.

The site of Frere's new Government House was south-west of Kirkee, close to the battlefield of 1817, and near a pass or *khind* between two hills dedicated to the elephant-god, Ganesh, which gave the house its name of Ganesh Khind. Although it was much closer to Poona than Dapuri, it was still regarded by some later Governors as too far out, being more than three miles from the city and five from the main cantonment. This meant, however, that the house could stand in magnificent seclusion at the end of a very long drive, surrounded by a park on the scale of a country estate.

Frere cannot have been so wedded to Gothic as the public buildings put up during his reign would suggest, since he chose an entirely different style for Ganesh Khind, a style to which it is hard to give a name. Certainly the house did not in the least resemble a 'modern French chateau', which was the standard description of later years. If the style derived from anywhere in Europe, it was from the shores of the Mediterranean or the Adriatic. Some of the detail, such as the arcading along the garden front, was Romanesque. The tall and slender flag tower, eighty feet high, which dominated the building, was a rather Victorian rendering of an Italian campanile. This Italian air was enhanced by a terrace and a fountain, and later by Florentine pots as well as by a copy of Michelangelo's David and a Roman emperor on either side of the entrance; yet the house bore the unmistakable stamp of British India. While most of it was two storeys high, it was so rambling and wide-spreading that it might have been the familiar Indian bungalow, magnified many times over, and embellished with Romanesque and Italianate trimmings. There were many ground-floor verandahs with plain arches of the familiar sort; there was not just one porte-cochère but two, side by side, on account of the rains; the grander being for guests, while the other was the Governor's private entrance.

From under the main porte-cochère, one passed into a series of large and lofty rooms, with plenty of marble and scagliola. Most impressive was the ballroom or banquetting hall, rising the full height of the house and surrounded by a clerestory at first floor level, which lit the bedroom passage running behind it. There was also a 'flower gallery' or winter garden, ninety feet long, which afforded a pleasant place for a walk when it was raining. The rooms contained several historic paintings; notably a picture by the eighteenth century artist James Wales of the signing of the treaty against Tipu Sultan, and a portrait of the last Peshwa.

Before Ganesh Khind was completed, the American Civil War came to an end; Europe was flooded with American cotton and Bombay suffered a crash as spectacular as the boom of the previous four years. As a result, Frere's original plan for the house was curtailed, making it lopsided. Even so, it cost £175,000 – nearly six times the sum raised by the sale of Dapuri. The building of this palatial new Government House was much criticized; the blind Radical politician, Henry Fawcett, referred to it in Parliament as 'a typical instance of the extravagance and insubordination of the Governors of Bombay'. Frere defended himself in an able minute, pointing out that he had built a very fine dwelling for future Governors, that he had acted within his legal powers, that he was not insubordinate and that he had not spent all the money at his disposal.

He might well have added that he himself derived no enjoyment from his palace, for it was not yet habitable when he left India in 1867. His successor, Sir Seymour FitzGerald, carried out the decorations and furnishings, and was in turn criticized for being extravagant; the Secretary of State taking particular exception to a £500 chandelier in the ballroom. FitzGerald maintained that the grand style of the house compelled him to furnish it appropriately. For all this lavish expenditure, nobody seems to have thought of putting in water-closets. There were just the homely Indian 'thunder-boxes', emptied by sweepers who carried their baskets up and down rickety iron staircases fixed to the outside of the house. This state of affairs lasted until after the First World War, when a newly-arrived Governor's wife, finding that there was a sweeper's staircase immediately outside her own sitting room, insisted on the house being provided with modern sanitation.

Again, for all its grandeur, the house had only three or four spare bedrooms, apart from the State Suite for Viceroys or other illustrious guests. When the Prince of Wales came to stay in 1875, there was not even enough room for such exalted members of his party as the Duke of Sutherland and Lord Alfred Paget, who were accommodated in a bungalow somewhere outside the park. The scarlet-clad coachman and syce of the Government House carriage that was to take them to their lodging had no notion where it was, and they went for a long drive without ever finding it.

The Prince's suite included none other than Sir Bartle Frere, who was able to admire his palace in all its glory. Already the gardens and grounds looked mature. Below the terrace, with its view over the undulating plain and strange scenery of the Deccan, were two splendid lawns bordered with beds of cannas and masses of English flowers. Beyond, in the park, the trees were growing up; though they were nothing to what they became a few years later, when the great banyan sheltered a colony of flying foxes. The grounds were looked after by a botanist, who also ran the nearby Botanical Gardens.

Despite its shortcomings, Ganesh Khind was consistently admired by later Governors, their families, Staff and guests. Some went so far as to call it the finest Government House in India, which, while being certainly untrue, shows what a grand impression the house gave. Frere's extravagance was more than justified when Parell was given up; from then onwards, Ganesh Khind was the only full-scale Government House in the Bombay Presidency. The bungalows on Malabar Point, which became the Bombay residence of the Governor, were hardly worthy of this role; though charming enough with their *moucharabya* work and carved Surat screens.

And delightful though it was to hear the waves and feel the fresh breezes on that narrow sea-girt promontory, Malabar Point was very restricted, hemmed in by the ocean and the great city of Bombay. It was only at Ganesh Khind that the Governors and their families could lead the country life so dear to most of them. At Ganesh Khind they could go for long rides; here, too, was kept the picturesque Governor's brake, drawn by a team of four matching blacks and used for driving to horse-shows and similar events. Governors were even able to farm; Lord Brabourne brought out a champion bull from England, which grazed in the park.

In an earlier age, Sir Richard Temple was able to enjoy his hobby of water-colour painting. One morning, however, when he had settled down in an attractive spot and was peacefully working at a picture, he was interrupted with the news that the dam of the Bombay waterworks was threatened by floods; so, with characteristic haste, he dropped his brushes and made for the train. His daughter, Edith, who was a very good waltzer, found Ganesh Khind a wonderful place for dancing partners. With so many young officers in the cantonments, Poona was every girl's paradise. Yet even in the eighteen-eighties, the plagues of India would sometimes strike down the gayest maiden as suddenly and as ruthlessly as they struck down Walter Savage Landor's sweetheart, Rose Aylmer, in the previous century. When Mountstuart Grant Duff, the then Governor of Madras, stayed with Lord and Lady Reay at Ganesh Khind in 1885, he was enchanted by a pretty girl named Helen Portman. A year later, Lady Reay told him in a letter that she had just been to see 'the little white and silver coffin' of Helen 'laid in a damp earth grave'. Edith Temple, who was afflicted with chronic dysentery, escaped a similar fate by leaving India. The young Government House doctor attributed her illness to an excess of dancing; one suspects he was jealous of her numerous beaux.

When this same doctor was playing tennis at Ganesh Khind with the daughter of the next Governor, the two of them had a friendly squabble; and the girl, who was normally very shy, gave him what he euphemistic-ally called 'a spank on the back with her bat'. At that moment there appeared the impressive bewhiskered figure of the girl's father, Sir James Fergusson; the doctor was covered in confusion, for it was not the thing for a mere medico to romp with a Governor's daughter. However, His Excellency turned out to be very pleased that his daughter's shyness had gone.

With the passing of the years, Poona regained something of the 'Eastern magnificence' which Lord and Lady Falkland had failed to find among the impoverished *sirdars* of their day, but it was an Eastern magnificence of a very Western sort. The rich Parsis now came for the season to their Poona mansions, of which the finest was Mr Bomanjee Dinshaw Petit's Garden Reach, a riverside palace built during the cotton boom by one of the Sassoons. Another Poona palace, at Yeraoda, across the river from the main cantonment, belonged to the Aga Khan. The Parsis – and the Aga Khan, when he was here – gave a cosmopolitan leavening to the entertainments at Ganesh Khind, their womenfolk providing an elegant contrast to the army wives, some of whom were elegant and some were not. One English lady of the early nineteen-twenties thought that nature would prevail over art and came to a fancy dress ball as a shrimp, wearing only a net, but the Governor, the formidable Sir George Lloyd, sent an ADC to ask her to leave.

Today, the army wives who live in the trim, latticed bungalows of the cantonments are Indian and as smart as their husbands. The rich Parsis, however, are less inclined to come to Poona; and Ganesh Khind has been turned into a university. A writer who visited the house a few years ago found it empty and deserted, as is so often the case with public buildings in India. 'We rattled doors, but no caretaker emerged; the shutters were all tightly closed. After walking about on the lawns, we sat down on the polished marble steps of the drawing room loggia. I felt that at any moment, the shadow of Lady So-and-So's niece would appear through one of the windows and summon us in to tea.'[1]

[1] Roderick Cameron, 'Poona Revisited' (*Country Life*, 12 June, 1958)

8

SIMLA

S IMLA was British through and through and the creation of the Raj in its nineteenth century heyday. It had no Mogul past, like Delhi or Lahore; it neither harked back to the Portuguese, like Bombay, nor even, like Calcutta, to the admittedly British but none the less exotic world of the eighteenth century 'Nabobs'. When, in 1819, a certain Lieutenant Ross built himself a thatched cottage on this remote mountain ridge in the north-western foothills of the Himalayas, it was virgin forest. Half a century later, it was the summer headquarters of the Government of India as well as of the Government of the Punjab. For six months of the year, the houses of timber and corrugated iron perched precariously on ledges among the deodars and rhododendrons, approached by zig-zag paths along the sides of precipices, were filled to capacity with officers and civilians, wives, daughters and unmarried sisters. The proverbial Simla life of fetes and gymkhanas, dances, flirtations and performances by the Amateur Dramatic Club, was already in full swing. By day, if it was not raining too hard, the fashionable – those of them who were not tied to the Secretariat – disported themselves on the Mall, a sinuous thoroughfare following the ridge westwards from the mountain called Jakko to the lesser heights of Observatory Hill and Prospect Hill, past the Gothic Christ Church and the spindly wooden verandahs of the Town Hall; or else, far below at Annandale, where a miniature race-course had been levelled out of a cup in the hills, they furiously schooled ponies, practised polo-strokes or cantered around for the sake of their livers.

When Lieutenant Ross built his cottage, the British had already decided that this would be a suitable place for a 'sanatorium' – as a hill station was then called – having captured the territory in the Gurkha War of 1815–16. The settlement grew rapidly during the eighteen-

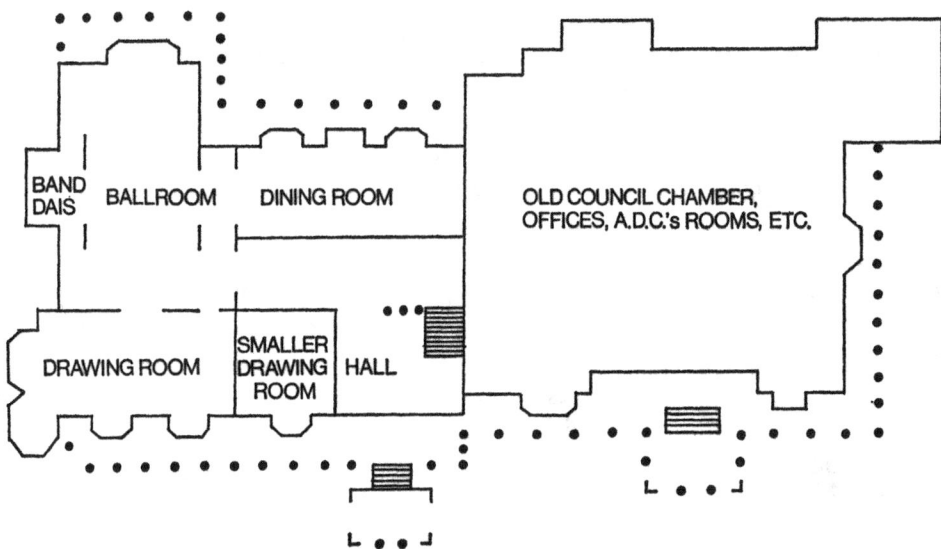

VICEREGAL LODGE, SIMLA ground floor

twenties, and was honoured by the presence of the Governor-General, Lord Amherst, in the summer of 1829. This set the seal on its popularity, and it henceforth became customary for each successive Governor-General to spend at least one summer at Simla as a health-cure. Lord William Bentinck had a house built for him here, which was gradiloquently named Bentinck Castle, one of the neighbouring peaks being afterwards known as Bentinck's Nose. His house, however, was not taken over by his successors, who, for the next thirty years, varied their Simla abode.

Lord Auckland lived at Auckland House on the hill to the north of Jakko, which was christened Elysium as a compliment to his two sisters, Emily and Fanny Eden. Emily thought it 'a jewel of a little house', but its mud roof leaked badly and it was full of fleas. She and her sister made it as nice as they could, and they set out to entertain there in a manner worthy of the Governor-General. 'How any dancing is to be managed at our parties we cannot make out', lamented Emily, for the society of the place consisted of eighty-six ladies to only twenty-eight gentlemen; Simla having already become the haunt of the grass widow. However, it was not quite as bad as it seemed, for the more dutiful wives would not go out when their husbands were away with the army. One with no such inhibitions was a Mrs James, who was Irish, very young and extremely beautiful. Emily thought 'little Mrs J' was 'such a merry, unaffected girl' and invited her often, making her a present of a pink silk gown as she was very poor, her husband being only a subaltern. A few years later, 'little Mrs J' appeared on the London stage as 'Lola Montez, the Spanish dancer'; she eventually became notorious throughout Europe for having caused the downfall of her elderly Royal lover, the King of Bavaria.

It was John Lawrence who, in 1864, instituted the annual migration of the Government of India to Simla as a way of getting more work done, and to be in closer touch with the Governments of the Punjab and the North-Western Provinces. At Simla, he did his best to escape from the Viceregal formality which he found so irksome; he even went in person to wish a Councillor's daughter happiness on her engagement, trudging up the hill to her house, accompanied only by a single red-coated *chaprassi* carrying a wedding present – a vast presentation inkstand which had clearly been a presentation to the Viceroy himself. With his simple tastes, Lawrence had no desire to build a proper Viceregal summer residence, but merely took over the house which had been occupied for a short while by his predecessor, Lord Elgin.

For the next twenty years, successive Viceroys made do with this modest dwelling, which went by the unlikely name of Peterhof. Lady Lytton compared it to 'a large rectory'; her husband was less polite and called it a 'pigsty'; while to Lady Dufferin it was the inevitable 'cottage'. Father Henry Schomberg Kerr, chaplain to the Catholic Lord Ripon, came nearest to the truth when he spoke of it as a 'shooting-box'. It was, however, a shooting-box in the Tyrol rather than the more familiar Scottish lodge, with one big chalet-like roof, gables at each end, and two tiers of wooden verandahs, the upper ones overhanging the lower. It stood at the top of the ridge a little to the east of Observatory Hill on what was the very watershed of India, so that a glass of water thrown out of a window on one side was said to find its way eventually into the Bay of Bengal, and on the other into the Arabian Sea. 'At the back of the house you have about a yard to spare before you tumble down a precipice, and in front there is just enough room for one tennis court before you go over another,' wrote Lady Dufferin. 'The ADCs are all slipping off the hill in various little bungalows, and go through most perilous adventures to come to dinner.' More serious than such 'perilous adventures' was the high incidence of typhoid among the

ADCs and other members of the Staff when they were here, which was attributed to the fact that the house was built on or near an old grave-yard.

Although Peterhof was a mansion by the normal standards of the Hills – with a ballroom, a drawing room, a dining room that seated more than twenty, a lesser dining room, a private upstairs drawing room, a study for the Viceroy and five bedrooms, one of which Lord Ripon used as a chapel – it was, for most of its illustrious tenants, the smallest house they had ever lived in. It had, moreover, many of the characteristics of the usual hill station house: the corrugated iron roof on to which monkeys jumped, the perpetual leaks, the falling plaster. And while it would have been spacious enough for a private individual, it was more cramped for Their Excellencies than the humbler dwellings round about were for the ordinary sahibs and memsahibs.

Not only did the Staff have to sleep in bungalows outside, but also any guests who happened to be there, and even some of the Viceregal children, if Their Excellencies had a large family. To be surrounded by 300 servants and an army of guards and policemen on a narrow hill-top could be oppressive; Their Excellencies were reminded even more forcibly of their position in Lawrence's rustic retreat than they were in Wellesley's palace. Lord Lytton complained that he could never be alone here; the sentries outside his window were too close, the ADCs, who had their meals in the house, too much on top of him; 'three un-pronounceable beings in white and red nightgowns' rushed after him if he walked about indoors, and if he set foot in the garden, he was 'stealthily followed by a tail of fifteen persons'. At night, the servants who slept in the passages in case they were needed took up even more space than they did in the broad corridors and verandahs of Government House, Calcutta.

For a ball, the whole house, including Her Excellency's private drawing room, had to be turned upside down. Doors were taken off their hinges and verandahs closed in to provide the maximum space. The effect was certainly cosy, with logs blazing in the fireplaces which were as large as the rooms were small, with many nooks and corners for sitting out. When Lord William Beresford was Military Secretary, he always made sure that there was a particularly secluded recess to which he could take the lady of his choice. Seeing the servants deeply en-grossed in arranging curtains and potted palms before a ball, somebody once asked them what they were trying to do; to which they replied that they were making a '*kissi ka waste* for Lord Brasspot-Sahib'.

At a fancy dress ball given by the Dufferins in 1886, 'Lord Bill', disguised as a Chelsea Pensioner, spent much of the evening in a shadowy nook with a Gad-fly whose wings made it difficult for her to dance. 'The poor old Pensioner did not like much light – it hurt his poor old eyes', another lady who was present observed roguishly many years later, going on to recall how a well-known hunting man had appeared as a baby, complete with what she described as 'frilled kicksey-wickseys'.[1] At the other end of the scale in the way of costumes, there was a 'White Lady of Avenel' whose own hair was loose and touched the ground. Even the Viceroy, who had started the evening in plain clothes, was impelled, on the spur of the moment, to get himself up as an Arab, which he did so well that Lady Dufferin failed to recognize him. Altogether, it was a most successful party; the rain held off, so that the *shamiana* or tent in which the supper was served did not get waterlogged, as it often did.

The Viceroy would hold Durbars in the *shamiana*, seated on his silver chair of State which had been brought from Calcutta. When His Excellency paid a return visit to one of the hill Rajas, this heavy silver throne would be lugged ahead of him up the precipitous paths. The entire Government of India, the military High Command, the Punjab Government, the neighbouring hill Chiefs and many other dignitaries were packed into a *shamiana* twenty feet by twenty on the tiny Peterhof lawn for the installation of Lord Ripon, who arrived in India during the summer of 1880 and came straight to Simla.

Lord Ripon's journey from Bombay was very hot. His chaplain, Father Kerr, was depressed by the knowledge that there were coffins in readiness at every station along the line; a necessary precaution in those days when people were liable to die during the course of a long Indian train journey. Having reached Ambala, the Viceregal party had to transfer into carriages and char-à-bancs for the forty miles to Kalka, where they transferred again into a fleet of tongas for the final sixty miles to Simla.

This progress up the winding mountain road, with the tonga-driver blowing a picturesque horn, greatly appealed to the previous Viceroy, the poetic Lord Lytton, when he first came to Simla in 1876. He was less attracted by Simla society. The ladies were too virtuous for his taste. 'I do miss the pleasant scamps and scampesses of pleasant France,' he

[1] Mrs Stuart Menzies, *Lord William Beresford* (London, 1917)

wrote to Lord Salisbury, 'and having seen virtue embodied in the form of Lady —, I don't agree with Schiller that if virtue were a woman, all the world would fall in love with her . . . I envy you the pleasure of living amongst so many naughty people.'

If Lytton is to be believed, a puritanical gloom hung over Simla when he first became Viceroy. 'Members of Council and Heads of Departments hold prayer meetings at each other's houses thrice a week, and pass the remainder of their time in writing spiteful minutes against each other,' he told a friend in England. 'The young ladies are not allowed to dance lest they should dance to perdition; and I believe that moonlight picnics were forbidden last year by order of the Governor-General in Council lest they should lead to immorality.'

One feels he exaggerated, mistaking for puritanism the simplicity of Simla life in his time. Society was still small enough for Lady Lytton to be at home for an hour each day to any ladies who cared to come and see her. She hoped in this way to share their joys and their sorrows: 'I got to know from the sadness in the faces those ladies whose children were parted from them, and far away in Europe.'

The Lyttons were the first really fashionable Viceregal couple to live at Peterhof. They not only brought with them the statutory French chef, but also an Italian confectioner named Peliti, who stayed on in Simla as the proprietor of Peliti's Grand Hotel. During their reign, some progress was made in the matter of building a more suitable Viceregal residence, which had long been in the air. Lord Lytton chose a site on Observatory Hill, where the Government had already acquired a considerable acreage; and from it he sent up a fire balloon, as he was wont to do on every possible occasion. A design for the new house was produced by Captain H. H. Cole of the Royal Engineers. Yet even to Lord Lytton, it seemed doubtful when, if ever, the house would actually be built. In his speech at the opening of the 1878 Simla Fine Arts Show, he referred to Cole's design as 'a prospect so distant that it is only possible to the eye of faith'. His successor, Lord Ripon, was not interested in building a new house; when the engineers told him that Peterhof was likely to slide down the hill, he replied: 'I think it will last for my time.'

Then came Lord Dufferin, a Viceroy who combined a romantic temperament with a love of architecture. He had long dreamt of building an enchanted castle, first on his Irish estate, then, when he was Governor-General of Canada, at Quebec; but neither his own resources, nor those of the newly-fledged Dominion, had been up to his soaring architectural fantasies. Now it seemed that his dream would at last come true, on the summit of Observatory Hill. Before embarking on the new house, however, he considered the possibility of enlarging Peter-hof; for he had a romantic weakness for buildings that had grown bit by bit.

In the end, it was decided that the Peterhof site was too cramped, as well as having been condemned as unsafe by the engineers – whose forebodings did not, in fact, come true. And so, having obtained the blessing of the Secretary of State (Lord Randolph Churchill) Lord Dufferin set out to crown Observatory Hill with his enchanted castle. It was designed by the local Superintendent of Works, Henry Irwin, in association with Captain Cole, and was in the Elizabethan style, with towers and cupolas to rise above the trees and delight Lord Dufferin's heart.

The new house was supposed to be ready by July 1886, but the difficulty of getting stone up the hill in bullock-carts caused even more than the usual delays, and to make matters worse, there was a strike of the cartmen. The following season, 1887, saw the shell partly roofed, but no more; one suspects that Lord Dufferin was not too disappointed, for the building works were now his chief hobby. He visited them morning and evening, rather to the dismay of the Public Works Department, since he was constantly making changes. He would take his family and his guests – including the Duke and Duchess of Connaught and the Duc d'Orleans – on hazardous tours of the fabric. 'We climbed up the most terrible places, and stood on single planks over yawning chasms,' wrote Lady Dufferin after one such tour in July, though she enjoyed watching the workpeople, 'especially the young ladies in necklaces, bracelets, ear-rings, tight cotton trousers, turbans with long veils hanging down their backs and a large earthenware basin of mortar on their heads' walking about on the rooftops 'with the carriage of empresses'. Sir Alfred Lyall, who visited Lord Dufferin in October, was impressed by 'his capacity of becoming absorbed in the details as he went over the building, as if he had nothing else to think about'.

When the Dufferins arrived in the spring of 1888 for their last Simla season, it was still not possible to see the front of the house for scaffolding; the drive was 'like a mountain torrent', and the boilers for the electricity generator – one of the first in India – were only then being dragged up the hill. Once the generator was in operation, however, it was possible for the work to continue after dark, by electric light; and so the house was ready by the end of July, enabling Their Excellencies to enjoy it for at any rate three months. They were delighted with the tall mansion of greyish stone, with its towers and cupolas, its porte-cochère liberally embellished with strapwork, its oriel windows through which could be seen the distant snow-capped ranges. Though its style was Elizabethan, it had, as people said, quite the air of a mediaeval castle, particularly when seen from near the entrance to the grounds, rising skywards from its wooded peak above the half-timbered guardhouse.

After Peterhof, the rooms seemed so grand and so plentiful that Lady Dufferin wondered how they would ever be filled. They were also very sumptuous, having been furnished and decorated by Maples of London. In the tremendous hall, which rose through the full height of the house, everything was of teak, walnut or deodar, elaborately carved and moulded: the massive staircase, the panelling, the chimneypiece with its Royal Arms and heraldic beasts, the arches and pillars of the first and second-floor galleries. A curtained archway at one end of the hall led into the ballroom, where the pale yellow walls were relieved by Jacobean pilasters and broken up with many recesses. From here, there was an impressive vista through another arch into the big drawing room, furnished with gold and brown silks. The dining room, also entered from the ballroom, was hung with Spanish leather in 'rich dark colours' above teak panelling decorated with strapwork and with the arms and coronets of almost every past Viceroy and Governor-General. There was also a Council Chamber, and a smaller drawing room furnished in blue; while on the first floor was the Viceroy's study, alongside Her Excellency's boudoir. The colouring of the latter was described by Lady Dufferin as 'a bright sort of brown'; whereas the former was suitably 'dark and serious-looking'.

An unusual feature, for India, was the large, white-tiled basement kitchen, very different from the traditional cook-house. An even greater novelty was the electric light; Lady Dufferin found it 'quite a pleasure to go round one's room touching a button here and there'. Yet another innovation was the indoor tennis court, similar to that which Lord Dufferin had built at Rideau Hall, Ottawa. Back in London, Lord Cross, who had succeeded Lord Randolph Churchill as Secretary of State, was less enchanted when faced with the bill for the new house, which finally came to well over £100,000.

Later generations seldom had a kind word for the Simla Viceregal

Lodge. It was variously and inaccurately likened to a Scotch Hydro, a lunatic asylum, Pentonville Prison, St Pancras Station and the mansion of a rich but tasteless German industrialist, though in fact its style was similar to that of numerous Victorian Elizabethan country houses in England, and it compared not at all badly with any of them. There was something of the flaunting and fragile air of genuine Elizabethan architecture about it which the Victorians usually failed to reproduce. This was because of its extra storey, made necessary by the hill-top site; while a characteristically Indian double verandah gave relief to the rather harsh texture of the stonework.

Such is the fickleness of taste that, a mere ten years after they had been so admired by Lady Dufferin, Lady Curzon lamented of the glowing interiors: 'Oh, Lincrusta, you will turn us grey! It looks at you with pomegranate and pineapple eyes from every wall.' She and Lord Curzon replaced some of the Lincrusta with damask; twenty years later, Lady Reading removed the strapwork in the dining room, pickled the panelling and did everything up in her favourite greys and mauves. But in spite of being redecorated many times over, the house kept its Victorian character. By the very end of the Raj, when fashion had gone full-circle, some of the younger ADCs began to find it rather charming.

Curzon's efforts to improve Viceregal Lodge – which also included raising the principal tower and introducing into the dining room a copy of the carved screen behind the Emperor of China's throne at Peking – did not alter the fact that he disliked Simla intensely. Like so many people before and after him, he felt it was not India. Even in his spacious and luxurious eyrie, surrounded by a hill-top garden of terraced lawns gay with banksia roses (maintained by 40 gardeners, together with 10 men employed solely for the purpose of keeping the monkeys from damaging the plants) and by many acres of steep but private woodland, he could not forget that he was on a narrow mountain ridge crowded with officials. And he had, moreover, to share that ridge with two other potentates, the Commander-in-Chief and the Lieutenant-Governor of the Punjab who, while being his inferiors, were exalted enough to be his rivals. There was room in Calcutta for both the Viceroy and the Commander-in-Chief, as well as for the Lieutenant-Governor of Bengal; but Simla was not large enough for three Lord Sahibs; certainly not when one of them was Curzon and another was Kitchener.

While the conflict raged between the Viceroy and the Commander-in-Chief, Simla society was divided into two camps; the followers of

Kitchener finding encouragement in the magnificent series of balls which he gave at the Commander-in-Chief's house, a half-timbered mansion named Snowdon on the other side of Jakko from Barnes Court, the rather grander half-timbered summer residence of the Lieutenant-Governor of the Punjab. Barnes Court, too, was at war with Viceregal Lodge for a period during the Curzon regime, owing to an unhappy quarrel between the Viceroy and the Lieutenant-Governor of the Punjab, Sir Mackworth Young. When Lady Young and the Viceroy were in adjoining boxes at a performance by the Amateur Dramatic Club, she gave him, as Curzon himself put it, 'a Medusa-like bow which would have frozen most people to stone'.

Curzon's feelings for Simla were improved neither by an earthquake in 1905 which wrecked Lady Curzon's bedroom and sitting room; nor by an equestrian farce that could easily have ended in tragedy at the bottom of a precipice. One day, as the Viceroy and Vicereine were riding down the drive from Viceregal Lodge and approaching the guard-house, the guard saluted with such vigour that both Their Excellencies' ponies bolted in alarm along the main road. The Viceroy, having mastered his steed, came back alone to speak to the guard, who, imagining that their first performance had been faulty, did a second and even more vigorous salute, which caused His Excellency's pony to disappear once again in the direction of the bazaar.

Such mishaps occurred all too frequently at Simla. In the days before the annual migration had become an accepted custom, Lord Dalhousie and the Lieutenant-Governor of the North-Western Provinces, James Thomason, both fell down a precipice when riding together. 'How delighted the newspapers will be!' Dalhousie wrote afterwards. ' "Oh, this comes of Governor-Generals (*sic*) and Lieutenant-Governors going into the Hills".' Lord Lytton met with a similar accident and was no less fortunate to escape serious injury, as were Lady Dufferin and her companions, who were caught in a landslide while out riding. It was customary at Peterhof, and then at Viceregal Lodge, to fire a salute every day at noon, but this had to be discontinued because of the danger of scaring horses. When Lord Ripon's first salute was fired, the dignified cavalcade of gold-laced notabilities riding homewards along the Mall after his installation ceremony was suddenly transformed into what an eye-witness described as 'a struggling mass of men and horses, all presenting the appearance of circus riders doing tricks'.[1] A portly

[1] Mrs Stuart Menzies, *op cit.*

General endeavoured to stop his Yarkundi pony from jumping over the railings and down the precipice; another gentleman was badly hurt while trying to discourage his horse in its attempts to climb a tree. Various people were seen disappearing into the distance on madly galloping steeds; the ground was strewn with topees and cocked hats with flowing plumes.

Viceroys and Vicereines who were unwilling to endanger themselves on horseback could use a carriage – and in later years, a motor – on the Mall, the only proper road in the place; this privilege being afforded to nobody else except for the two lesser Lord Sahibs and their wives, but if they wished to deviate from the single thoroughfare, they were obliged to walk, or go by *dandy* – a form of litter, consisting of a hammock slung to a pole – or rickshaw. When Lady Dufferin, her daughter and another girl went for a rickshaw outing, there was, as she recalled, 'a small regiment of nineteen men in scarlet liveries pulling and pushing our three machines'. Even with this abundant supply of manpower, it was not possible for more than one person to sit in each rickshaw, which made such expeditions rather unsociable. And for all but the most insensitive, much of the pleasure was taken out of a rick-shaw ride by the puffings and pantings of the *jhampanis* as they pushed and pulled the vehicle and its occupant up a steep hill. People were particularly sorry for the *jhampanis* of a seventeen-stone, flaxen-wigged General's lady who lived at Simla soon after the First World War; they were known as the Faith Team, because faith moves mountains. There was, however, a particular fascination in going in a rickshaw up the long, steep drive of Viceregal Lodge before a ball, when 'the twinkling lights of other rickshaws could be seen like moving necklaces strung along the hillside, above and below'.[1] Then, for certain ladies, there was the added pleasure of being tucked into their rickshaws by young and good-looking ADCs after the party was over. 'I'm sure you'll agree that Captain A. tucks you into your rickshaw most perfectly,' one Simla lady of the eighteen-nineties declared to another, when discussing the rival merits of two particular 'Aides'.

Apart from the problem of getting about the place, there was the effort of travelling to and from Simla, which, even at the end of the Raj, was hardly less cut off from the rest of India than it had been in the time of Lady Dufferin, who felt that she had never before lived in such an out-of-the-way place, even though she had travelled in many of the

[1] Iris Butler, *The Viceroy's Wife* (London 1969)

remoter parts of Canada. Modern science, if anything, made the journey less pleasant, at least for the privileged, for instead of the leisurely progress up the hill in tongas, there was five hours of discomfort in the Motor-Rail, a cramped little train driven by petrol which went round the bends of the narrow-gauge line from Kalka to Simla with a motion that was misery to all but the strongest stomachs. On their arrival at Simla, the Viceregal party had to face an official reception and much hand-shaking while trying to get over their queasiness and get used to the thin air, which continued to tax peoples' strength even after they had grown accustomed to it, so that, in the words of Lady Dufferin, there was 'something of the vampire' about the Simla climate: 'it extracts your strength, and you know nothing about it until some very slight ailment reveals the melancholy fact.'

The Simla climate was, in itself, far from ideal. When the season opened, in April, it could be unpleasantly cold, with hail and sand storms. In May, it was hot and dusty, and the deep ravines smelt of urine. Then the monsoon broke, and there were many weeks of rain, mist and grey skies, when books, shoes and everything else of leather became coated with mildew. It was only in September, when the Rains were over, that Simla was really delightful. 'A clean atmosphere, in which every line and shadow stood out sharp and unmistakable . . . a sun perpetually shining out of a cloudless sky; and in the great distances the ridges of snow mountains catching all the changing lights until these faded into darkness with the last rose-coloured rays of the setting sun' was how Lord Halifax remembered it, thirty years after he had reigned at Viceregal Lodge as Lord Irwin. The whole country was washed clean by the monsoon, so that there was a delicious smell of fresh pine needles, mingling with wood-smoke.

Notwithstanding the rain, the thin air, the epidemics and the 'venomous chill' peculiar to the place with which everybody sooner or later was laid low, the inhabitants of Viceregal Lodge managed to enjoy life, except, perhaps, for the hard-working Viceroy. As well as the constant gaieties at Viceregal Lodge itself, there were entertainments at Snowdon and Barnes Court. There were the balls held by the Knights of the Black Heart, a society of eligible bachelors and gay grass widowers. There were balls given by Councillors and Generals and by many lesser folk. Modern dance music was quick in coming to Simla. During a conversation about it at the Viceregal dinner-table, an ADC mentioned a tune called 'I shall remember your kisses when you have forgotten my name'. The Vicereine, who was not quite listening, asked him to repeat the name of the tune, whereupon he became flustered, and said: 'You will remember my kisses, Your Excellency, when I have forgotten your name.'

By the beginning of the present century, Simla society had grown to twice what it was in the Lyttons' time; so that Lady Minto found Vice-regal Lodge too small. There were now 800 guests at the State Ball, whereas the parties at Peterhof in the old days had seldom been for more than 400. To cope with this increased scale of entertaining, the domestic staff at Viceregal Lodge had risen to 800, almost as many servants as at Government House, Calcutta.

As well as the civilians and the military, who had an assured place in society, there was a large unofficial population filling the hotels and boarding-houses during the summer season; with, needless to say, a preponderance of unattached women. Some of them managed to get invited to Viceregal Lodge, others did not. On one occasion, a lady who had been unsuccessful in this respect appeared at a Viceregal party, telling the ADC that she had forgotten to bring her invitation card. The Military Secretary took the matter up, and requested her to send him the card for inspection. To his surprise, she duly sent him a card which appeared to be quite in order, so he sent it back to her with an apology. Later, however, it was found that her servant had engaged in a financial transaction with a clerk in the Military Secretary's office. By that time, the lady had returned to the Plains, taking the card with her to show to her friends.

Perhaps the heyday of Viceregal Lodge was the period between 1912, when the Viceroy deserted Calcutta for Delhi, and 1929, when the New Delhi Viceroy's House was ready for occupation. During those years, it was the chief Viceregal residence; for at Delhi there was only a glorified bungalow and a camp. To make up for Lady Reading's mauves and greys, the house was enriched with pictures, furniture and trappings brought from Government House, Calcutta. The silver State howdah – which had been used by Lord and Lady Hardinge of Penshurst for their entry into Delhi in 1912, when a bomb was thrown at them – stood at the foot of the staircase. In the drawing room, there was the portrait of Lady William Bentinck, the only Governor-General's wife to have been honoured with a portrait at Government House; in the ballroom, there were the two even more historic portraits of Louis XV and Queen Marie Leczinska, which were taken from the French settlement of

Chandernagore when it was captured by Clive and Admiral Watson in 1757.

From the journal of Yvonne FitzRoy, a charming and intelligent young lady who was secretary to Lady Reading, we get a lively picture of Viceregal Lodge in this period; when the guests staying in the house ranged from King Albert and Queen Elisabeth of the Belgians to Melba. 'For a lady who declares she had heat stroke yesterday and palpitations to-day she is quite remarkably spry,' Miss FitzRoy wrote of the latter, whose rendering of *Home, Sweet Home* reduced the Commander-in-Chief, Lord Rawlinson, to tears. She recorded the mishaps as well as the triumphs. One day the lift stuck, with the Viceroy in it; he had to climb down a ladder, and 'descended with a crash' onto the 'devoted head' of Lady Reading's nurse. Then there was the lady at a large dinner party who had too much to drink, and collapsed backwards as she curtsied to Her Excellency 'with an exclamation of mild surprise and the comment, "I knew I should do that" '. No less disconcerting was the behaviour of the *purdah* Begum of Dera who, during one of Lady Reading's *purdah* parties, suddenly dashed outside 'to say her prayers to the setting sun or to have a fit', and met the entire Viceroy's Band on the doorstep. At this same party, the *purdah* ladies were entertained with a cinema show; many of them had never seen one before and turned their backs to the screen, so as to be more sociable.

Simla, so uncompromisingly British, was now favoured by an increasing number of rich and prominent Indians; apart from those who were here merely because they were in the Government. Some of the Princes had Simla houses; others came and stayed at Viceregal Lodge. Among the latter was the Maharaja of Patiala, who amazed Miss Fitz-Roy by the amount he consumed at luncheon: three poached eggs and rice, four thick slices of mutton and vegetables, two large helpings of chicken curry, and plum tart. 'And yet,' she added incredulously, 'he is thinner.'

Lady Reading liked giving parties that were both dazzling and exotic. There was the Moonlight Revel of 1923 when the garden was turned into an Old English Fair with booths, merry-go-rounds, a baked potato stall and an Aunt Sally. The high spot of the evening was when the Viceroy, the Governor of the Punjab and the Commander-in-Chief went down the chute together. Most spectacular of all was the Feast of Lanterns, a year later. All the guests wore Chinese costume; the ballroom was hung with scarlet, the hall with bright blue; the monsoon mist was pierced by rows of Chinese lanterns along the verandah. A seven-foot dragon with motor lamp eyes made its appearance, and out of it came a pretty girl who did a Chinese dance. Then Miss Megan Lloyd George in Burmese garb entered in a rickshaw, pulled by Miss FitzRoy and another young lady dressed as *jhampanis*. When this cabaret was over, the guests danced to such tunes as *The Junkman's Holiday, Behind the Lacquer Screen* and *Pagoda Bells*.

Miss FitzRoy describes the preparations for an earlier festivity which Lady Reading supervised herself. Whilst a bower of magenta bougain-villea, scarlet geraniums and purple Canterbury bells was being con-structed for the band, six boys walked up and down the ballroom floor pulling a flat sledge loaded with a heavy granite slab on which sat a very old man, turbaned and cross-legged, scattering chalk. It was much the same performance as Ella Druitt had watched at Government House, Madras, in the eighteen-seventies; it had been repeated countless times on the floors of Government House ballrooms all over India. But this morning there was a difference. In the midst of the furniture moving and the flower arranging, Her Excellency and the attendant ladies and ADCs peeped into the hall to catch a glimpse of the visitor who was being received by the Viceroy. They saw 'a slim, spare figure in the coarse white wrappings of the Hindu holy man'. It was Gandhi, the living symbol of an India in which Vicereines and State Balls would no longer have a place. Before the end of the Reading regime, Gandhi's Muslim counterpart, Mohammed Ali Jinnah, had also appeared within the portals of Viceregal Lodge. He came to dinner, bringing his pretty and fascinating wife: 'with less clothes and more golden brown skin showing than I have ever seen before,' as Her Excellency put it, noting how 'all the men raved about her' and 'the women sniffed'.

Gandhi and Jinnah both had their way; with the result that not only have the British gone, but an international frontier now cuts off Simla from Lahore, whence came a large part of its summer population. Simla is now the capital of a new Indian province called Himachal Pradesh; the head of the province does not, however, live at the former Viceregal Lodge, which is used as an Institute of Advanced Studies. When an eminent Irish scholar visited Simla a few years ago, he was put up there, together with his daughter. It was vacation time; the two of them were alone in the great house and, surprisingly enough, there were no servants. So the daughter heated up baked beans for her father in the echoing Viceregal kitchen.

9

GOVERNMENT HOUSE
ALLAHABAD

LLAHABAD, at the meeting of the Ganges and the Jumna in the
plains of Hindostan, was not the most distinguished of Indian
cities, although it boasted of some fine mosques and a Mogul
fort. To Lady Dufferin, it was 'brown and dusty and muddy looking';
even the magnificent public park – named in honour of Prince Alfred,
who visited Allahabad in 1870 – which formed the eastern boundary of
the wide-spreading European quarter, seemed as if it were only 'struggling to be green . . . and only managing it by contrasting itself with
the asphalt tennis courts'. For her, as for others, the redeeming feature
of the place was Government House, which stood in shady grounds
adjoining Alfred Park to the eastwards, its high and large rooms opening
on to what she considered to be the prettiest flower garden she had seen
in India.

Lady Dufferin described the house as of 'the bungalow type', but it
was a palace among bungalows; a sort of British-Indian Sans Souci or
Grand Trianon, a single-storey version of Government House, Calcutta, with two wings instead of four. Nevertheless, it was originally
intended to be merely temporary. Although Allahabad was the capital
of the North-Western Provinces for a brief period after they were
separated from Bengal in 1834, it was deserted in favour of Agra before
any Government House could be built; and did not finally become the
capital until 1859. During the eighteen-sixties, the Lieutenant-Governor
lived at Lowther Castle, a house rented from a local Nawab and not
quite up to its name; while plans were afoot for building a proper
Government House in Canning Town, the new civil station which was
then being laid out. Lieutenant Cole, of the Royal Engineers, who later

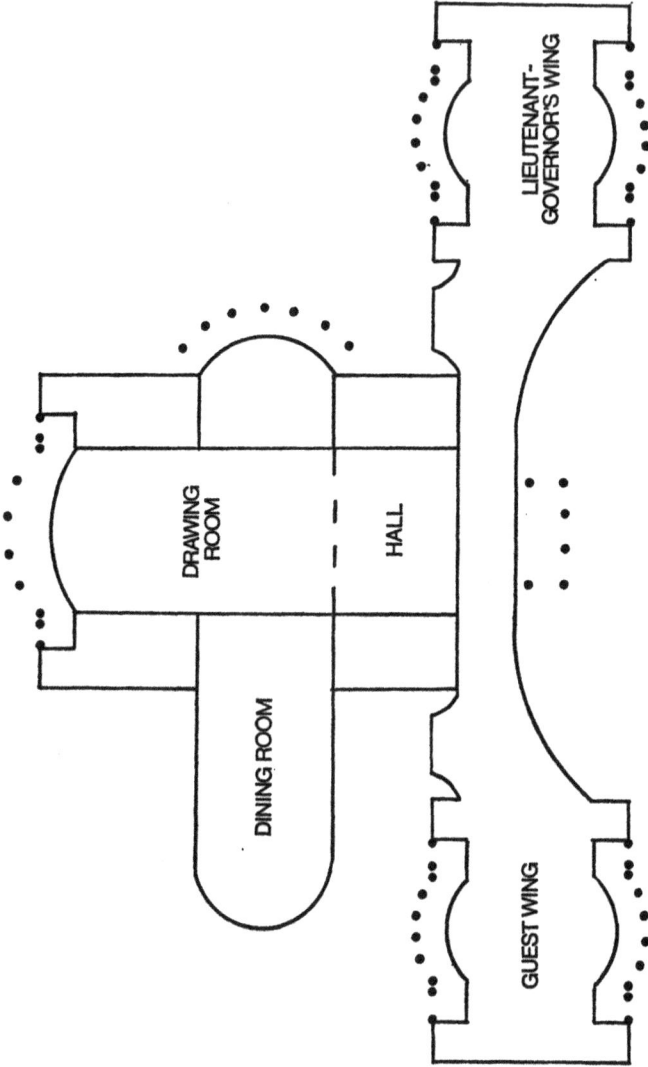

DINING ROOM

DRAWING ROOM

HALL

LIEUTENANT-
GOVERNOR'S WING

GUEST WING

GOVERNMENT HOUSE, ALLAHABAD

had a hand in the Simla Viceregal Lodge, produced designs for a house in the Italian style, which he estimated would cost about three lakhs. The Government of India had, however, set the limit of the expenditure to be incurred on the new house at one lakh only – rather less than £10,000. With the frugal John Lawrence as Viceroy, there was no question of this limit being exceeded; in fact Cole's design was turned down by the Viceroy himself.

Meanwhile, Sir William Muir, who became Lieutenant-Governor in 1868, was clamouring for better accommodation. It was therefore decided that Lowther Castle should be enlarged, so as to provide an adequate Government House for the time being, until money was easier and Cole's Italianate mansion – or its equivalent – could be erected in Canning Town. But before this could be done, Lowther Castle had to be bought by the Government, and the Nawab asked too high a price. So instead, the Government bought the adjoining property, which belonged to a local bank but had been used for some time by the 107th Regiment as its Mess. It stood a little way to the east of Canning Town, in a locality which was regarded as unhealthy. For this reason, after the Mutiny, the cantonment was removed from here to the other side of the new civil station. The neighbourhood was, however, greatly improved when Alfred Park and the Government House grounds had taken the place of the old cantonment.

The building acquired by the Government was an impressive single-storey block dating from the eighteen-thirties or 'forties, in the traditional British-Indian Classical style with a portico on each side. As would be expected of an old officers' mess, it had some very fine public rooms but few bedrooms. So two wings were added in 1869, joined to the main block by curving corridors. Their cost, together with the cost of buying the property and putting up various outbuildings, came to just over the stipulated lakh, which seems cheap, even by the standards of those days. The local Public Works Department had assured the Government of India that the wings would be 'perfectly plain', yet this did not prevent them from having the same rich Classical ornamentation as the main block, with a semi-circular portico on each of their façades. So well did they match the centre that the house looked as if it had all been built at the same time. And while the wings trebled the length of the principal front, it did not appear unduly low, in the way that over-sized bungalows generally do.

In fact, this so-called bungalow was higher than many two-storeyed houses since all the main rooms rose into clerestories. It was particularly high at the centre, where there were two great rooms separated from each other by an open Venetian arch, so that they really formed one vast hall running from east to west through the whole depth of the house; though the more westerly of the two was usually furnished as a drawing room. At right angles to these two central rooms was the long dining room, which reminded Lady Dufferin of a church: 'especially when a church is hung with *punkahs*.

One of the wings contained the private rooms of the Lieutenant-Governor and his family, the other was for guests. The bedrooms, being on the ground floor, were, in the cooler months, full of the scent of roses; but it was often difficult to sleep in them, owing to the peacocks which inhabited the garden. Not content with making a noise outside, these birds would put their heads through the open clerestory windows and shriek down into the rooms below, which drove one Private Secretary to distraction; though as well as being decorative, they were useful in that they killed and swallowed snakes.

The idea of building a grander Government House in Canning Town was eventually dropped, and what had been intended as a makeshift became permanent. During the years that followed, the house underwent few changes. A ship's mast was planted in front of it as a flagstaff, surrounded by a formidable array of cannon; a somewhat incongruous feature, since both the great rivers were at least two miles away and out of sight.

At first, the great reception rooms looked rather bare. Sir Alfred Lyall, who became Lieutenant-Governor in 1882, asked his sister, when she was on a visit to Venice, to obtain for him some '*large* copies of good pictures of the Old Masters' to cover the walls. 'I don't want *religious* subjects, or naked creatures, goddesses, or angels,' he told her; and he specified that they should cost no more than £100, which would come out of the Government House furnishing allowance. 'The pictures look very well and uncommon in India, and people gaze at them much,' he wrote, after their arrival a few months later; though *Judith with Holofernes' Head* and one or two others were, in his opinion, 'too dark and indistinct' for the rooms at Government House, which as well as being vast were dimly lit owing to the necessity for keeping out the sun. When his sister went to Florence in the following year, he commissioned her to find him a 'large central picture' with 'a striking effect'. Lyall's art collection was later augmented by two enormous Burmese figures, and by a series of portraits of the Begum Samru and her family, acquired after the sale of the Begum's old home at Sardhana in 1893. Henceforth, visitors to Government House were greeted by the awe-inspiring gaze of that remarkable old lady, originally a Kashmir dancing-girl, whose husband, the European soldier of fortune, Walter Reinhardt, known as Samru, massacred sixty Englishmen at Patna in 1763, but who, in her widowhood, became a staunch friend of Britain and a great benefactress of the Christian missionaries, having won territories and riches as the commander of her late husband's private army.

Lyall could spare some of his furnishing allowance for pictures, since an earlier Lieutenant-Governor, Sir John Strachey, had left the house well furnished in other respects, spending substantial sums of Government money on chintzes, damasks and carpets. 'My new carpets are really beautiful,' he wrote in 1875 to his brother. 'I could not bear Lady Muir's English filth.' It certainly seems perverse that Lady Muir should have imported inferior English carpets in preference to all that was offered by India or Persia, particularly as her husband was a distinguished Orientalist. One suspects, however, that Strachey exaggerated their inferiority, for there was something slightly malicious in the way in which he spoke of his predecessors at Government House, and indeed of other people as well. Not for nothing was he the uncle of the yet unborn Lytton, whom he must have resembled in appearance as well as in character, having, in the words of Wilfrid Scawen Blunt, a way of 'sitting with his head on one side like a sick raven'. He took pleasure in reports of how Lady Muir was shocked at the godlessness of his regime: 'I am told that she compares Government House in its present state to Sodom and Gomorrah. "Think my dear" she was heard to exclaim, "that in that room where every Sabbath we used to have our hymns and our prayers, the only sounds now heard are those of profanity and Sabbath-breaking". A Lieutenant-Governor who has dinner parties on Sunday and who never goes to church because he thinks it wicked to give a bad example is indeed a change.'

When, however, the Prince of Wales and his party descended on him during the cold weather of 1875–6, it was Strachey's turn to be shocked. Or rather, it was his wife's turn. 'The Prince's tastes are low and childish enough,' wrote Kate Strachey, who was no less critical of humanity than her husband was. 'As for HRH's moral character, Major Bradford told Auckland Colvin that he was bad as possible. . . . He has set all

Calcutta by the ears with his *particular* attentions to Milly. He asked himself to luncheon with her at her lodgings in Ballard's Buildings and went there with four of the most rowdy of his set.' To make matters worse, the lady in question – who notwithstanding her doubtful reputation must have been quite somebody to be able to correspond with the wife of a Lieutenant-Governor – sent Kate Strachey 'a rather silly letter' saying how 'a God had descended into her first floor back'. Kate was no less critical of certain members of the Prince's party than she was of HRH himself. She found Lord Aylesford, the celebrated 'Sporting Joe', 'a coarse oafish creature', while Lord Alfred Paget was 'a horrible coarse-looking man, drinks brandy and water all day. He is made a complete butt among them and called "Old Beetroot" even by HRH, who descends to silly coarse jokes on occasions'.

Thus we see the Prince of Wales's set and the serious-minded Victorian official world brought into closer and lengthier contact with each other than ever they were at home. The Stracheys had some reason to be jaded, for the Prince stayed longer with them than he did with anybody else in India, not just at Allahabad but also in camps at Agra, Benares and in the Himalayan foothills. Nevertheless, they seem from the very start to have regarded the Royal visit as a nuisance rather than an honour. 'I am afraid I am giving you a great deal of trouble,' wrote Kate in the previous July to a relative in England, asking him to send her an extra supply of sheets, pillowcases and towels. 'But I cannot help it, it is all the horrid *Prince*.'

In October, she was writing minute instructions to her brother-in-law, General Sir Richard Strachey, on the subject of crockery. 'The dimensions of HRH grow constantly, and we have been obliged to order from Goode a quantity more china. Goode has been told to let you know immediately whether he can send off, not later than first December steamer, dinner plates etc of our old blue and gold china pattern, or whether in consequence of the necessity of making it on purpose he would be obliged to send the plates of *another* pattern. It is very important that we should know this as soon as possible . . . Please, therefore, directly you hear from Goode, to telegraph through Reuter . . . if you send the one world "old", we shall know Goode has been able to send our old pattern. If you send the word "new", we shall know that a new pattern is coming.'

'With exchange at 1s. 9d. and Prince of Wales, money is very *tight*,' Kate complained in January, after playing hostess to the Royal party at

Benares, though Strachey had already been given a private assurance by the Viceroy that he would be reimbursed for the cost of the Prince's visit. 'Otherwise we should have gone to gaol,' Kate declared when telling her brother-in-law the good news. The Prince came to Allahabad in March, on his way back to Bombay. Every room in Government House was occupied, and the grounds were full of tents, for the Viceroy, Lord Northbrook, was also staying, in order to take leave of the Prince before he returned to Europe.

Face to face with the Prince, even the Stracheys fell beneath his spell. 'He is, of course, thoroughly selfish and inconsiderate,' wrote Kate. 'On the other hand, he has the gift of extremely pleasant manners, a charming smile, and can make himself most agreeable . . . John curses and swears directly his back is turned, but admits that when he is present in the flesh he is so good natured and polite and *likeable* that one cannot help liking him.' And whatever she thought of some of the other members of the suite, she could not help liking Prince Louis of Battenburg whom she described as 'an exceedingly handsome and gentleman-like naval officer, very fond of music'.

When the Prince had left Allahabad, Kate felt there was cause for self-congratulation. '*We* really did everything most perfectly and beautifully for HRH. They *all* said they never had such comforts anywhere as with us. The bedrooms were all most comfortable and were luxurious. Nurse and I accomplished all this domestic part ourselves. The food and drinks were delicious.' But she added ruefully: 'The way they all drank was awful – between seventy and eighty dozen of champagne in a fortnight, fourteen dozen of soda water in a day.'

Perhaps it was the thought of how much her guests were drinking that made her remark wearily, at the height of the Royal visit: 'The game is just not worth the candle, and whether it is old age or not, I nowadays positively dislike so-called gaieties, balls etc.' Although she and her husband had a considerable sense of their own importance, one doubts if they were really cast for Government House life. Indeed, after only two years as Lieutenant-Governor, Strachey reverted to being a Member of Council, at the request of the new Viceroy, Lord Lytton. As the Viceroy's *eminence grise*, he was far more in his element than as ruler of the North-Western Provinces.

The next Lieutenant-Governor, Sir George Couper, would certainly not have agreed to cut short his term of office in this way. When the Viceroy, Lord Ripon, fell ill during a visit to Allahabad and was obliged to stay on at Government House for much longer than had been originally intended, Couper 'chuckled with delight, calculating that . . . he had established such a claim on the Viceroy's gratitude as would make absolutely certain his recommendation for a year's extra Lieutenant-Governorship'. Thus wrote Sir Alfred Lyall, having himself suffered the same experience with Lord Dufferin at Lucknow, observing that nothing was 'more dangerous than to have the Viceroy and party tied by the leg in your house. They get very sulky over the bad luck of the thing, and they get utterly bored with you and your household'. It goes without saying that Couper failed to obtain his extension. He had enjoyed a long enough innings, having previously been Chief Commissioner of Oudh, which was joined to the North-Western Provinces when he became Lieutenant-Governor. Nevertheless, he was 'very loth to leave his Oriental pomp and big-wig privileges', so that when Lyall, who was his successor, stayed with him at Government House before his departure in April 1882, the atmosphere was frigid.

For the next five years Government House was the home of that great administrator, who was also a poet. At first he felt uneasy in his high position, the very pinnacle of the Indian Civil Service. 'We live in this huge house quietly', he wrote a few days after his arrival, when it was too hot for much entertaining. 'Here, as Lieutenant-Governor, I am such a big man that no one comes near me; sometimes I think I shan't stand five years of the life; anyhow I am rather depressed. Cora does me much good, being obstinately cheerful, and obviously enjoying the position.' Cora Lyall was the very best sort of Memsahib. Comely, sociable, good at riding, archery and croquet, she had been happy to share numerous hardships with her husband during his past career. To complete the family party at Government House, there were two daughters, Sophy and Eva. Her father found Sophy 'distracting as a young lady; constantly late, wardrobe all wrong, etc.' He was, however, proud of her 'literary taste'.

It was difficult for Lyall, in his position, to indulge his own taste for literature. He had little time for writing poetry, and if he did write anything, he could not publish it without attracting more attention than was deemed proper. 'It doesn't do for Lieutenant-Governors to be scribbling verses in reviews,' he remarked ruefully, after the appearance of his poem, the 'Amir's Message', in the *National Review* had been greeted with headlines by the Indian Press. He craved intellectual pleasures which he found singularly lacking in Allahabad, where the dinner table conversation was limited, as he put it, to 'remarks about the weather and lawn tennis . . . so long as you are civil it doesn't in the least matter what one talks about'. For him, there was little to choose between the Government House dinner parties – 'always exactly alike, due mixture of army and civilians' – and the balls. 'We had a ball last night which did very well,' he wrote in January, 1884, 'but what's the use of filling your rooms with military and civilians and their wives – you ask everybody, so it's no favour; you can't talk intimately with anyone, so it's not society.' On another occasion he wrote: 'How *much* superior society at Simla and Calcutta is to all else in India. The provincial people seem to me very different.'

But while complaining that he had no friends at Allahabad, and worrying about his inability to save money, Lyall grew attached to his kingdom. 'I think a Lieutenant-Governor's business as pleasant as can well be imagined,' he wrote in 1887 to his brother James, who had been appointed Lieutenant-Governor of the Punjab. Up to now, James had been Resident at Bangalore, and he and Alfred had shared consignments of champagne from Europe, thirty dozen at a time. The two brothers were neighbouring monarchs – ruling between them a population of seventy million – for only a very brief period, for when James obtained his Lieutenant-Governorship, Alfred's time was running out.

With his introspective nature, Alfred Lyall was well aware of the transience of his position. 'They gave us a parting dinner and dance at Allahabad,' he wrote, after his final departure in November 1887, 'and I made a speech that was liked. We went off honourably, there were many sayings of regret, especially for Cora, who is very popular. In a month we shall be virtually forgotten.' As for the prospect of leaving India, he was, like many of his kind, pulled in opposite directions. He knew he would miss the Indian people, to whom he was devoted; he dreaded saying goodbye to his old servants. He was sorry to see the last of Government House: 'I regard pensively the lawn tennis court where I shall never play again.' Yet in many ways he looked forward to his new life at home; it grieved him when an old colleague died after enjoying only five years of English life, making him wonder if 'all the risks and countless drawbacks of an Indian career were worth it' – a question to which, in his heart, he would have answered unhesitatingly in the affirmative. He hoped to visit Italy; up to now, he had only known it in the canvasses sent by his sister to decorate the walls of

Government House. He dreamt of high society and brilliant conversation, while being doubtful as to what sort of figure he would cut in the great world.

He had, paradoxically, been introduced to that world at Allahabad, which, being on the main railway line from Bombay to Calcutta, was a regular stopping-place for distinguished official visitors and illustrious tourists. Lyall liked what he saw of these people, who, stimulated by his intellect and attractive personality – and also, no doubt, by the spacious comforts of Government House after dusty nights and days in an Indian railway carriage – gave him of their best. Lady Goldsmid, 'two-thirds Italian and very much so in manner and talk', he described as 'most vivacious and amusing, with a turn of flirtation tempered by the fact of having eight daughters in ten years'. He found 'intellectual capacity and a sympathetic nature and high culture' in Wilfrid Scawen Blunt, though also *'restlessness'*. Lord Rosebery, who sat up half the night with him over cigars, was very pleasant, if inscrutable; his rich wife was less pleasant, so that Lyall afterwards remarked: 'I guess he pays for his millions.' Prince Frederick Leopold, brother of the Duchess of Connaught, who stayed at the same time as the Roseberys, was 'very well bred' and 'very well turned out'.

Yet Lyall had no illusions about his fashionable guests. 'I am bound to own that there is an air of distinction about these great families,' he wrote, when recounting the Roseberys' visit, 'especially in the evening, which makes them. But what on earth is the good of my entertaining all these folk? I shall scarcely see one of them again; perhaps Lady R will send me a card to some huge London "at home".'

The most exalted of Lyall's guests, the Connaughts, were no passing tourists, for the Duke was soldiering in that part of India. Lyall noted how the Duke's disgust at the quarters provided for himself and his Duchess at Meerut – 'an old bungalow with the usual rickety chairs and tables, and a few rascally servants to cook their meals' – was 'evidently deepened' by the contrast with Government House. 'He kept on saying that this was a palace, that it was the first time he had been decently comfortable, etc etc . . . the truth being that these simple royalties expect everything to be done for them somehow.' When Lyall invited them to stay in his luxurious camp at Agra, they could not make up their minds. 'These folk have a way of saying neither yes nor no, and in a high polite manner doing very coolly precisely what suits themselves,' he observed with some irritation; though on the whole he found them pleasant enough, particularly the Duchess; and he took comfort in the fact that they had behaved no less casually to the Viceroy.

With the opening of the shorter railway route from Bombay to Calcutta across central India, Allahabad was less frequented by visitors. With the removal of the Government of India to Delhi, it ceased to be a stopping-place for the Viceroy and high officials on their way to and from Simla, as it had been when Calcutta was the capital. Delhi also attracted the illustrious tourists, who having stayed there with the Viceroy, usually penetrated no further into the United Provinces – as the North-Western Provinces were called after 1902 – than Agra and perhaps Lucknow. Only those venturing as far as Benares came to Allahabad, among them being the eighty-year-old Clemenceau, who spent a day at Government House in 1920, arriving from Benares in a shabby brown suit with a patch on the seat of his trousers and carrying 'the conventional tourist's white and green lined umbrella'. He particularly admired the portrait of the Begum Samru, and when told the story of how she had a slave girl, of whom she was jealous, buried alive, and her own bed put over the grave to prevent the girl from being rescued, he was delighted and kept exclaiming: 'C'est magnifique! I love her, she is after my own heart.' His host, Sir Harcourt Butler, thinking he would like a rest, had prepared a suite of rooms for him, complete with the latest French illustrated papers and several new French novels, even though he was not staying the night; but the old politician never went near them, preferring to go sightseeing in a Government House car.

Sir Harcourt Butler, as well as having a particular affection for Lucknow, disliked Allahabad, where he was dogged by misfortune. When he came in February 1919 for the All-India Tennis Tournament, it rained. When he gave a 'firework dinner' for the Chief Justice in April of the same year, he developed a temperature of 103°; so having drunk the King's health immediately after the soup, he retired to bed, leaving his guests to enjoy the delicious food, the dancing and the illuminations. On another occasion, his ADC, who had just recovered from jaundice, developed dysentery, while he himself was covered in prickly heat, even though he had unearthed an old plunge-bath beneath the Government House gentlemens' cloakroom into which he plunged twice daily. Yet another sojourn was spoilt for him by a severe cold, which, together with the ceaseless cries of the peacocks and jackals, made it impossible for him to sleep. On the other hand, he had to admit that the male society of Allahabad was more intelligent than that of Lucknow, though he condemned the women as 'fairly awful', and he also found that he could get a better game of bridge here.

Allahabad resented Butler's preference for Lucknow; particularly so when Lucknow was given three days to Allahabad's one in the programme of the Prince of Wales's visit during the cold weather of 1921-2. The Allahabad worthies made what Butler regarded as 'the most absurd proposals' to detain the Prince in their city; it was even suggested that he should 'unveil a column which has been unveiled for six or seven years'. Unfortunately, however, this column incorporated medallions of George V and Edward VII which had recently been tarred over, and it proved impossible to get the tar off in time. The fact that Allahabad was strongly Congress meant that it was not the best place for the pomp and circumstance of the Raj; though in 1923, when the Viceroy and Vicereine, Lord and Lady Reading, came here in state, many Congress supporters turned out to greet them, feeling that if they stayed away it would benefit Lucknow.

Sir Harcourt Butler's efforts on behalf of Lucknow bore fruit in that although Allahabad remained the official headquarters of the provincial Government, the Legislative Council was established at Lucknow, and his successors regarded the Lucknow Government House as their chief residence. Government House, Allahabad, was deserted except for occasional brief visits. It had always been rather impersonal, never really winning the affections of its inhabitants in the way that some of the other Government Houses did. Even in the last century, the Lieutenant-Governors spent a great deal of their time away from it: at Lucknow, at the hill station of Naini Tal, or touring their wide-spread dominions. For the last twenty years of the Raj, it had ceased to be a home altogether, and was merely the glorified version of what it became after Independence – a 'Circuit House', for the accommodation of high officials on tour. Yet for the Governor and his family and Staff, there was something rather magic about going to this Sleeping Beauty palace, where the peacocks gave their unearthly shrieks and the beady eyes of the Begum Samru followed one around the dim, lofty rooms.

10

GOVERNMENT HOUSE
LAHORE

I FIRST became aware of 'the divinity that doth hedge a king' on the occasion when the Governor of the Punjab was my parents' guest. It was one of those outdoor functions such as were held almost daily during the Lahore winter season, with lots of handshakes, the Police Band playing selections from the *Maid of the Mountains* and a tea which while being quite admirable in its way – lettuce and tomato sandwiches, curry puffs, little iced cakes and Nedou's toffees – never varied from one afternoon to the next. Even I, at the age of five, had come to take these entertainments rather for granted, having at times been allowed to accompany my parents to them. But to have such a festivity at one's own home, and with the rare honour of the Governor's presence, was different.

For days beforehand, my *ayah* and I watched the preparations: the pitching of the blue and yellow striped *shamianas*, the planting of the flags and the hanging of the bunting. On the afternoon itself, we watched the Police Band unloading their trumpets and trombones, while other policemen stationed themselves along our drive and in the road outside. And then came the great moment: the band struck up *Rule Britannia* and the Governor's black limousine hove into sight, the Union Jack fluttering proudly above its radiator, preceded by a motorcycle outrider and followed by a police escort in an open tourer. I still expect a large black limousine flying the Union Jack to drive up whenever I hear *Rule Britannia* played; the fact that it does not being a stark reminder that Britannia no longer rules the waves.

Later that afternoon, I was summoned to the shiny leather sofa where the Governor and my mother sat in state, and as I approached I

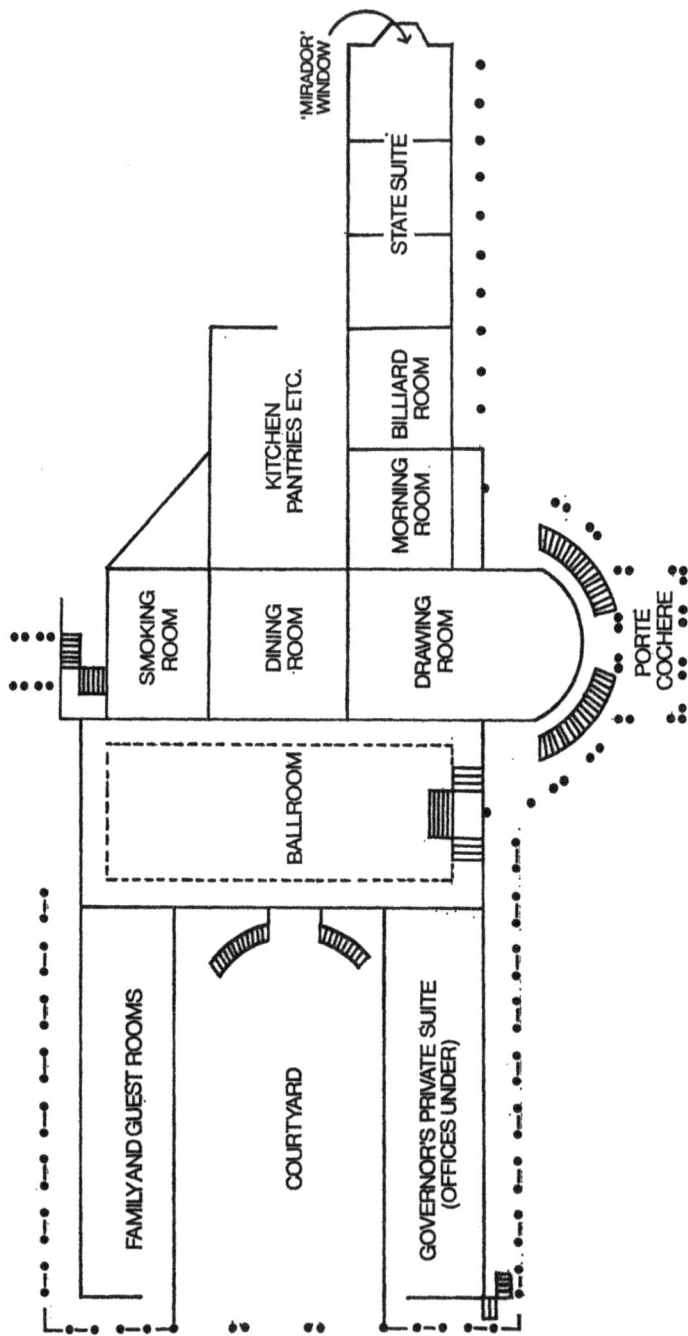

GOVERNMENT HOUSE, LAHORE principal (upper) storey

Labels within the figure:

'MIRADOR' WINDOW

STATE SUITE

BILLIARD ROOM

MORNING ROOM

KITCHEN PANTRIES ETC.

SMOKING ROOM

DINING ROOM

DRAWING ROOM

BALLROOM

PORTE COCHERE

FAMILY AND GUEST ROOMS

COURTYARD

GOVERNOR'S PRIVATE SUITE (OFFICES UNDER)

asked in a loud voice, 'Is that the Governor?' My mother afterwards said that she had expected me to follow this up by remarking, 'Hasn't he got a funny face!' Whereas my question was not in any way derogatory, but simply to satisfy myself that the kindly gentleman who was about to take me on his knee was indeed His Excellency, the autocrat of twenty million souls, for I had not been close enough to observe him properly as he emerged from his car. Once I had made sure of the identity of my new friend, I settled down to enjoy my few moments of proconsular favour. The fact that he looked like any other middle-aged gentleman and was dressed in an ordinary grey morning suit was not in any way a disappointment; on the contrary, it made him more real. I knew there were mightier monarchs than the Governor of the Punjab, for I had spent my earliest years under the shadow of Buckingham Palace, but Kings and Queens were insubstantial beings who half dwelt in the world of story books. *They* did not drive to my home in a big black limousine with a flag and a motorcycle in front and a car full of policemen behind. *They* did not allow me to sit on their knee.

Having made the acquaintance of the Governor, I began to take notice of Government House. Not that I could see very much of it, for it lay hidden among the trees of its enormous compound, behind a long, fortress-like wall topped with broken glass, though if one looked hard enough one could catch a glimpse of pillars and verandahs and an octagonal tower from which the flag flew when the Governor was in residence. I longed to go past the sentries and policemen who guarded the main gate on the Mall and explore the forbidden world within, envying my parents when they went off there to garden parties, dinners and balls, from which they would bring me back dance programmes, embossed with a gold lion and with a little pencil dangling from the corner.

I particularly envied them when the Viceroy and Vicereine, Lord and Lady Linlithgow, came to Lahore, for during the week of the Viceregal visit they went to functions at Government House almost every day. My father also took his Indian officers there for a select little tea party with the Viceroy – no small honour for them, though in fact they did not enjoy it, for not only did the Viceroy spend most of the time talking to my father about mutual friends in Scotland, but he ate no tea, so that they, too, felt constrained to eat nothing, and resented being thus deprived of their curry puffs and iced cakes. The only Viceregal function to which I was taken, the Presentation of New Colours to the

3rd Battalion, 17th Dogra Regiment, was not held at Government House. It turned out to be the most memorable of the week's events owing to a dust-storm, which caused the front part of the *shamiana* to collapse on top of the Viceroy. The rest of us, in the less volatile main body of the tent, were treated to the spectacle of him crawling out from under the fallen canvas. Lord Linlithgow's own account of that occasion, written to the King, is quoted in his son's recent biography of him: he speaks of how 'a high wind and dust storm could not mar the very high level of the drill', but regarding the collapse of the tent he remains tactfully silent.

With the advent of a new Governor, who had grandchildren of my age, the portals of Government House were at last opened to me. The reality surpassed my expectations. The grounds were an endless paradise of trees, lawns and flowers, in the midst of which the house lay like a great white ship, lapped by waves of potted plants. It was, however, a ship that had grown through the ages, for while the central octagon tower might have been the squat funnel of a liner, the Moorish *mirador* window which confronted the visitor approaching from the main gate on the Mall made that end of the house resemble the stern of a galleon. The house was in fact a regular hybrid: one side of the principal front had verandahs with pointed Gothic arches, the other side was Classical, while the centre was in the massive but unassuming style of an old Punjab officers' mess, with a lofty porte-cochère carried on pillars of no recognizable order.

Compared with our simple and straightforward bungalow, it was impressively large and of a fascinating complexity, particularly in the interior, where the rooms extended in many directions, and it was possible to get from one part of the house to another in a variety of ways. There were also numerous ways of going in and out, since there was nothing like a front door or hall in the ordinary sense. Sometimes we went up one or other of the two red-carpeted staircases of polished wood which curved to the left and right under the big porte-cochère; one of them leading to the ballroom, the other to the drawing room by way of an anteroom decorated with swords and guns arranged in patterns. Sometimes we entered the ballroom by way of the balustraded Baroque steps in the three-sided courtyard enclosed by the Classical part of the house. Or we may have used the stairs under the back porch which led up to the smoking room; or one of several smaller staircases at the ends of the verandahs.

The route we took was dictated by my friends' governess, who shepherded us to whichever room or verandah had been appointed for our tea; there was no question of exploring the house unattended. But as we always seemed to have tea somewhere different – doubtless in order to keep us as far away as possible from wherever the grown-ups happened to be – I became familiar with most of the main rooms, which smelt deliciously of polished teak and contained a wealth of intriguing objects ranging from antlers, weapons and an elaborately carved and gilded State howdah to framed photographs of bejewelled Maharajas and bewhiskered Lieutenant-Governors. There was the great echoing ballroom, with its richly moulded teak panelling, its springy floor and its gallery; it was at a lower level, so that each of the double doors leading out of it – which, like the doors of the other principal rooms, had pairs of red-coated *chaprassis* stationed by them, who opened them for us as we passed through – were approached up a little flight of steps. There was the drawing room, large and light and chintzy, a contrast to the very masculine smoking room, where the arms of the leather chairs and sofas were fitted with ashtrays mounted on miniature saddles, complete with chromium-plated stirrups. There was the morning room and the billiard room. But the most wonderful room of all was the dining room, a high, domed chamber in the Mogul style, decorated with niches and arabesques. It was in the very centre of the house, beneath the octagon tower, which concealed the dome from outside; so that to pass from one or other of the adjoining rooms, with their decidedly English character, into this survival from the days of Shah Jahan, came as a complete surprise.

It was in fact the upper storey of the tomb of Muhammad Kasim Khan, a cousin of Akbar the Great, and dated from about 1635. The room below, which was the tomb proper, served for a number of years as the kitchen, when the cooks would use the sarcophagus as a table. In spite of being built round a tomb, the house had a happy and friendly atmosphere. There were no unpleasant ghosts, apart from an elemental which used to haunt the grounds near the main gate early this century. Thus it would seem that the spirit of Muhammad Kasim did not object to later generations feasting in his tomb, if indeed the sarcophagus contained his bones, for according to some accounts, he was buried elsewhere. He probably feasted here himself, having built the tomb in his own lifetime, as was customary, and used it as a house of pleasure until he died. As he was a great patron of wrestlers, the ground near by was the scene of many wrestling matches, which continued to be held here long after his death; so that the tomb came to be known as Kushtiwala Gumbaz, or the Wrestlers' Dome.

In the early nineteenth century, when Lahore had become the capital of the Sikh ruler, Ranjit Singh, a house of octagonal form was built around the tomb by a military commander named Ram Singh. It was then not unusual for tombs to be turned into dwellings: thus, another of Ranjit's henchmen, the Italian General Ventura, inhabited the tomb of the dancing-girl, Anarkali. After the British annexation of the Punjab in 1849, Ram Singh's house was occupied briefly by Major Macgregor, the Deputy-Commissioner; being subsequently chosen by Sir Henry Lawrence as his home.

Henry Lawrence had the intense energy and deep religion of his brother John, but he was less down-to-earth and more of a romantic. As head of the commission which took over the government of the Punjab when it became British territory, he set out to bring law, order and prosperity to a province as large as England, Scotland and Ireland put together, stretching as far as the North-West Frontier, being helped in his task by his brother John, and by a team of brilliant young men like Nicholson, Abbott and Edwardes. By his side was his wife, Honoria, pretty and lively, Northern Irish like himself, and with an Irish wit to temper her evangelical sense of duty which was every bit as strong as his, though ill-health impaired her energy. She was also unconventional; when the stiff-boned Victorian dresses grew unbearable in the hot weather, she would go about in a long grey flannel petticoat and high-necked cotton bodice: 'perfectly decent of course, but not presentable', as the wife of one of her husband's colleagues described it.

At first the Lawrences lived in the old Residency, close to the tomb of Anarkali; they found it uncomfortable and moved temporarily to a smaller house. Having then decided to take over the house of Ram Singh, they rebuilt it all but the tomb. The new house was the same shape as its predecessor, this being probably dictated by the shape of the *chabutra* – the twelve-foot-high platform round the base of the tomb – on which it stood. 'If we have not got a *paragon* of a house, we have at least an *octagon*,' Honoria wrote to her elder son Alick, then at school in England, in March 1851, when the new house was 'springing up quickly'; and she drew him a plan, so that he could see what it would be like.

The octagon was single-storeyed, consisting of four large rooms backing onto the four sides of the tomb, and four smaller rooms of a triangular shape. It was surrounded by an outer octagon of verandahs and bathrooms – a bathroom for every bedroom, 'for here we should be very uncomfortable if we did not actually go into a bath every day', as Honoria explained to her son. Each of the principal rooms had a fireplace, which was not only essential in the Lahore winter, but served, in hot weather, to hold the 'thermantidote' – a primitive air-conditioning device in which a fan, turned by a man or a bullock, blew air through wet *cuscuss* matting.

Thanks to this appliance, the rooms were kept at eighty when the inside temperature of most houses was over ninety. And as the house stood in open country, a couple of miles to the south-east of the old walled city of Lahore, the Lawrences found it cooler and fresher than their previous home in the Residency quarter, which was nearer the city. It was also delightfully peaceful. 'I can be out of doors as much as I like without meeting anyone,' wrote Honoria. 'I can mount my pony and toddle about to my heart's content.' The only drawback was that Henry now lived two miles away from his office, having previously slept, ate and worked under the same roof; Honoria found it 'a great privation' to be thus parted from him.

He was, however, able to do some work at a desk in the tomb-turned-dining room, to which the food was brought from a detached cook-house in the garden by way of the drawing room or one of the bedrooms. The drawing room also occupied the same position as it did in later years, facing west and opening onto a verandah which ran round three sides of the octagon, with a view across the fields to where the domes and minarets of the city rose above a distant pall of smoke. The Lawrences' bedroom faced south. 'Your first impression would be of a naked, comfortless look in the room,' Honoria told her son. 'It is a large one, thirty-two feet long by twenty-two feet wide, and twenty-two feet high. *Only five* doors, for our object was not to have many. Ceiling bare beams and rafters; walls bare lime, coloured grey; floor covered with chintz; bed without curtains or posts or anything to harbour dust or insects, standing in the middle of the room, a red screen shutting it out from the door that leads into the large centre room. A yawning chasm is now where in winter the fireplace stands, and inside this chasm are turning four large fans, like the sails of a windmill, bringing cool air into the room.'

In the adjoining triangular room to the eastwards slept the

Lawrences' younger son Harry, aged six, and their infant daughter Honie, together with several other children, whose parents were away in the *mofussil*. One of them, Willy Levinge, had run wild and could speak no English until he was taken under Honoria's wing. There was also Marianne, a child from the barracks, rescued from 'a drunken and depraved father'. The other bedrooms were usually no less crowded, whether it was with more children, or with brothers, sisters and in-laws of Henry and Honoria – of whom there were many then in India, not counting the John Lawrences, who had their own house on the other side of Lahore – or with Colonels or clergymen and their respective wives, or with Henry's 'young men'. Honoria's letters are full of references to Nicholson and Abbott, and she told her Rugbeian son of 'a very good sample of Rugby' who was staying, the young Richard Temple, destined to become one of the most dynamic figures in the India of the next generation. There was even an illustrious visitor from England, who seems to belong more to the Government House of later days: Lord Stanley, son of the Prime Minister, Lord Derby. Honoria considered him 'a young man of great energy and intelligence', while deploring the poor figure he cut in the saddle: 'He lamed Papa's favourite horse for want of knowing how to manage him, and was sadly annoyed – indeed, I suspect frightened – when Nicholson, or Lumsden, or any of the young men with Papa, proposed a scamper.'

Honoria gave Alick an account of 'our hot weather way of life'. The day starts at four in the morning, and before five the children, 'who begin to have a white look with the heat, though they continue well and as merry as crickets', have all gone outside. 'On the elephant go Honie, Mona, Billy and Marianne with Dhyze and a *chaprassi*. Harry and John go out to ride if they like, otherwise they play in our own grounds, harnessing a goat to a little carriage, working in the garden, visiting the stable, or anything they like. After six they are confined to the western side, where this tall house casts a shadow for many yards, where they play, but they must be in the house by seven. Meantime Papa and I have got up and generally sit in the beautiful western verandah to read and write and I *potter* about the house, seeing after the many things so large a family require, and very happy and thankful thus to be able to occupy myself.

'At eight o'clock Bell comes to teach the children, and lessons go on, interrupted by prayers and breakfast, till two o'clock.' Then, 'one by one, children and attendants drop off, so that about two or three o'clock there is a lull all over the house . . . after three, the little voices are heard again, and then Harry and John go to my large bath which I used in the morning tepid, and which is now cold for them, and great fun have they there, so that they are fresh and clean and comfortable for our four o'clock dinner. Then play till near six, go out again as in the morning, home soon after seven, tea and bed. And the seniors do not sit up much later. I am rejoiced when we have day dining, for it breaks off Papa's work much earlier than would otherwise be, and enables us to go to bed betimes, avoiding all candlelight work.'

This busy, well-ordered life was all very well in May. The Lahore June, which is as hot as May and oppressively overcast, brought 'a lassitude inexpressible – week after week, day and night passed in a bath of perspiration'. Then, quite unexpectedly, came the Rains: 'At nine o'clock this morning . . . we were closing every cranny to keep out the fiery wind, and were panting, even under the *punkah*. The children had on only white muslin pyjamas and *kootas* (loose drawers and long shirts) and I was gasping to myself: "three months of this!" Our Bible lesson this morning was from Kings, and the children well understood what I talked to them about heat and drought. I did not think that relief was so near, but at ten o'clock there came "a sound of abundance of rain" – first an angry, howling, hot wind, twisting the trees about, and then the blessed moisture – every door opened, a clear cool air filling the house, and the children, in their English clothing, rushing about, wild with delight at getting out.'

In July, Harry had a bad attack of fever and was sent to Simla to convalesce. He fell ill again after his return, and was in danger of death; Honoria herself was also ill that autumn. But they both recovered to enjoy the delights of a Lahore Christmas – the clear, frosty mornings, the log fires blazing where a few months earlier the fans of the thermantidotes had turned; twenty-five people staying in the house and a constant influx of 'comers and goers'. After church on Christmas Day, the Indians came to pay their respects: the officers presenting their swords to be touched, the civilians offering *nazars* of a few rupees laid on a white handkerchief; and all of them bringing trays of fruits, flowers and sweet-meats. To one of these Indian visitors, Henry gave 'a handsome Bible'.

Honoria felt that the five 'delightful' cold weather months were well worth the four 'fearful' months from May to September, which in any case she found less unbearable than the English winter. Her letters convey the poetry of those cold weather months in Lahore. There was a glorious evening when she and the children went to the Ravi river, on the far side of the city, to meet Henry, who was returning from camp. 'The late rains had swept away the bridge of boats, and now the river was covered with ferry boats, the banks gay with parties waiting to cross. The winding stream flowing away to the west seemed almost to meet the setting sun, which made it one sheet of gold – for though running with great swiftness, it was as smooth as glass . . . Herds of bullocks, buffaloes, sheep were waiting by the brink, and every few minutes a clumsy flat-bottomed boat pushed off with a freight of bipeds and quadrupeds.' Across the river, the four minarets of Jahangir's tomb cast long shadows. 'Presently I saw two horsemen dashing down the sandy bank opposite, leaping into a boat, jerking their horses after them, and then pushing across. I soon recognized Ibrahim, one of our followers . . . in time of quiet a lazy, troublesome fellow, but when anything is to be done, all activity; and at all times a most handsome, well-dressed, picturesque fellow. He soon landed, dressed in close-fitting scarlet cloak, leather breeches, jack-boots, a voluminous turban and a shawl-girdle with dagger. On his wrist sat a falcon and I longed for a picture of him as he came up, made obeisance, and reported his master's approach.'

The next time Henry went into camp, Honoria and the children went with him. Harry, Honie and a friend's child were rigged out in fur coats and long jack-boots so that Honoria called them the Three Bears. Our baggage,' she wrote, 'will go on five elephants, twenty camels, six mules, and very likely some cattle. We take two large tents, two smaller, two yet smaller, three or four very small for servants. We shall have from twenty to thirty servants with us, also horsemen, soldiers, and provisions of all kinds. This sounds a vast preparation, yet our camp is not a third of what most people would take – not a tenth, hardly a twentieth, of what the Governor-General or Commander-in-Chief requires.'

Enjoyable though the tour was, Honoria declared when it was over: 'I am right glad to return to my own pleasant dwelling, which I now feel to be *home*, and where I should be well content to pass the rest of my days . . . But indeed I rarely think about the future of this life, every year makes me feel the utter futility of our arrangements.' Her fatalism was justified, for less than a year later, Henry was ordered to leave Lahore and take up a post in Rajputana. But even before this bombshell, the Lawrences' 'pleasant dwelling' was overshadowed by the impending departure of Harry to school in England. He had to go; he was far behind most English boys of his age in book-learning. Yet in other ways he was so much more advanced. 'He can pluck and curry a bird, and bake *chapattis* to eat with it,' wrote his mother. 'He can run and leap and climb, and tell a tale and translate it too.' He could ride anything: 'He was greatly surprised to find Lord Stanley hesitate about mounting a strange horse, and still more about riding a camel.'

Harry's grief was piteous when the time came to say goodbye. His departure, however, served to lessen Honoria's sorrow at leaving the house of which she had grown so fond; now she almost felt glad to leave, for 'every spot here would be to me full of my darling'. But Henry was heartbroken at having to leave the Punjab and its people. On the day they left, he and Honoria knelt down together for a last prayer in their bleak, dismantled bedroom. Outside the house, a tearful crowd of Sikh and Muslim Chiefs were assembled to do him homage; they formed 'a living funeral procession' behind the Lawrence's carriage for most of the thirty miles to Amritsar. Certainly the Lawrences left their earthly happiness in the Wrestlers' Dome; for almost within the year, Honoria was dead. Henry survived her only to die a hero's death in the Residency at Lucknow three years later.

Although John Lawrence took over the administration of the Punjab from Henry, he did not move into his brother's house, which did not become the permanent residence of the head of the province until the time of his successor, the chubby, bespectacled Sir Robert Montgomery, known as 'Pickwick'. Montgomery was an Ulsterman like the Lawrences – he was also, incidentally, the grandfather of Lord Montgomery of Alamein – and his features belied his resolution, for it was a decisive stroke on his part, in John Lawrence's absence, which saved Lahore during the Mutiny. In 1859 the Punjab had been constituted a Lieutenant-Governor's Province, so that the old home of Henry and Honoria Lawrence became Government House.

In order that the house should be a suitable residence for His Honour the Lieutenant-Governor, Montgomery enlarged it considerably; rebuilding the outer octagon of verandahs and bathrooms to provide more rooms, and doubling the size of the drawing room by means of a bowed projection. These additions overflowed the old *chabutra* or platform, so that various rooms were fitted in beneath them at ground level, giving the house the appearance of being two-storeyed. The Lawrences' octagon rose above the additions of the Montgomery regime, enabling the original rooms to be lit by clerestory windows; while above that again rose the octagonal tower concealing the dome.

The effect was slightly that of a Moorish fort; with covered balconies, like *mirador* windows, projecting on either side. The frontispiece, however, was unmistakably British-Indian: a semi-circular verandah masking all but the top of the drawing room bow, shaded in the middle by a vast porte-cochère. Two curving wooden staircases rose from under the porte-cochère to the main storey of the house; but arriving guests could, if they wished, pause in a rather dark hall beneath the drawing room before making their ascent. This hall was in the nature of a dead end, leading only to the cloakrooms – where, in the closing days of the Raj, a resourceful ADC incarcerated a visiting English Member of Parliament, who had drunk so much as to be unfit to appear at dinner.

The house remained as Montgomery left it for the reigns of the six succeeding Lieutenant-Governors. The gentlemen accompanying the Prince of Wales, who stayed here early in 1876 as the guest of Sir Robert and Lady Davies, found it 'very comfortable'. When one reads of Government House at the time of the Prince's visit, it is hard to realize that Henry and Honoria Lawrence and their simple, patriarchal way of life had only been gone twenty-three years. A guard of honour of a hundred picked men of the 92nd Highlanders – with blue noses and knees, for it was very cold – were drawn up outside, pipes playing. Upstairs in the drawing room, the Prince stood in the midst of his Staff and held a succession of levees similar to those which he had held in Bombay, Madras and Calcutta, except that the people he received in audience were more picturesque – the Lahore Municipality resplendent in brocade robes, turbans of gold tissue and coils of emeralds, rubies and pearls; the Chiefs of the tiny Hill States dressed far more brilliantly, and with more extravagantly-clad followers, than the rulers of much greater importance who had done homage to the Heir-Apparent earlier in his tour.

The Prince of Wales was not the first Royal visitor to Government House; his brother, Prince Alfred, had stayed here in 1870. And the house had seen the State visits of several Viceroys, ever since John Lawrence came in 1864 to stay with his old friend Montgomery and to hold a great Durbar for all the Punjab Chiefs whom he knew so well. The pattern of these Royal and Viceregal visits to Lahore varied only in minor details – for Prince Alfred, a 'conversazione' was held at Government House, which must have been a rather unusual form of enter-tainment; while the Prince of Wales had the rare privilege of meeting an elderly Thug at Lahore Gaol who claimed to have murdered more than 250 people. Otherwise it was the same: the Durbar or reception for Their Highnesses of Kashmir, Fardikot, Jind and Bahawalpur and all the lesser Chiefs; the elephant ride through the old city, the visit to the Fort or Mogul palace, to see the sunset over the Ravi which had held Honoria Lawrence spellbound; the tea party at Jahangir's Tomb and the evening of Arabian Nights enchantment at the Shalimar Gardens, with all the pools and fountains lit up. There was also a more European evening at the fine Classical assembly rooms across the Mall from Government House, built during the eighteen-sixties as a memo-rial to John Lawrence and Montgomery.

These rooms were used by the Lieutenant-Governor when he gave a ball or other large function; just as the Governors of Madras and, in earlier years, the Residents at Lucknow held their grand entertainments in detached Banquetting Halls; but the Lahore assembly rooms were different in that they were not private to the Lieutenant-Governor, being used by the whole British community. Over the years, the civil-ians deserted the old Residency quarter for this neighbourhood, so that Government House, which had been out on a limb in the days of Henry and Honoria Lawrence, became very central, with the Mall leading in one direction to the cantonment, and in the other to the shops, the Secretariat and the Law Courts.

Even in the present century, when many more buildings had sprung up, the Mall had, for much of its length, the aspect of a drive through parks and gardens. In the eighteen-eighties, it appeared to Lady Dufferin that there was no 'town' in Lahore, but avenues of trees, luxuriant foliage and roses growing in incredible profusion. Trees made it no longer possible to see the old city from Government House.

The Dufferins paid more than one State visit to Lahore. On the first occasion, their host and hostess at Government House were Sir Charles and Lady Aitchison, who, according to Sir Alfred Lyall, kept 'a very bourgeois ménage'. The second time the Dufferins came to Lahore, Aitchison had been succeeded by Alfred Lyall's younger brother, James, one of the most popular and successful Lieutenant-Governors the Punjab ever had. Compared with the rather stuffy Lady Aitchison, the new Lady Sahib seemed gay and dashing. After breakfast, she peram-bulated round the garden of Government House on a camel, which had a side-saddle fitted to its hump. Lady Dufferin could not resist having a ride herself, and as the camel got up she was first of all nearly thrown over its tail, then only just avoided being thrown over its head.

The Government House camels were broken to harness. Those of the Prince of Wales's suite who fancied themselves as whips were impressed by the way in which the driver and postillions managed a team of six camels harnessed to a brake, while noting how 'the leaders had a knack of turning round now and then to see what those who were behind were about'. As well as the brake, there was the State Camel Carriage, which existed in the time of Montgomery and was to be a feature of Government House right down to the outbreak of the Second World War; with a postillion in scarlet on each camel and a driver in scarlet on the box. At the Lahore Races, the Lord Sahib and Lady Sahib drove in it down the course Ascot-fashion, escorted by Lancers and preceded by kettle drums on another camel. The Camel Carriage was put at the disposal of guests; but after a long drive in it on a hot day, when the smell of the six camels could be rather overpowering, they were usually glad to exchange it for the victoria. When Sir Louis Dane was Lieutenant-Governor, shortly before the First World War, the Camel Carriage was mostly used by his young daughters, who on one occasion raced the brake of the 12th Lancers in it. It was also lent to take the infant Dorothy Butler, daughter of the Deputy-Commissioner and sister of Richard Austen Butler, to her christening.

Government House boasted of elephants as well as camels; the *hatikhana* stood a little way to the east of the house, adjoining the stables. Long after the Viceregal *hatikhana* was redundant, the Lieutenant-Governors of the Punjab continued to use elephants for touring in remoter districts and also for riding through the narrow streets of the old walled city of Lahore, and along the even more tortuous ways of cities in the *mofussil*. Sir Henry Durand, a brilliant soldier and administrator of commanding presence who became Lieutenant-Governor in 1870, was killed when the howdah of his elephant was crushed going under an archway at Tonk, near the Frontier. As late as the nineteen-twenties, there was still one elephant in the Government House *hatikhana*; she was called Primrose and did duty at children's parties, as well as taking distinguished visitors through the city. There was a time when she disturbed the inhabitants of Government House every night with her trumpetings; it was then discovered that a syce was stealing her grain. In the eighteen-nineties there were two other elephants called

Peter and Steady Joe. 'Peter quite frolicsome,' remarked Sir James Lyall, when he returned to Lahore on a visit in 1894, less than two years after his retirement.

Revisiting the scene of his past glory – something which former Lord Sahibs seldom did – made Lyall aware that the glory of a Lieutenant-Governor was very transient. He was, it is true, met by thirty Indian gentlemen at the station; but when he arrived at Government House, Sir Dennis Fitzpatrick, who had succeeded him, only gave him a perfunctory greeting before starting for a ride on Peter with his daughters. Left to his own devices, Lyall walked across the Mall to see his portrait, which had recently been added to the gallery of Lieutenant-Governors in the Lawrence Hall. When, a day or two later, he visited the Nawab of Bahawalpur at his Lahore residence, he drove there not in a Government House landau, but in a *tikka ghari* or hackney-carriage. He felt ashamed of his conveyance when the Nawab received him with a guard of honour and all ceremonies, though it must have helped to restore his self-esteem.

Lyall's visit to his old capital was not improved by the weather, which was cold and grey, so that Government House looked, as he thought, 'dreary'. The new wing, with its Gothic verandahs, which had been built onto the south side of the octagon in 1892, seems to have made little impression on him; it had been planned when he was still Lieutenant-Governor, but he had asked for the building to be deferred until after his departure. It contained ADCs' quarters and additional bedrooms as well as a Durbar Hall on the upper floor with ornate panelling and a projecting *mirador* window facing south. One of the old covered balconies from the octagon appears to have been re-erected and glazed to form this Moorish feature, which is believed to have been put up under the supervision of Lockwood Kipling, father of Rudyard and Principal of the Mayo School of Arts, whose pupils carried out frequent restorations of the frescoed arabesques and Mogul motifs in the dining room. Although they only dated from a few years back, having been copied from a mosque in the old city, these frescoes perished quickly in the Lahore climate.

Improvements and alterations to Government House continued during the later 'nineties and the opening years of the present century, being held up from time to time owing to financial stringency in the Punjab. Rooms were floored and panelled in teak. Electric light was installed in 1903, and electric fans a year later. The house had possessed a tiled bathroom with running water as far back as 1887, which would have been very advanced for India; now the plumbing was extended. In 1905, during the reign of Sir Charles Rivaz, a north wing, containing offices, was added in anticipation of the visit of the Prince and Princess of Wales, the future George V and Queen Mary, towards the end of that year. It did not balance the south wing, being Oriental rather than Gothic. So easily does the history of a Government House become garbled, that the south wing also came to be associated with a Royal visit, that of the Duke of Clarence; and it was subsequently known as the Duke of Clarence Wing, though in fact the Duke's visit was in 1890, two years before the wing was built. The addition of the wings entailed the rebuilding of parts of the old octagon; but other parts remained, notably the former bedroom of Henry and Honoria Lawrence, and the triangular room adjoining it where their children had slept. These rooms, together with other rooms on either side of the drawing room and dining room, were the bedrooms of the Lieutenant-Governor and his family: in the Danes' time, the triangular room was occupied by their youngest daughter; it was rather dark, and was abandoned after she had suffered a bad attack of malaria there.

The building of a garage in 1907 for the Lieutenant-Governor's newly-acquired Daimlers was followed by a pause. Sir Louis Dane, who became Lieutenant-Governor in 1908, preferred to concentrate on the garden and grounds. He created a wilderness of bamboo overhanging a pool; he improved the artificial hill or mound – formed out of old brick-kilns – to the west of the house, crowning its summit with a graceful Mogul pavilion, to which garden party guests could ascend by way of a spiral path.

At the foot of the mound was an indoor swimming bath, housed in a Classical structure with Doric columns. It dated from many years before, and must have been one of the first full-scale swimming baths in India. Soon after it was built, it was the scene of a tragedy on which Flora Annie Steel based an incident in one of her novels. A young officer, eager for a swim after a hot game of tennis, dived into it without realizing that it contained no water and was killed.

A cypress avenue ran from the swimming bath to the other end of the grounds, passing the front of the house. Apart from this avenue – which was subsequently felled – the garden was informal. Stretches of lawn were shaded by palms, shishams, blue and lemon-scented gums, and other trees, with groves of tamarinds screening the boundary wall.

25   Government House, Lahore, 1869.

26   Government House, Lahore.

27   Government House, Lahore, Sir Robert Montgomery in the camel carriage, with the camel brake and attendants.

28   Government House, Lahore, the garden, looking towards the mound.

Everywhere else was a kaleidoscope of colour, with clouds of gypso-phila to provide relief; verbena covered the rockeries at the foot of the mound, roses grew between the cypresses of the avenue and night-scented stocks filled the downstairs rooms of the house with their fragrance. The grounds were maintained by sixty *malis*; the head *mali* was believed to do well for himself by selling the surplus produce of the enormous kitchen garden.

The first two decades of this century were the golden age of the Lahore Government House. The Lieutenant-Governors who reigned during this period were the cream of the Indian Civil Service in its late-Victorian prime. It still seemed that the Raj would endure, with the British and the Indians ruling India in partnership. Those Indians who were known to be actively anti-British were few enough not to matter; and some of them were easy to deal with. Lady Dane was frowned upon because she insisted on entertaining Sawrula Devi, a lady of notoriously subversive opinions; but it had the effect of keeping her quiet for as long as the Danes were in the Punjab. When they left, Lady Dane's seditious friend presented her with a complete edition of the Veda, in Sanskrit.

People like the Danes found it easier to understand Indian rebels than British socialists. Sidney Webb, when he came to stay, did not make a good impression, though Beatrice, who was with him, was thought attractive. It was seldom, however, that itinerant socialists disturbed the calm of Government House in those Edwardian days. Globe-trotting European royalties and British noblemen in search of big game were the more usual guests; the most illustrious being the German Crown Prince, who every evening would slide down the bannisters of one or other of the curving staircases under the porte-cochère. Then, of course, there were the Maharajas and Nawabs, and the polo teams from British and Indian cavalry regiments who were always put up at Government House when they came to Lahore to play in a match. The entertaining was constant throughout the winter months, with one or two State dinner parties of thirty or forty guests every week; it reached a climax at Christmas, when the lawns on either side of the house were covered with tents. Henry and Honoria Law-rence had known the joys of Christmas in the crisp, bright winter weather of Lahore. Since their time, Lahore Christmas Week had grown into an institution, to which people came from all over the Punjab, and from other parts of India as well. Kipling wrote of how, as the festive season approached, there were sahibs and memsahibs joining the Lahore train at almost every station along the line: 'with racquets, with bundles of polo-sticks, with dear and bruised cricket-bats, with fox-terriers and saddles.'

The Lieutenant-Governor still held his larger entertainments in the Montgomery and Lawrence Halls. In 1913, however, a *chaprassi* was killed near these assembly rooms by an anarchist's bomb meant for the British gathered there of an evening; and so, in the following year, the new Lieutenant-Governor, Sir Michael O'Dwyer, built a ballroom at Government House, to the north of the drawing room and dining room. To replace the bedrooms on this side, which were thus swept away, the north wing was rebuilt on a much larger scale and in a simple Classical manner with Doric columns; and a parallel wing was added to the eastwards. This formed a pleasant three-sided courtyard, into which, during a ball, the guests could descend by impressive Baroque steps from the ballroom, and then pass through a colonnade into the garden, where the supper tables were arranged beneath trees decked with coloured lights. The Lord Sahib's private suite was on the upper floor of the more westerly of the two wings, with his office below; the upstairs rooms in the other wing were for his family and guests. It was a convenient arrangement, except that to get from the bedrooms to the reception rooms entailed a walk along an open verandah, which in the depths of the Lahore winter could be rather cold. Of the remaining bedrooms in the centre of the house, some were turned into extra reception rooms, others became domestic offices. The kitchen, having been previously moved from an outside cook-house into the lower chamber of the old tomb, was now brought upstairs. Henry and Honoria Lawrence's bedroom became a magnificent pantry, lined with presses containing enough china and glass for the most elaborate of Edwardian banquets.

The 1913 bomb outrage heralded a period of unrest in the Punjab during the First World War and immediately afterwards, with conspiracies and disturbances following each other in bewildering succession. O'Dwyer dealt with them quickly and effectively; he was a man of great courage, tempering firmness with an Irish humour. He also had the quick wits of a keen hunting man. He would go out with the Lahore Hunt not only on Thursdays, but on Sundays as well, which some people thought was a bad example. To them he replied that, on the contrary, he was setting a good example; for he always left the hunt, even in the middle of a good run, so as to be back for ten o'clock Mass. This meant that he generally appeared in his pew beneath the pulpit of the Catholic Cathedral in his hunting clothes.

O'Dwyer was a great Lieutenant-Governor, devoted to the Punjab and its people, among whom so much of his life was spent; and up to the end of 1918, when he was due to retire, he was popular with all but a few extremists – as is testified by the success with which he mobilized the resources of his Province in the war effort. Unfortunately for himself, he agreed to stay on a few months longer, which meant that he had to deal with a serious outbreak of violence in April 1919. He did so according to the old Punjab maxim that 'the man who is most ready to use force at the beginning will use least in the end'. Even a year earlier, he would probably have been thought to have acted rightly – by the majority of Indians, as well as by the British. But Indian opinion, during the past few months, had undergone a sudden change. To make matters worse, some of O'Dwyer's military colleagues went further than he himself would have gone; characteristically, he stood by them. So he acquired that reputation for harshness which caused an Indian fanatic to assassinate him many years later in London.

Although the worst of the 1919 troubles were at Amritsar, thirty miles away, there were also serious riots in Lahore. O'Dwyer woke up one morning to the 'ominous cries' of a mob of ten thousand, advancing along the Mall in the direction of the civil station. He immediately ordered all women and children to be brought into Government House, where they remained under the protection of his entirely Indian guard until more troops arrived.

When, later in the year, O'Dwyer finally handed over to Sir Edward Maclagan, who from being Lieutenant-Governor became Governor, things were back to normal. The Maclagans enjoyed a peaceful reign; though after the kidnapping of an English girl on the Frontier, their ten-year-old daughter Pamela went about with an armed guard and two *chaprassis*, as well as her *ayah*, which made her feel very important. Her greatest moment, however, was when she was allowed to stay up for the ball given in honour of the Prince of Wales, who came to Lahore early in 1922; the Prince waltzed with her in the garden for a long time. Her parents were less charmed, for they knew that several eminent Lahore ladies would thereby be deprived of their rightful privilege of dancing with him.

The Prince caused his host and hostess other worries during his stay at Government House. On his arrival, he stipulated that the sermon on Sunday should not take more than ten minutes, and that dinner every night should not take more than twenty minutes. It was easy enough for the Governor to telephone the Bishop about the sermon, but when Lady Maclagan broke it to the head butler that he and his minions would have to serve dinner to forty-eight people in twenty minutes, that dignitary was horrified. So by way of compromise, she told him to provide a buffet in the ballroom, to which those who did not get enough at dinner could afterwards repair. On the night of his departure, the Prince sat on in the drawing room listening to gramophone records and playing a swannee-whistle even after it was time for him to go. The Royal train was waiting; the other trains were all held up; there were Cuttack Dancers, picturesque tribesmen with flaming torches, lining the route from Government House to the station. But still His Royal Highness showed no sign of making a move.

In preparation for the Prince's visit, an imposing State Suite was made by dividing up the Durbar Hall in the south wing, which had become the Council Chamber when the Legislative Council was established in 1897, and was no longer needed for this purpose after the Council had been reconstituted in 1921. Apart from the Prince himself, ten gentlemen of his suite were fitted into the house, though this meant that the ADCs were turned out of their rooms and went under canvas, along with the lesser members of the suite. There was a second-class camp for such people as clerks and police inspectors, as well as for the Prince's head motor mechanic and his head valet, his second valet and the valets of the suite being relegated to the third-class camp.

Government House entertained Royalty once again in 1925, when Prince and Princess Arthur of Connaught came to stay. The Princess sprained her ankle playing tennis and was carried into the house single-handed by the Governor, Sir Malcolm Hailey, whose muscles were as powerful as his intellect. Hailey was a tremendous walker, and even the spacious compound of Government House was not large enough for him. One day, he managed to escape from the ADCs and the *chaprassis*, and walked out of the gates and along the Mall, accompanied only by his dog. It was pouring with rain, but so hot that he took no mackintosh and let his shirt and shorts get soaked. Eventually he met a procession in protest against something, and being interested to know how the police really dealt with such a gathering, he joined it. Nothing happened; but next day he was delighted to read in the police report that the procession had been joined by 'a disreputable European with a dog'.

During the Hailey regime, Lahore was treated to the novel spectacle of a flying Lady Sahib. The airman, B. M. Leete, who had flown out from England in a Moth, offered to take Lady Hailey up; she eagerly accepted. The story of what ensued is best told by Lady Hailey herself. 'We were coming down after a jolly flight over Lahore and Government House, with some glide stunts, and side-way stunts; we started coming down, and were just near the aerodrome, when I heard a click . . . at once our nose went straight downwards, and we landed on it; and slowly, with a crackling, breaking noise, turned a somersault . . . Soon some Tommys came with stretchers, and were very inclined to pull me out, but I cheerily said, "Wait a bit, lads, I can manage, I'll ask for a hand when I want it". So I crawled out. They were all concerned, but my one concern, when I had ascertained that the pilot was all right, was the poor broken machine, such a jolly little aeroplane.' As soon as Leete had acquired a new aircraft, Lady Hailey showed that she still had confidence in him as a pilot by making him give her flying lessons.

When the Haileys were in Lahore, I was not yet born; but the Government House of their time was very much the Government House of my childhood. Many of their servants were still here to dance attendance on my friends, the Governor's grandchildren – 'The Government House servants can jolly well clean me up, what else are they there for?' the little girl said loftily, when she muddied herself in an obstacle race at our bungalow. Not much can have been done to the furnishings in the past decade, for they had a pleasantly antiquated air; a welcome change from the prevailing modernity of the ordinary Lahore dwellings. No less antiquated was the Governor's own special car. For all of its age, I thought it very grand as, from my vantage point on the 'Breakfast Verandah' under the porte-cochère, I watched His Excellency enter it, with one red-coated *chaprassi* to hold open the door, and another to arrange the rug over his knees. At the wheel, with a fresh white cover on his peaked cap, sat Mr Eves, the Governor's chauffeur, an important personage whose many other duties ranged from looking after the swimming bath to dressing up as Santa Claus. On the occasions when I rode in a Government House car, I did not have the honour of being driven by Mr Eves, but had to make do with an underling, a magnificent uniformed Punjabi named Kizah, who was really more impressive. The car, too, was newer, and even larger, than His Excellency's. It was a memorable experience to drive along the Mall in this great limousine, with, above the radiator, the silver Punjab lion and the flag – admittedly furled.

I sometimes felt, however, that the Governor's grandchildren gave themselves airs on account of this lordly equipage; and it gave me considerable pleasure to see them outdone. Not by me; but, still better, by a little girl who, I flattered myself, entertained feelings for me that were more than just friendship. She was staying at Government House for the winter months, her parents being away in some remote Princely State where her father was Resident. The Governor's grandchildren treated her very much as an inferior: after all, what was a mere Resident – and a minor one at that – to the Governor of the Punjab? She endured their bullyings with sweet resignation; and then, one day, when I was fortunately present, her mother drove up in a magnificent Rolls, borrowed from her father's tame Maharaja. It was a car which put the entire Government House fleet in the shade; but my lady-love wisely refrained from rubbing this in; she simply let the Rolls speak for itself.

Far less effective was the attempt by another little girl to score off the Governor's grandchildren. She suddenly said, in a rather forced way: '*My* grandfather was the Governor of a *very large* province, and he had *State elephants.*' I always wondered where that province could have been; but it was bully to her as regards the elephants, for Primrose, alas, was now dead. The *hatikhana* was empty; the State howdah stood in a corner of the ballroom, and was a wonderful thing to get in and out of, with its shiny red leather seats and its gilded Royal Arms, For some of the other young visitors to Government House, the howdah was less of a marvel than the water-closets, since 'thunder-boxes' were all they knew. One boy was so intrigued with the flush that he broke it. I was more blasé in this respect, for we had water-closets in our bungalow, as well as a bath which was the actual twin of the one installed at Government House for the Prince of Wales. The Government House closets differed, however, from any others that I knew in being not of porcelain but of a gleaming metal. I now suppose this to have been aluminium, but at the time, I had more romantic ideas. My ayah had once told me that the King-Emperor's lavatory was of gold. Could this, I wondered, be really true, and could the Governor's closets be therefore of silver?

Certainly my friends' grandfather remained a very regal and remote figure; familiarity with Government House did not in any way breed familiarity with him. One saw him from a long way off, walking in the garden, followed by two red-coated *chaprassis*; it was not quite up to Lord Auckland's 'tail of fifteen joints', but in the same manner. It was only after my friends and their grandfather had departed from the scene – their lights fled, their garlands dead – that I once again had the privilege of conversing with a Governor, as I had when that earlier Governor sat on the sofa with my mother. His new Excellency possessed neither grandchildren nor children of my age, but he and his wife gave children's parties, to which I was always invited, for my behaviour, unlike that of some of the other boys of Lahore, was known to be up to Government House standards. Not that I was by nature particularly well behaved, but Government House still held the same fascination for me as when I first went there. To jump on the seats of the howdah, to slide down the bannisters – had I then known that the German Crown Prince had done so, it would have made no difference – or to meddle with the ancient, horned gramophone which the ADC brought into the ballroom for musical chairs, seemed to me like sacrilege.

The giver of childrens' parties was my last Governor, for we left India before he did. In later years, architecture having become one of my chief passions, I often wondered how I would find Government House if ever I returned there; whether I would be disappointed, or whether it would still have something of its former magic. It seemed that, as the house of the Governor of West Pakistan, it was continuing in its old role. I heard that the Queen stayed there, and also the Shah of Persia.

Eventually I found myself back in Lahore. I was introduced to one of the Governor's ADCs, who said he would be delighted to show me and my wife round Government House on a certain day. The day came, and I felt a thrill of expectancy as we drove up to the familiar gate on the Mall. There, our way was barred by several of Field-Marshal Ayub Khan's stalwarts. I told them we were expected; they knew nothing about it. One of them disappeared into the little lodge where my father used to sign The Book at the beginning of each season, and telephoned the house; he then emerged to inform us that the Governor and all his staff, including my ADC, had gone away on tour; they would not be back for several days, by which time we would ourselves have departed. I argued with the guard, I remonstrated, I cajoled; the *subadar* did more telephoning, but it was to no avail. There was nobody there senior enough to take the responsibility of letting us in. Through the gate I saw a tantalizing vision of lawns and flowering trees, and of the house itself, just the same as ever: the octagon tower, the porte-cochère, the Gothic verandahs. I was back thirty years in the past, before I first gained admission to those hallowed precincts; Government House was once again the mysterious, forbidden world of my early childhood.

II

GOVERNMENT HOUSE
NAINI TAL

I T was not until 1839 that the British discovered a lake hidden among
wooded peaks in the Himalayan foothills which according to the local
legend had grown out of a hole dug by the goddess Naini. Forty
years later, the hill station of Naini Tal, summer capital of the North-
Western Provinces, had grown up around the lake – in defiance of the
goddess, who had forbidden the place to strangers – so that the fearful
landslide of September 1880, which buried the Victoria Hotel, the
Assembly Rooms and the Library, together with a great many people,
might have been her way of punishing this invasion of her privacy.

One is certain that Sir John Strachey, Lieutenant-Governor from
1874 to 1876, was not in the least afraid of the goddess's wrath when he
built himself a large new Government House here; though he sited it
well out of the reach of landslides, 1,200 feet above the lake on a lofty
peak to the southwards, remote from the rest of Naini Tal, just as Naini
Tal was remote from the rest of India. 'Fancy Government House at
Simla perched on the top of Jakko, and then add some 500 feet to Jakko
and you will have an idea of our situation,' wrote Sir Alfred Lyall, when
he first took up residence in the house in 1882. According to Lyall,
Strachey chose the site for three reasons that had nothing to do with
landslides; because he 'insisted on living where he could see the snows,
a sort of tyrannical caprice'; 'to show his contempt for the rest of official
humanity'; and 'because he liked doing singular and remarkable things'.
For all his poetic nature, Lyall did not consider that a far-distant view of
Nanda Devi, India's highest mountain, made up for being cut off from
Naini Tal society, and felt 'savage at Strachey every day'.

He admitted, however, that the house itself was 'probably the best

185

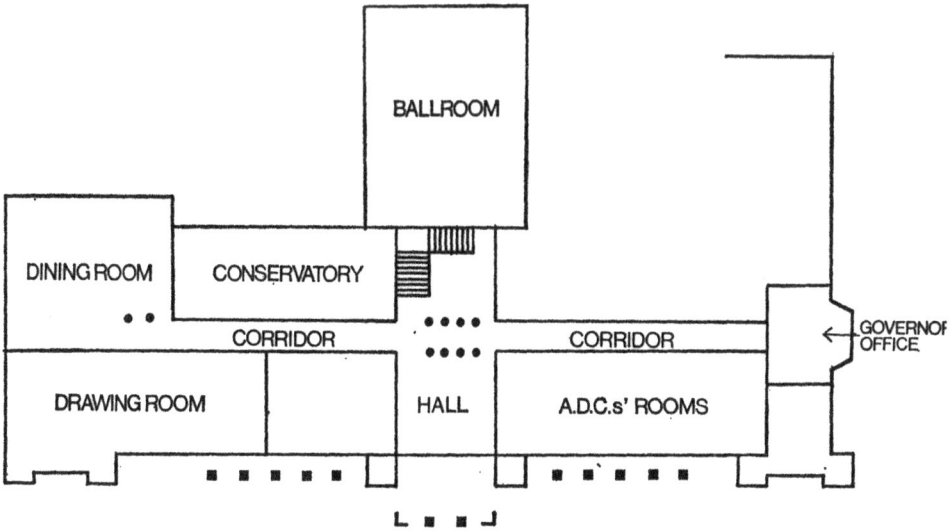

GOVERNMENT HOUSE, NAINI TAL ground floor

on the Himalayas'. A few years later, most people would have agreed that it had lost this title to the new Viceregal Lodge at Simla; yet a few years later again, when fashions had changed, the floridly Elizabethan Viceregal Lodge was decried as a monstrosity, whereas the architecture at Government House, Naini Tal, was thought to be at any rate innocuous. It was basically what was known in India as Public Works Department Gothic, enlivened by a liberal application of watered-down Baronial and with a certain amount of Swiss Chalet thrown in. These elements were combined to produce a long, two-storeyed mansion, with a row of battlemented turrets, some square, others octagonal, a Gothic porte-cochère and verandahs, and a complex of roofs. The whole effect was pleasant if uninspired; the yellow-grey stonework looked a little too new, even after the rains of half a century, but it was softened by creepers.

The porte-cochère and verandahs were the only Indian features in what was meant to come as close as possible to the popular notion of a country house in England – or perhaps Scotland, for some of the turrets originally had pepper-pot roofs. It was an expression in stone of all the nostalgia aroused in the sahibs and memsahibs by the climate and scenery of the Hills, and by such reminders of 'Home' as the smell of damp leaves and pine needles. Such Britishness also helped to keep out

186

the sinister side of India, which is felt no more strongly than in the Himalayas, where the mountains and valleys seem haunted by a multitude of malign spirits.

'Living in a house which is all Gothic arches, one realises the perfection of the Greeks in architecture,' wrote Sir Harcourt Butler during his first season at Naini Tal. 'The arch springs, it is in motion, never at rest. It is difficult to rest in a room all arches.' One passed beneath the Gothic arches of the porte-cochère into the hall, and then through more Gothic arches into the long passage running from one end of the house to the other. There were yet more Gothic arches between the passage and the top-lit Baronial staircase of dark wood which led up to the bedrooms and had a landing overlooking the ballroom, at the back of the house; and more arches again between the passage and the dining room. The dining room, drawing room and conservatory lay to the left of the hall; in the opposite direction, the passage led to the ADCs' room and the Lord Sahib's office. Such was the length of the passage that to walk up and down it satisfied the craving for exercise of that tireless walker, Sir Malcolm Hailey, when the weather was too bad even for him to venture out of doors.

It was all somewhat institutional and typical of Victorian domestic architecture at its more austere, with an almost complete lack of portraits and other paintings. We must remember, however, that most of the houses in an Indian hill station such as Naini Tal were not only bare but gimcrack and poky. By contrast, Government House would have looked tremendously large, and well-finished, with its profusion of polished woodwork. Colour would have been lent to the rooms on formal occasions by the uniforms of the Staff and the military guests and at all times by the liveries of the servants. Thus we must picture the dining room not as it appears in old photographs – the dull expanses of panelling relieved only by a few stags' heads – but as it looked to the company going in to dinner: the long table with its damask cloth, its display of glittering plate, its glasses and its napkins, cunningly folded to resemble fans, or exotic birds, the *khitmagars* in white, scarlet and gold, at least one for each member of the party, all drawn up in a line and saluting, as was the custom in the Government Houses of the North-Western, or United, Provinces, where more ceremonial was observed than in any other provincial Government Houses, apart from those of the Presidencies. We must think of logs blazing in the ponderous slate fireplaces, particularly when the Governor was spending Christmas here, as he did in later years, though the weather was then usually so mild that it was a tradition to have drinks out of doors on Christmas Day. We must, above all, think of the rooms as being full of flowers.

Flowers grew splendidly at Naini Tal, and nowhere better than in the compound of Government House, not only in the beds and borders of the garden, but throughout the surrounding forest. They followed each other in gorgeous succession, from the arrival of the Lord Sahib and Lady Sahib in April, when the garden was fragrant with lilies-of-the-valley and the slopes were scarlet with rhododendrons, until just before their final departure in October, when the chrysanthemums were in bloom and the hill near the house was a mass of pink and white cosmos. At other times, mauve orchids lined the paths, and wild white clematis covered the jungle shrubs.

In between the cedar-clad slopes and the great banks of hydrangeas was a good stretch of what Sir Harcourt Butler proudly described as 'beautiful English grass'; a more spacious lawn than the Viceroy possessed in his cramped hill-top garden at Simla. After the Rains, it looked intensely green, as did everything else in the garden, the tree-trunks being covered with moss, and with ferns that gave an exotic touch to the familiar English oaks, beeches and chestnuts. In another level place, with a stupendous backdrop of mountains, was an outdoor swimming pool, where the gentlemen – and in later years, the ladies too – would disport themselves in bathing dresses and solar topees. Elsewhere in the grounds there was an eighteen-hole golf course, which in Butler's time started to slide down the hill. The course was duly altered, and Hailey adorned it with a Doric temple where he and his successors would breakfast.

The garden and golf course took up only a part of the Government House compound, which was so large as to be more like an estate. There was a farm, providing the house with milk, meat and poultry, and there were many acres of forest and jungle, inhabited by panthers and wild deer. Paths wound their way up hill and down, providing Hailey and others of his energy with several miles of walks. To Lady Reading's secretary, Yvonne FitzRoy, setting off along one of these paths during her first visit to Naini Tal, it seemed 'like a park at home' – until she suddenly came to a landslip, and a sheer drop of hundreds of feet. 'The drop was fathomless, for a smoke of cloud curled below us, and immense jagged rocks, on the top of one of which two golden eagles had nested, towered up on either side,' she wrote in her journal. 'Only far below the cloud was torn away in the centre, and like a stage picture, the plains stretched away for sixty incredibly lovely miles.' From other places in the grounds there were glimpses of the lake, while from the garden, there was a wonderful view down a valley.

After Naini Tal, Simla seemed, to Lyall, 'suburban and shoppy'. The Viceroy could not venture out of his own grounds without coming under the gaze of passers-by, whereas the Lord Sahib of the North-Western Provinces and his family could walk and picnic in the hills outside the Government House compound and still enjoy complete privacy. Hailey liked to climb at least four hills every week-end; when the week-end was over, the ADC who had accompanied him was generally in a state of exhaustion. One disadvantage of being surrounded by so much forest was, in dry weather, the possibility of fires. 'We have nearly been burnt out of Naini Tal,' wrote Butler in May 1921, when the hillsides all around had been ablaze. The fires had been started deliberately, a sign of the prevailing unrest.

Then there was the isolation of which Lyall complained. Lieutenant-Governors and their wives, who, unlike the Stracheys, did not wish to keep entirely to themselves, had to be constantly making the long journey down the hill to the 'Flats' by the lake, where the Polo Ground, Parade Ground and Assembly Rooms were situated, and then up one of the more heavily-populated hills on the far side. With the advent of motors, it became easy enough for the Lord Sahib and Lady Sahib to go where they pleased, provided the road was not too bad, but since they were the only couple in the station to whom a motor was permitted, it still meant that whenever they gave a dinner, a ball or a garden party, their guests had to make the weary trek up the hill by rickshaw, pony or *dandy*. People staying at Government House, and members of the Staff, relied on these primitive forms of transport like everybody else, though they were able to use the Government House rickshaws, which were painted white and pulled by *jhampanis* in livery. When Yvonne FitzRoy and nine others went one evening to a play, it took sixty men to convey them there, in two rickshaws and eight *dandies*.

But however arduous the journey to and from Government House, people were prepared to make it. 'We . . . wander about our lofty ridges in a rather solitary manner', Lyall lamented, but almost in the same breath he spoke of 'heavy dinner parties' and a ball. 'Private theatricals go on here with much vigour,' he reported during the following season, adding: 'It is a queer idea that a lady may show her legs and hips on the stage; when if she did it in her own drawing room, people would be disgusted.' Even Lyall's rather unsatisfactory daughter, Sophy, showed signs of enjoying herself at Naini Tal and her father noted that she was 'developing with immense rapidity under the influence of Indian gaieties'. She refused, however, to respond to the attentions of 'a very pleasant and gentlemanly Major of Infantry' aged forty-seven or forty-eight. Though he felt 'she might have done much worse than take him', Lyall saw that the situation was hopeless, but his wife Cora, who had herself fallen rather in love with the highly agreeable Major, 'was *very* anxious to persuade Sophy to do likewise'. Lyall himself, while complaining that nobody in Naini Tal took the slightest interest in literature, and expressing his 'contempt for the women ever plunging about in lawn tennis courts, and dancing incessantly with *les militaires*', got so carried away at the Birthday Ball of May 1885 that he 'took a lady out into the garden and smoked cigarettes with her, much to Cora's wrath – but one must be horrid now and then'.

Sir Harcourt Butler had less fun at the fancy-dress Victory Ball of 1919, sitting on a dais in plain clothes, engaged in dull conversation. 'Never did I see such a queer lot of people or dresses, or apologies for dresses,' he declared in a letter to his mother. Balls were not his favourite form of entertainment, for he regarded himself as 'not young enough nor old enough to dance'. He preferred his Sunday lunches, which became a regular feature at Naini Tal during his time, luncheon being 'followed by a stroll to the view or to the fowls and stables and back to the front door' where his guests' rickshaws, *dandies* and ponies awaited them. It was all over in an hour. He also much enjoyed giving a childrens' party. Electricity had recently been installed at Government House, enabling a light to be put under the water of the goldfish pool in the conservatory, which was a great success. A chute was contrived from the staircase leading down to the ballroom floor; there were 200 balloons and at the end of the party His Excellency presented each child with a signed photograph of himself – costing, as he told his mother, 'about sixpence each'.

Butler was at his best when important and interesting people came to stay, which happened quite often now that there were motors, Naini Tal being only a twenty-mile climb by road from the end of the railway at Kathgodam, known to the British as Curse-the-dog. He was a magnificent host, and being himself fond of his food – as was testified by his ample figure – took a close personal interest in the details of his table; how many chickens had hatched, how his sea-kale was doing, how fared his trout, which were kept in a tank and fished out in an old tennis-net for breakfast, luncheon or dinner, though he felt it was a bit much when the official in charge of Government House started a correspondence about the sixty dozen corks sent for bottling the latest supply of whisky having arrived two short. His gastronomic efforts were of little avail in feeding that brilliant but vicious ruler, the Maharaja of Alwar, who refused all made-up dishes lest they contained a bit of the cow, and would not even eat Cheddar cheese because it was made with rennet, but they were much appreciated by his European guests. 'They all liked my cooking and the short meals,' Butler told his mother after being visited by the Viceroy and Vicereine, Lord and Lady Reading. 'My dinners were, as usual, five courses only.'

Lady Reading had already heard that Butler's establishment at Naini Tal was the most luxurious in India, a reputation well borne out by this visit, though her fashionable young secretary, Yvonne FitzRoy, reckoned Simla could teach Naini Tal a thing or two as regards dances. The Vicereine's health was very frail, but she blossomed under the genial attentions of 'Harkie', and on the big night 'looked wonderful' in a dress of blue and silver. 'Sir Harcourt, in spite of his gouty toes, became most gallant,' reported Miss FitzRoy, who thought, during dinner, that her own toe was being pressed by her neighbour, the Finance Member of the United Provinces Government. It turned out, however, to be a fox-terrier.

Had she stayed at Government House a few years later, when the dog-loving Lady Hailey was chatelaine, she would never have suspected the gentleman alongside her, but would immediately have attributed it to one of her hostess's Pomeranians. Lady Hailey had six or seven of these dogs, and when leading her luncheon party guests into the dining room, she would first of all take them into the conservatory, so that they could watch the Pomeranians having *their* luncheon. The dogs' dishes were laid by the goldfish pool, but before being allowed to eat, they had to stand to attention at a word of command from their mistress. When Lady Hailey drove out in the Government House motor, her Pomeranians would sit behind her on the folded-back hood. If the chauffeur took a corner too fast, one or more of them would fall off and get left behind in the road, but they were inevitably picked up and restored to their mistress by social climbers, who hoped thereby to gain the entrée to Government House. The dogs would also be taken for outings in a rickshaw, accompanied by another of Lady Hailey's pets, a small bear.

Disliking the formality of Government House life, Lady Hailey would from time to time escape into the Himalayas, to shoot and explore; she was awarded the Gold Medal of the Royal Geographical Society for her journeys. But while she was happiest in camp, with her horses, her dogs and her guns, she entered whole-heartedly into the gaieties of Naini Tal, which went on unceasingly from April to October, culminating with Naini Tal Week when every house and hotel in the place was full. The whole society of the United Provinces converged here during the summer, whereas in the cold weather it was split up between Lucknow, Allahabad and other centres such as Agra. A vast number of military also spent their summers here. The more dashing of the young officers, including the Governor's ADCs, formed themselves into a coterie known as the 'Matelots' – the Naini Tal equivalent of the 'Black Hearts' at Simla – which held dances and organized elaborate pranks as well as moonlight expeditions up Cheena, the mountain dominating Naini Tal to the northwards. The nautical name alluded to the fact that sailing on the lake was the chief Naini Tal activity, even more than tennis, hill-climbing and dancing. There was a yacht club, and the Governor had a private boathouse; Butler recorded with some pride that his boat had won two cups, though not with him in it. But while the lake was beautiful, it was also sinister. Every year a fatal sailing accident occurred near a rock on which stood a Hindu temple, and the bodies of the victims were never recovered.

It was as though the goddess Naini were claiming an annual tribute of human life. And there were other and less dramatic ways in which she punished the British for invading her domain. Like most hill stations, Naini Tal was not as healthy as might have been expected. The climate was cool, but also damp; it would rain for days on end, and for days everything would be shrouded in an ocean of mist. Lyall suffered from long bouts of neuralgia when he was here and during his last season he was laid up and in pain for two and a half months with 'a big carbuncular abcess' under his left thigh, 'spreading all ways like a jellyfish'.

Almost worse than ill-health was the ennui of the Hills, that claustrophobic feeling engendered by life in an Indian hill station. 'I feel cut off from all my familiar friends and honourably detained on top of a mountain,' Lyall complained after being at Naini Tal for less than a month. Two years later, when returning here from a visit to the Plains

29   Government House, Naini Tal.

30   The Viceroy's House, New Delhi.

31 The Viceroy's House, New Delhi, Lord and Lady Wavell receiving a Tibetan mission in the Durbar Hall, March 1946—a familiar scene of the Raj enacted for perhaps the last time.

in July, he regretted having to leave 'the heat and the natives', and declared with feeling: 'There is nothing so stupid or unreal as this hill station life, where a lot of officials eat, drink and play together.' Now that the officials have gone for good, together with the Hill Captains and the tennis-playing women, the spirit of Naini may at last be at rest. But knowing the Himalayas, one suspects that the present Indian inhabitants of Government House, and of all those smaller houses across the lake with names like Balmoral, Braemar, Tara Hall, Primrose Cottage and Woodbine Lodge, are sometimes troubled by spirits that are no less disquieting and not a hundred years old.

12

THE VICEROY'S HOUSE
NEW DELHI

T HE decision to make Delhi the capital of India instead of Calcutta was proclaimed at the Durbar of 1911 by the King-
Emperor himself, as he addressed the assembled multitude from
beneath a gilded pavilion on the edge of that great plain, scattered with
the tombs of forgotten dynasties, where the Imperial city was to be
built. New Delhi could not have been more splendidly or more fittingly
launched. Yet the project did not arouse much enthusiasm. The Calcutta merchants objected to their own city being deprived of its pride
of place; the officials and their wives were dismayed at this plan 'to
banish the Government of India to the crumbling graveyards of Delhi',
as Lord Curzon put it. Indian politicians criticized the scheme on the
grounds of cost, though the more nationalistic among them should have
welcomed it, remembering – as indeed, most of their countrymen did –
the old superstition that the move of the seat of government of a ruling
power to Delhi was inevitably followed by its downfall.

This belief was firmly based on history. From the eighth century
onwards, successive capitals rose up here, then fell into ruins, some of
them leaving monuments, such as the Kutb or the Purana Kila, others
vanishing without trace beneath the plain. The surviving Mogul city,
containing the Palace or Red Fort and the Jami Masjid, was the newest
of these former capitals, having been founded as late as 1638 by Shah
Jahan, whose dynasty had previously been seated at Agra and Lahore.
The glories of Mogul Delhi lasted a mere seventy years, until the death
of Aurungzeb in 1707. After that came a century and a half of decline
and defeat. The city was sacked by the Persian, Nadir Shah; it fell into
the hands of the Marathas and was eventually captured by the British,

194

THE VICEROY'S HOUSE, NEW DELHI principal floor

VICEROY'S PRIVATE SUITE (FORMERLY GUEST ROOMS)

CLERKS

VICE-ROY'S OFFICE

NORTH COURT

BALLROOM

STATE DRAWING ROOM

STATE LIBRARY

WEST GARDEN LOGGIA

STAIRCASE COURT

STATE DRAWING ROOM

DURBAR HALL

VESTIBULE

STATE DINING ROOM

STATE DRAWING ROOM

STATE SUPPER ROOM

SOUTH COURT

GUEST ROOMS (FORMERLY VICEROY'S PRIVATE WING)

MILITARY SECRETARY AND A.D.C.s'

who allowed the descendants of the Moguls the title of King and some semblance of royalty until Bahadur Shah sided with the insurgents in 1857 and was banished to Rangoon. Having been the scene of stirring events during the Mutiny, Delhi afterwards sunk into obscurity as a provincial city of the Punjab, being temporarily brought back to life in 1877 for the Imperial Assemblage which proclaimed Queen Victoria Empress of India, and in 1903 for the Durbar celebrating the Coronation of Edward VII, when Lady Curzon appeared in her celebrated peacock dress.

The Government of India did not wait for its new capital to be built, but almost as soon as the 1911 Durbar was over, moved into a gigantic camp and shanty town to the north of the old city, the Viceroy occupying an imposing bungalow built to accomodate Lord Curzon when he came for the Durbar of 1903. When the Viceroy and Vicereine, Lord and Lady Hardinge of Penshurst, made their State entry into Delhi on an elephant, a bomb was thrown at them, badly wounding the Viceroy. It was hardly an auspicious beginning, but it could not damp the boyish high spirits of the architect who was already at work choosing the site of the new capital and laying out its avenues. At the age of forty-three, he had landed the commission of which every architect dreams: to design a great city from scratch, and to build a palace on a heroic scale, something never before vouchsafed to an English architect, not even to Wren. It was a happy coincidence that he was the son-in-law of Lord Lytton, the Viceroy who had presided over the Imperial Assemblage, that first landmark in Delhi's regeneration, a regeneration to which he was about to give visible form.

He was, of course, Edwin Lutyens, who now stands out as the leading English architect of the present century, but who in 1912 would have been by no means the obvious choice for a commission like New Delhi. His work, up to then, had been almost entirely confined to building country houses for imaginative and discriminating private clients and he had little experience of public buildings. While he understood the proportions of Classical architecture better than any of his contemporaries, he showed an originality in his handling of it that sometimes verged on what has been described as 'naughtiness', a naughtiness well in keeping with his puckish nature. This would hardly have recommended him to officialdom, which would have preferred the weaker but stodgier Classicism of Sir Aston Webb, Reginald Blomfield or Herbert Baker.

The Viceroy's House at New Delhi thus differed from all the other Indian Government Houses in being by a famous architect, rather than by an unknown military engineer or a nameless functionary in the Public Works Department. It also stood apart from the others on account of its size, which far exceeded even Government House, Calcutta. The length of each of its two main fronts was about 600 feet; the top of the dome was 180 feet from the ground; the whole house covered four and a half acres and enclosed twelve courtyards. Wellesley's palace cost just over £60,000; seventy years later, the Lieutenant-Governor of the North-Western Provinces spent less than £10,000 on Government House, Allahabad. The Viceroy's House cost more than a million sterling.

It was, in fact, a palace to compare with Versailles, Schönbrunn, Caserta and the other palaces of the world, the latest of a great line and also, one fears, the last. As such, one can only be grateful that Lutyens was chosen to design it, rather than any of the other leading architects of the period, who would almost certainly have produced something uninspired, however impressive; whereas he produced a building that had both power and beauty. Its architecture was a fusion of East and West, not in the superficial way of so many nineteenth and twentieth century Indian buildings, but in combining the strict proportion and grandeur of line of the European Classical tradition with the shapes, colours and water-effects of Mogul India. The Mogul features were not just borrowed in order to give the building a suitably Oriental air, but they served the important purpose of counteracting the brilliant tropical sunlight, which makes European architectural forms appear flat, and subtle Western colours seem palid.

As well as giving a sculptured solidity to his façades by means of boldly projecting wings, advancing and receding surfaces and colonnaded loggias, Lutyens made use of the blade-like Mogul cornice known as the *chujja* to cast a definite shadow along them. He gave emphasis to his skyline by means of the little roof pavilions called *chattris*, as well as by the dome, which rose with Imperial might from the centre. For strong colour, he used the blood-red Dholpur sandstone which the Moguls had used before him, contrasting it with cream-coloured stone from the same quarries. He also followed the Moguls in getting movement and an extra dimension from water. There were oblong pools in the gigantic forecourt before the east front, a criss-cross of waterways and fountains in the formal garden which stretched westwards from the other side of the house and merged into the plain; fountains in some of the courtyards, fountains even on the roof – a solecism, in that the flatness of the surrounding country betrayed all too clearly that they were mechanical, rather than fed from higher ground, as all good fountains should be. A more successful Lutyens pleasantry was the order of his own invention which he used for the capitals of the columns. These incorporated stone bells, since there was a legend that so long as the bells were silent, the dynasty would reign.

Work on the house did not really begin until after the 1914–18 War, and it was not ready for occupation until 1929. Throughout the nineteen-twenties, Lutyens, now knighted, was a familiar figure in Indian high-life, with his puns and his pranks and his funny drawings. To be taken by him to see 'the ruins', as he delighted in calling the unfinished walls of his palace, became a popular form of entertainment. He even planned to take Lady Reading and her entourage for a ride around the works on the light railway which carried the stone; the trucks were to be furnished with armchairs and decorated with scarlet bunting and tea was to be served, but it all had to be cancelled at the last minute owing to Her Excellency's departure on tour.

During these years, Lutyens added the All-India War Memorial Arch to his original scheme, framing the two-mile vista to the house along King's Way. He also designed Delhi residences for many of the Princes, so many that when, at a later date, somebody admired one of these mansions in his presence, he remarked casually: 'I'm not sure if that's not one of mine.' Unfortunately, however, Lutyens was not the only architect involved in New Delhi. He had entrusted the two Secretariats, which the Government wanted in a hurry, to Herbert Baker, thereby meeting what he afterwards characteristically referred to as 'my Bakerloo'. Not only did Baker insist on putting the Secretariats, which were even larger than the Viceroy's House, but architecturally inferior, on the flat-topped hill or eminence which Lutyens had intended to be occupied by his palace alone. He also allowed, or even encouraged, officialdom to make the gradient of the roadway between them steeper than it should have been. Lutyens protested, but the officials remained obstinately wedded to the steeper gradient for reasons of economy – a saving of £8,000 in a project running into millions – and also because it would entail a few less steps for the clerks crossing from one Secretariat to the other. As a result, the approach to the Viceroy's House along King's Way, that splendid ceremonial avenue lined with canals and parks, was ruined. At a certain stage, as one drove towards the house, the façade began to disappear, until by the time the Secretariats were reached, the top of the dome was all that showed above the sea of asphalt.

Only further on did the house begin to reappear, to be seen in its full glory at the entrance to the forecourt, where the wrought-iron screen was flanked by piers with sculptured elephants and stone sentry boxes sheltering mounted troopers of the Bodyguard. One now appreciated the great length of the house, but not until one had passed the Jaipur Column and was really close to it did one become aware of its height, so that to arrive at the foot of the steps leading up to the portico was like arriving at the steps of St Peter's.

Immediately inside the portico was the circular Durbar Hall, rising into the dome, its walls lined with white marble, its floor of porphyry, and with columns of yellow jasper in the four apses. The thrones faced the entrance from beneath their canopy of crimson velvet; this was the climax of the two-mile approach. From here onwards, the axis divided, one corridor leading to the hundred-foot-long State Dining Room, with its teak panelling, its portraits of Viceroys, its display of gold plate and its table for more than a hundred people, the other to the Ballroom. For all its great size, the latter was originally rather dull; Lady Willingdon, the second chatelaine of the house, enlivened it with brightly-coloured arabesques and Mogul motifs, painted on the walls and ceiling by Italian artists. These enrichments aroused the wrath of Lutyens and his admirers, but they were allowed to stay, unlike Lady Willingdon's painted decorations elsewhere in the house – described as 'wild duck falling into Dorothy Perkins roses' – which were obliterated by her successor, Lady Linlithgow. The Ballroom and the State Dining Room were separated by a loggia in the middle of the west front, behind which was one of the most pleasing features of the interior: a grand staircase open to the sky, so that its cornice framed an oblong of azure blue by day and of stars by night. The largest of the three State Drawing Rooms, which was even longer than the State Dining Room, faced westwards across this Staircase Court, so as to have a view of the garden through the loggia.

The entrance beneath the portico was in fact at first floor level, and only intended to be used by personages arriving in state. All other guests, as well as Their Excellencies and the household, entered on the floor below, driving through arches into the North and South Courts. When there was a large function, the guests drove along tunnels joining the two courts, which deposited them on either side of a battery of cloakrooms situated beneath the centre of the house, from which they ascended to the principal floor by a choice of two grand staircases. All this ingenious planning did not prevent a Governor's daughter from getting locked in the lavatory when arriving for one of the first State Balls to be held in the house. She only managed to escape by climbing over the partition and into the neighbouring cubicle, besmearing her dress with whitewash in the process.

Along the western side of the lower floor ran the 'Semi-State' rooms, which were used on all but the grandest occasions. They had a certain monotony about them, the typical Lutyens theme of panelling, coffered ceiling and architectural marble chimneypiece repeating itself rather too often, albeit with variations. Monotonous, too, were the corridors, which were of infinite length and appeared to run in all directions. Lutyens, who seems to have preferred his vistas to be along corridors rather than through *enfilades* of rooms, made the most of them, so that they had receding perspectives of arches faced with a fawn-grey marble, and floors of white and coloured marble pavement, but the effect was somewhat heavy – more like a sumptuously-appointed office building than a palace. In fact, Lutyens' carefully planned and beautifully finished interiors are less satisfying than the grand simplicity of Government House, Calcutta. In the same way, it has to be admitted that the plaster façades of Wellesley's palace are better architecture than the magnificent elevations of the palace at New Delhi, though this is not so much a criticism of Lutyens as a sign of how even the finest of early twentieth-century buildings did not quite come up to a building of average quality dating from a hundred years earlier.

The Viceroy's House followed Government House, Calcutta, in consisting of a central block with four wings, though the ranges and corridors joining the wings to the centre were straight and not curving, while the two northern wings were joined together, enclosing the North Court. The south-east wing was for the Military Secretary and the ADCs, the north-east wing for clerks and the north-west wing for guests. The south-west wing contained the private rooms of the Viceroy and his family. Her Excellency had a bedroom forty feet long, together with a dressing room, while His Excellency had two bedrooms as well as a dressing room downstairs, but these rooms, instead of facing westwards over the garden, faced south and overlooked what was in fact the tradesmens' entrance. There was a further disadvantage in that the Viceroy's bedrooms were an exceedingly long walk from his main office on the north side of the house. He was, however, provided with two more offices in the south-west wing; Lady Reading, on being shown the plan, 'courteously refrained from asking Sir Edwin if he was supposed to keep his papers in all three'. The Willingdons simplified matters by moving into the north-west wing, having found the Viceregal bedrooms in the south-west wing too large. Subsequent Viceroys adhered to this arrangement, and the south-west wing was given over to guests. As such, the Viceroy's House was unique among Indian Government Houses in having enough accommodation for even the largest of house-parties. There was the Dufferin Suite and the Curzon Suite, the Clive Bedroom and the Minto Bedroom and a host of others, each named after a Viceroy, or lesser personage – even Lord Bill was commemorated by the Beresford Bedroom – and each with its own telephone number. Since the first-floor rooms in the wings were lower than the State apartments in the centre of the house, there were extra rooms above them, which were allotted to less eminent guests, as well as being used as nurseries, and for European servants. The Indian servants occupied separate quarters in the Viceregal Estate. Here, in what was virtually a town, fanning out on either side of the garden, but invisible from it being below the level of the hill, lived nearly 6,000 people; for as well as the actual servants, clerks, gardeners, grooms and motor mechanics, the band, the Bodyguard, the sepoys who did sentry duty at the side entrances and the police who patrolled the grounds, numbering altogether the best part of 2,000, there were wives, children and other dependents.

Beneath the entire house ran a basement, containing the kitchens as well as the full range of domestic offices that one would have expected to find in the largest country mansion of Edwardian England. There were sculleries, dairies, bakeries, game-larders, wine-cellars, coal-cellars, and linen rooms, rooms for confectioners and rooms for pastry-cooks. In addition, there were rooms that would have been unusual in an English house: a tailor's shop, a room for overhauling camp equipment, and a room for the Viceroy's Press. The latter was as much an institution here as it had been in Calcutta, putting out a constant stream of menus and seating plans, together with leaflets marked 'confidential' which gave all the forthcoming Viceregal arrangements – from a Durbar to a visit to the dentist – as well as the movements of the house party and Staff.

The house was thus designed to cater for every detail of Viceregal life; there was to be none of the makeshift that characterized Government House, Calcutta, even after Curzon's improvements. Edwin Montagu wondered whether future Viceroys and Vicereines would, nevertheless, outgrow it, just as Viceregal Lodge at Simla, which Lady Dufferin had found too large, was too small for Lady Minto twenty years later. For the Liberal Montagu, who speeded the Indians along the road to self-determination, to have envisaged a Viceregal establishment of the future, is indeed strange; most people, even before the Viceroy's house was completed, realized that the life for which it was designed would not last much longer.

When Lord Irwin arrived back at New Delhi in 1929 to take up residence in the house for the first time, there was an attempt to blow up his train. Not much damage was done, and the Viceroy remained suitably unperturbed. 'I heard the noise and said to myself, "that must be a bomb",' he afterwards wrote. 'But as nothing happened, I went on reading Chaloner.' Nevertheless, it was a portent; and as a further portent there was the slight figure of Gandhi arriving at the Viceroy's House a few months later for a series of interviews with Lord Irwin. Almost every servant in the house managed to find some urgent task near the door through which he entered; and he, thinking they were ordinary people assembled there to meet him, greeted them as such, much to the disgust of the ADCs and other members of the Staff. 'I remember Gandhi squatting on the floor and after a while a girl coming in with some filthy yellow stuff which he started eating without so much as by your leave,' wrote a high official who was present at one of these meetings, adding that he would have liked to have seen this happening to Curzon.

In fact, the house knew the full splendours of the Raj for a mere ten years, until the Second World War put an end to grand entertainments. It was a swansong, and a brief one; yet magnificent for all that. A visiting French nobleman[1] has left an account of a State Ball in the Willingdons' time. He was escorted by one of the ADCs – 'fair-haired youngsters who looked charming in their dress suits faced with sky-blue lapels' – to the foot of the open staircase, which seemed to him 'the most handsome staircase in the world'. There were two of the Bodyguard on each step, 'motionless as two grim giants hewn in stone'; the gold costumes of the maharajas mingled with the shining lustre of saris, the red,

[1] Baron Jean Pellenc, *Diamonds and Dust* (London, 1936)

blue and silver of uniforms, the glitter of diadems and the 'flaxen coiffures of the young Englishwomen'; while high overhead was the 'starlit splendour of the Indian night'. Ascending the stairs, he found himself advancing across the marble floor of the Durbar Hall, 'highly polished as a mirror', to where, flanked by *chobdars* with maces, stood the Viceroy, 'a charming representative of the English aristocracy who looked his royal part to proud perfection', and 'his smiling vivacious wife, who with prodigious sleight of mind found something to say – infallibly the right and fitting thing – to every one of us'. Then on into the ballroom, with 'sweet wafts of orange blossom' coming through the open windows.

Even more splendid was the scene when the elderly Willingdons had been replaced by the towering figure of Lord Linlithgow, immensely handsome and in the very prime of life, with his tall and graceful consort by his side. For an Investiture, they entered the Durbar Hall to a fanfare of trumpets, preceded by their Staff in scarlet and gold and followed by solemn little Indian boys, sons of maharajas or nawabs, carrying their trains. The corridors beyond the apses were lined with the Bodyguard; there were 600 people in the hall itself, waiting to be invested, together with 400 spectators.

Then there were the banquets held during sessions of the Chamber of Princes, when every other guest at the long table was the ruler of a State. The gold plate glittered in its crimson-lined niche, the lustres glinted, the scarlet and gold *khitmagars* moved deftly against the teak-panelled walls, and from an adjoining room came the music of the Viceroy's Band. The Band played every night, even when there was only a small party in the Semi-State Dining Room downstairs, and by a long-standing custom, the company always went into dinner to the strains of *The Roast Beef of Old England*, which Lord Linlithgow and his family used to sing in a rousing chorus when there were no official guests.

Whatever might have been said about Lutyens' palace being only suited to great occasions, it provided a pleasant enough background for the day-to-day life of the Viceregal family, as well as for the party of handsome and high-spirited young ADCs in attendance on them. 'In spite of its size, it was essentially a liveable-in house,' recalled Lord Halifax, the former Lord Irwin, shortly before his death. 'Admiration and affection for it steadily grew together, and every day that we lived there, we came to love it more.' The Irwins had watched the house growing to completion during the first three years of their Viceroyalty; they had helped to furnish it, and had supervised the planting of the garden. In their day, the trees were still small and the creepers had not yet covered Lutyens' stone pergolas, but they were able to enjoy 'the riot of colour from the best of Western flowers' which grew in tropical profusion, softening the formal pattern of lawns and waterways in the main Mogul garden, running wild in the more English setting of the walled garden beyond. During the spring and autumn months, luncheon was served out of doors in the shadow of the house, or beneath the colonnade of the swimming pool, and there would also be dinner under the stars. Although Delhi could at times be very hot – a perspiring Lutyens had once suggested that the new capital should be called Oozapore – it was a dry heat, far less enervating than the humidity of Calcutta. In winter, the climate was crisp and bracing; log fires crackled in Lutyens' elegant fireplaces.

If the climate of Delhi was pleasanter than that of Calcutta, so was the atmosphere. One did not feel oppressed by the ghosts of the past, even though the surrounding plain was strewn with crumbling tombs. Lord Irwin and the Commander-in-Chief, Sir Philip Chetwode, would go for early morning rides across the plain, accompanied by their respective daughters, and with a single Indian ADC in attendance. In November, the mimosa trees and tamarinds were in flower; in spring, the corn was green; but at other times, the plain was burnt brown by the sun. They would pass the bullocks turning their wheels, and the processions of camels bringing in the crops. Sometimes they would have their breakfast among the fallen masonry of one of the tombs. That there was open country immediately beyond the Viceregal Estate was not the least of the advantages possessed by New Delhi over Calcutta, where, for many years, the inhabitants of Government House had only been able to ride on the Maidan. These morning rides, and a game of tennis in the afternoon, provided the Viceroy with much-needed exercise, for as often as not he spent the rest of the day and the greater part of the night at his desk, pausing only for meals. Lord Linlithgow even worked at breakfast, which he had with his Private Secretary; and he would retire after dinner to his study on the ground floor overlooking the garden and stay there till the small hours.

During the War years, and the couple of years that followed, life at the Viceroy's House went on as before, though it had lost much of its glitter. There were still the luncheon and dinner parties of fifty or a hundred, but with fewer courses and no band after 1942. Galaxies of Princes still came to stay, including the elderly Maharaja of Kapurthala, who was so punctilious about his appearance that he had men stationed at intervals along the corridors to dust his shoes as he walked from his bedroom in the south-west wing to join the assembled company for dinner. There were also periodic house-parties of Governors, who came to confer with the Viceroy, and there were important personages from England who had to be put up, notably the Cabinet Delegation which descended on Lord and Lady Wavell in 1946 and stayed for several weeks. During those weeks, the Viceroy not only had to cope with the machinations of Sir Stafford Cripps, but every evening after dinner he was obliged to listen to A. V. Alexander singing his way solo through a repertoire that consisted of music hall ditties such as *Lady of Laguna* and *My Old Dutch*, interspersed with revivalist hymns. It was very different from Harcourt Butler's cheery sing-songs of twenty years earlier.

One at least among the numerous adherents of Mr Attlee who flocked to the Viceroy's House during the fevered months before Independence managed to endear himself to the overworked Viceroy and his household. This was the Governor-designate of Bengal, the former railwayman, Sir Frederick Burrows, who, together with his wife, was stranded here for some days owing to riots in Calcutta. The absence of afternoon tea, which the Wavells and their household had given up as a good example, India being then in the throes of a food shortage, proved so great a hardship to Lady Burrows that a kind young ADC took her to the tea-shop in Connaught Circus and plied her with tea and cakes. He was worried, however, lest someone should recognize the Viceregal car and put it about that the self-denial which the inmates of the Viceroy's House pretended to practise was mere hypocrisy. As a further piece of self-denial, Their Excellencies and the rest of the party adopted an exclusively vegetarian diet when Congress Hindus came to luncheon or dinner. With the worsening of the political situation, Congress supporters absented themselves altogether from the Viceroy's House – it must have been some small consolation to Wavell, in the midst of all his troubles, to be spared those highly-coloured dishes composed mainly of chopped-up nuts that stuck in the throat.

Though Congress stayed away, there were plenty of other Indians at Their Excellencies' hospitable board. In March 1946, a Tibetan mission, which had come to present gifts to the Viceroy and Vicereine, was entertained to luncheon. The presentation took place beforehand; the Tibetans, nine colourful figures in robes and head-dresses, accompanied by sixteen retainers bearing the carpets and vessels of silver that were to be offered, made their way with dignity up the great steps and advanced across the floor of the Durbar Hall to where Their Excellencies awaited them on their thrones. It was a scene that would have been familiar to Emily and Fanny Eden; it had been enacted countless times in the past. But it was a scene that would hardly ever be witnessed again.

Within less than twenty years after Lord Irwin had taken up residence in the newly-completed Viceroy's House, the last Viceroy, Lord Mountbatten, had departed. Nevertheless, in the India that replaced the Raj, Lutyens' palace has managed to keep some of its glory. A reigning Queen of Great Britain has even stayed beneath its roof, an honour not vouchsafed to it in the days when Her Majesty's father and grandfather were Emperors of India. As the home of a modern democratic President, it is certainly on the large side, but the Indians have been wise enough to maintain a Presidential establishment worthy of the setting. Scarlet-clad guards still sit on their chargers beneath the stone sentry boxes, *khitmagars* in white, red and gold line the corridors.

When I visited the house in 1967, it was easy to imagine myself back in Viceregal days. I did, however, notice certain differences. The President's throne stood solitary in the Durbar Hall where formerly there were two; and as though to provide him with the feminine support which his Viceregal predecessors had derived from Her Excellency, there was the statue of a Hindu goddess standing behind it. In the adjoining corridors, there was a faint smell of joss-sticks. And in the State Dining Room, portraits of Gandhi and former Presidents had ousted a few of the Viceroys. But those responsible for the house had, with rare good sense, left the rest of the gallery of Lord Sahibs intact. There was Hardinge of Penshurst, but for whom New Delhi might never have been; there was Willingdon, 'the eternal Head of Pop', resplendent in grey frock coat and spats, the Star of India on his breast. There was even Ellenborough, the only one of the whole long line who could in fairness have been called bombastic. The idea of that Governor-General, who wanted to turn the old royal family out of the Palace at Delhi and 'come Aurungzeb' in it himself, sharing a room with the Mahatma, was just the sort of thing that would have appealed to

Lutyens. And there, not far away, was the bust of the 'architect of this house', as the inscription modestly called him, standing in the sunlight, against the glowing red stonework of the open staircase. After the faces in the portraits – the self-assured solemnity of the British, the slightly worried earnestness of the Indians – he seemed to be chuckling.

GLOSSARY OF INDIAN AND OTHER
EASTERN WORDS

ayah, a child's nurse; a lady's maid.

bheestie, a water carrier.

chabutra, a raised platform round the base of a Mogul tomb or other building.

chapattis, a form of unleavened bread eaten with curry.

chaprassi, a liveried servant, who combined the functions of a doorman, messenger and personal attendant.

chobdar, a ceremonial mace-bearer.

chunam, a stucco made of burnt sea-shells which polished like marble

dandy, a kind of litter.

dhooly, a box on poles, carried on men's shoulders.

dhoti, a loose cotton garment worn by Indian men.

farman, an order, decree or edict.

ghat, a step or steps leading down to a river.

hatikhana, a stable for elephants; an elephant stud.

jemadar, an upper servant.

jhampani, a rickshaw coolly.

khitmagar, a servant whose functions resembled those of a footman.

maidan, a large open space or plain, usually adjoining a city.

mali, a gardener.

mirador, a projecting oriel window in the Moorish style.

mofussil, the country, as distinct from the town; the hinterland; the territory of a province away from the provincial capital.

mohur, a gold coin formerly current in India, and worth about 15 rupees, or rather more than £1.

moucharabya, carved and moulded lattice-work.

munshi, a teacher, particularly of languages.

nautch, a performance by dancing-girls.

nazar, a token offering at a durbar or similar ceremony.

punkah, a fan, especially one hanging from the ceiling of a room and pulled by a cord.

serai, in this sense, the palace of the local governor in a provincial city of the old Turkish empire.

Glossary

shamiana, a large tent or marquee, principally used for parties and other functions.

shikar, big game shooting.

sirdar, a noble.

subadar, a senior non-commissioned officer in the army.

Taluqdar, a great landowner of Oudh.

tykhana, an underground room in a house in Upper India, occupied during the hot weather.

THE LORD SAHIBS

The Rulers of British India, who lived at Government House, Calcutta, from 1803 to 1912, at Barrackpore from 1801 to 1912, at Peterhof, Simla, from 1864 to 1888, at Viceregal Lodge, Simla, from 1888 to 1947 and at the Viceroy's House, New Delhi, from 1929 to 1947.

Note. For the sake of simplicity, the title of Governor-General is used throughout this book for all holders of the office up to 1858, and Viceroy for all those who came after; whereas the full designation was Governor-General of Bengal from 1774 to 1834, Governor-General of India from 1834 to 1858 and Viceroy and Governor-General of India from 1858 to 1947.

Earl of Mornington, afterwards Marquess Wellesley, 1798–1805
Marquess Cornwallis, 1805
1st Earl of Minto, 1807–1813
Earl of Moira, afterwards Marquess of Hastings, 1813–1823
Lord Amherst, afterwards Earl Amherst, 1823–1828
Lord William Bentinck, 1828–1835
Lord Auckland, afterwards Earl of Auckland, 1836–1842
Lord Ellenborough, afterwards Earl of Ellenborough, 1842–1844
Sir Henry Hardinge, afterwards Viscount Hardinge, 1844–1848
Earl of Dalhousie, afterwards Marquess of Dalhousie, 1848–1856
Viscount Canning, afterwards Earl Canning, 1856–1862
8th Earl of Elgin, 1862–1863
Sir John Lawrence, afterwards Lord Lawrence, 1864–1869
Earl of Mayo, 1869–1872
Lord Northbrook, afterwards Earl of Northbrook, 1872–1876
Lord Lytton, afterwards Earl of Lytton, 1876–1880
Marquess of Ripon, 1880–1884
Earl of Dufferin, afterwards Marquess of Dufferin and Ava, 1884–1888
Marquess of Lansdowne, 1888–1894
9th Earl of Elgin, 1894–1899
Lord Curzon of Kedleston, afterwards Earl and Marquess Curzon of Kedleston, 1899–1905

4th Earl of Minto, 1905–1910
Lord Hardinge of Penshurst, 1910–1916
Lord Chelmsford, afterwards Viscount Chelmsford, 1916–1921
Earl of Reading, afterwards Marquess of Reading, 1912–1926
Lord Irwin, afterwards Viscount and Earl of Halifax, 1926–1931
Earl of Willingdon, afterwards Marquess of Willingdon, 1931–1936
Marquess of Linlithgow, 1936–1943
Viscount Wavell, afterwards Earl Wavell, 1943–1947
Viscount Mountbatten of Burma, afterwards Earl Mountbatten of
   Burma, 1947

Governors of Bengal (the new Presidency set up in 1912) mentioned in
this book

2nd Earl of Lytton, 1922–1927
Lord Brabourne, 1937–1939
Richard Casey, afterwards Sir Richard Casey and Lord Casey, 1944–
   1946
Sir Frederick Burrows, 1946–1947

Governors of Madras mentioned in this book

Thomas Saunders, 1750–1755
George Pigot, afterwards Sir George Pigot and Lord Pigot, 1755–
   1763 and 1775–1777
Sir Thomas Rumbold, 1778–1780
Sir Archibald Campbell, 1785–1789
2nd Baron Clive, afterwards Earl of Powis, 1799–1803
Lord William Bentinck, 1803–1807
Sir Thomas Munro, 1820–1827
Sir Charles Trevelyan, 1859–60
Sir George Ward, 1860
Sir William Denison, 1861–1866
Lord Hobart, 1872–1875
Duke of Buckingham and Chandos, 1875–1880
Mountstuart Grant Duff, afterwards Sir Mountstuart Grant Duff,
1881–1886
Hon. Robert Bourke, afterwards Lord Connemara, 1886–1890
Lord Ampthill, 1900–1906

Hon. Sir Arthur Lawley, afterwards Lord Wenlock, 1906–1911
Lord Willingdon, afterwards Viscount and Earl and Marquess of
Willingdon, 1919–1924

Governors of Bombay mentioned in this book who lived at Parell from
1719 to 1885, and at Poona (Dapuri and Ganesh Khind) from 1829 onwards

Charles Boone, 1716–1720
William Hornby, 1771–1784
Sir Evan Nepean, 1812–1819
Hon. Mountstuart Elphinstone, 1819–1827
Sir John Malcolm, 1827–1830
Sir Robert Grant, 1834–1838
Viscount Falkland, 1848–1853
Lord Elphinstone, 1853–1860
Sir Bartle Frere, 1862–1867
Sir Seymour FitzGerald, 1867–1872
Sir Philip Wodehouse, 1872–1877
Sir Richard Temple, 1877–1880 (did not live at Parell)
Sir James Fergusson, 1880–1885
Lord Reay, 1885–1890
Lord Willingdon, afterwards Viscount and Earl and Marquess of
Willingdon, 1913–1918
Sir George Lloyd, afterwards Lord Lloyd, 1918–1923
Lord Brabourne, 1933–1937

Residents at Hyderabad mentioned in this book

Major James Achilles Kirkpatrick, 1797–1805
Captain Thomas Sydenham, 1806–1810
Henry Russell, afterwards Sir Henry Russell, 1811–1820
Sir Charles Metcalfe, afterwards Lord Metcalfe, 1820–1825
Colonel Cuthbert Davidson, 1857–1862
Sir Richard Temple, 1867–1868
John Graham Cordery, 1883–1888
Trevor Chichele Plowden, afterwards Sir Trevor Chichele Plowden,
1891–1900
Michael O'Dwyer, Acting Resident, 1908–1909

Colonel Alexander Pinhey, afterwards Sir Alexander Pinhey, 1911–
1916
Stuart Fraser, afterwards Sir Stuart Fraser, 1916–1919
Lennox Russell, afterwards Sir Lennox Russell, 1919–1925
Duncan Mackenzie, afterwards Sir Duncan Mackenzie, 1935–1938
Sir Arthur Lothian, 1942–1946

Residents at Lucknow mentioned in this book
Major John Baillie, 1811–1815
Mordaunt Ricketts, 1822–1829
Colonel John Low, afterwards Sir John Low, 1831–1842
Lieutenant-General Sir James Outram, 1854–1856
(Oudh annexed, 1856)

Chief Commissioners of Oudh mentioned in this book
Lieutenant-General Sir James Outram, 1856–1857
Sir Henry Lawrence, 1857
John Sherbrooke Banks, 1857
John Strachey, afterwards Sir John Strachey, 1866–1867
Sir George Couper, 1871–1876
(The Chief Commissionership of Oudh was amalgamated with the
Lieutenant-Governorship of the North-Western Provinces in
1876.)

*Lieutenant-Governors of the North-Western Provinces, called the United
Provinces after 1902, and Governors of the United Provinces* mentioned in
this book. (Lived at Government House, Allahabad from 1869 onwards;
Government House, Lucknow, from 1876 onwards; and Government
House, Naini Tal, from 1875 onwards)
Sir Charles Metcalfe, afterwards Lord Metcalfe, 1834–1838 (origi-
nally styled Governor of Agra)
James Thomason, 1843–1853
Sir William Muir, 1868–1874
Sir John Strachey, 1874–1876
Sir George Couper, 1876–1882
Sir Alfred Lyall, 1882–1887
Sir Harcourt Butler, 1918–1922 (Governor from 1921)
Sir Malcolm Hailey, afterwards Lord Hailey, 1928–1930 and 1931–
1933

Nawab of Chhatari, 1933
Sir Malcolm Hailey, afterwards Lord Hailey, 1933–1934
Sir Maurice Hallett, 1939–1945

British Rulers of the Punjab mentioned in this book

Sir Henry Lawrence, President of the Board of Administration, 1849–1853
John Lawrence, afterwards Sir John Lawrence and Lord Lawrence, Chief Commissioner, 1853–1859

Lieutenant Govenors

Sir John Lawrence, afterwards Lord Lawrence, 1859
Sir Robert Montgomery, 1859–1865
Sir Henry Marion Durand, 1870–1871
Sir Robert Davies, 1871–1877
Sir Charles Aitchison, 1882–1887
Sir James Lyall, 1887–1892
Sir Dennis Fitzpatrick, 1892–1897
Sir William Mackworth Young, 1897–1902
Sir Charles Rivaz, 1902–1907
Sir Louis Dane, 1908–1913
Sir Michael O'Dwyer, 1913–1919
Sir Edward Maclagan, 1919–1921

Governors

Sir Edward Maclagan, 1921–1924
Sir Malcolm Hailey, afterwards Lord Hailey, 1924–1928

MANUSCRIPT SOURCES

Letters from Sir Harcourt Butler to his mother and other papers, 1918–22. Harcourt Butler Collection, deposited at the India Office Library
Letters of Dr Robert Druitt and his daughter, Ella, to Mrs Isabella Druitt, 1872–4. India Offic eLibrary
Journal and papers of Hon. Mountstuart Elphinstone, 1819–27. Elphinstone Collection, deposited at the India Office Library
Journal of Yvonne FitzRoy, 1921–6, deposited at the India Office Library
Letters of Honoria Lawrence to her son, 1851–3. Henry Lawrence Collection, deposited at the India Office Library
Letters of Sir Alfred Lyall, 1882–7. A. C. Lyall Collection, desposited at the India Office Library
Journals of Sir James Lyall, 1892–4. A. C. Lyall Collection, deposited at the India Office Library
Letters of Sir John and Lady Strachey, 1866–7 and 1874–6. R. Strachey Collection, deposited at the India Office Library
Letters of Sir Richard Temple, 1867–8 and 1877–80. Sir Richard Temple Collection, deposited at the India Office Library

India Office Records
North-Western Provinces Public Works Department Proceedings, 1868–9
Punjab Public Works Department Proceedings, 1887–1914
Simla Correspondence with the Secretary of State, 1884–7

BIBLIOGRAPHY

Barlow, Glyn, *Story of Madras*, London, 1921
Birkenhead, Earl of, *Halifax*, London, 1965
Blunt, Wilfrid Scawen, *India under Ripon: a private diary*, London, 1909
Briggs, Henry George, *The Nizam, his History and Relations with the British Government*, London, 1861

215

Buck, Edward J., *Simla, Past and Present,* Bombay 1925

Butler, A. S. G. and others, *The Architecture of Sir Edwin Lutyens,* London, 1950

Butler, Iris, *The Viceroy's Wife,* London, 1969

Curzon of Kedleston, Marquess, *British Government in India,* London, 1925

Denison, Sir William, *Varieties of Viceregal Life,* London, 1870

Diver, Maud, *Honoria Lawrence,* London, 1936

Dodgson, D. S., *General Views and Special Points of Interest of the City of Lucknow,* London, 1860.

Douglas, James, *Book of Bombay,* Bombay, 1883

Dufferin and Ava, Marchioness of, *Our Viceregal Life in India,* London, 1890

Durand, Sir H. M., *Alfred Lyall,* Edinburgh and London, 1913

Eden, Hon. Emily and Hon. F. H. *Letters from India,* London, 1872

Eden, Hon. Emily, *Up the Country* (Introduction and notes by Edward Thompson), Oxford, 1930

Edwards, Michael, *The Orchid House,* London, 1969

Falkland, Viscountess, *Chow-Chow* (ed. H. G. Rawlinson), London, 1930

Glendevon, John, *The Viceroy at Bay,* London, 1971

Gordon, Sir Thomas, *A Varied Life,* London, 1906

Graham, Maria, *Journal of a Residence in India,* Edinburgh, 1812

Graham, Maria, *Letters on India,* London, 1814

Grant Duff, Sir Mountstuart, *Notes from a Diary,* London, 1899

Halifax, Earl of, *Fullness of Days,* London, 1957

Hare, Augustus, *The Story of Two Noble Lives,* London, 1893

Hay, Sidney, *Historic Lucknow,* Lucknow, 1939

Heber, Reginald, Bishop of Calcutta, *Narrative of a Journey through the Upper Provinces of India,* London, 1828

Heber, Reginald, *An Account of a Journey to Madras and the Southern Provinces, 1826,* published as an addition to the aforementioned work

Howes, Peter, *Viceregal Establishments in India,* New Delhi, 1949

Inglis, Hon. Lady, *Diary of the Siege of Lucknow,* London, 1892

Jacquemont, Victor, *Letters from India, 1829–1832,* (translated with an Introduction by Catherine Alison Phillips), London, 1936

Knighton, William (anon.), *The Private Life of an Eastern King, by a member of the household of his late Majesty, Nasir-ud-din,* London, 1855

Lawley, Hon. Lady, and Penny, F. E., *Southern India,* London, 1914

Lawrence, Sir Walter R., *The India We Served,* London, 1928

Lothian, Sir Arthur, *Kingdoms of Yesterday,* London, 1951

Love, H. D., *Descriptive List of Pictures in Government House and the Banquetting Hall, Madras,* Madras, 1903

Bibliography

Love, H. D., *Vestiges of Old Madras*, London, 1913

Maitland, Mrs J. C., (anon.), *Letters from Madras, by a Lady*, London, 1843

Mecham, Clifford Henry, and Couper, George, *Sketches and Incidents of the Siege of Lucknow*, London, 1858

Menzies, Mrs Stuart, *Lord William Beresford*, London, 1917

Mersey, Viscount, *The Viceroys and Governors-General of India*, London, 1949

Montagu, Hon. Edwin, *An Indian Diary*, London, 1930

Nilsson, Sten, *European Architecture in India, 1750–1850*, London, 1968

O'Dwyer, Sir Michael, *India as I knew it*, London, 1925

Parkes, Mrs Fanny, (anon.) *Wanderings of a Pilgrim in Search of the Picturesque*, London, 1850

Pellenc, Baron Jean, *Diamonds and Dust: India through French Eyes*, London, 1936

Power, Maud, *Wayside India*, Waterford, 1907

Reed, Sir Stanley, *The India I knew*, London, 1952

Reed, Sir Stanley, *The Royal Tour in India, 1905-6*, Bombay, 1906

Rivett-Carnac, J. H., *Many Memories*, Edinburgh and London, 1910

Roberts, Emma, *Scenes and Characteristics of Hindostan*, London, 1837

Russell, William Howard, *The Prince of Wales's Tour*, London, 1877

Steegman, Philip, *Indian Ink*, London, 1939

Temple, Sir Richard, *Men and Events of my Time in India*, London, 1882

Temple, Sir Richard, *Journals kept in Hyderabad, Kashmir, Sikkim and Nepal*. London, 1887

Temple, Sir Richard, *The Story of my Life*, London, 1896

Thompson, Edward, *Life of Charles, Lord Metcalfe*, London, 1937

Valentia, George, Viscount, *Voyages and Travels*, London, 1809

Wakefield, G. E. C., *Recollections*, Lahore, 1942

Waters, Lieut.-Colonel George, *Travel Reminiscences*, n.p. (193-)

Woodruff, Philip (Philip Mason), *The Men who Ruled India*, Vol. I, 'The Founders', London, 1953; Vol. II, 'The Guardians', London, 1954

INDEX

For Product Safety Concerns and Information please contact our EU
representative GPSR@taylorandfrancis.com
Taylor & Francis Verlag GmbH, Kaufingerstraße 24, 80331 München, Germany